Arranging *and* Describing
Archives *and* Manuscripts

ARCHIVAL FUNDAMENTALS SERIES III
Peter J. Wosh, Editor

1 **Leading and Managing Archives and Manuscripts Programs**
Peter Gottlieb and David W. Carmicheal, Editors

2 **Arranging and Describing Archives and Manuscripts**
Dennis Meissner

3 **Advocacy and Awareness for Archivists**
Kathleen D. Roe

4 **Reference and Access for Archives and Manuscripts**
Cheryl A. Oestreicher

5 **Advancing Preservation for Archives and Manuscripts**
Elizabeth Joffrion and Michèle V. Cloonan

6 **Selecting and Appraising Archives and Manuscripts**
Michelle Light and Margery Sly

7 **Introducing Archives and Manuscripts**
Peter J. Wosh

Arranging *and* Describing
Archives *and* Manuscripts

Dennis Meissner

SOCIETY OF
American
Archivists

CHICAGO

The Society of American Archivists
www.archivists.org

© 2019 by the Society of American Archivists
All rights reserved.

Printed in the United States of America.

Library of Congress Control Number: 2019942807

ISBN: 978-1-945246-07-4 (paperback)
eISBN: 978-1-945246-09-8 (epub)
eISBN: 978-1-945246-11-1 (pdf)

Graphic design by Sweeney Design, kasween@sbcglobal.net.

Table of Contents

FOREWORD: The Evolution of a Book Series vii
    Peter J. Wosh

1   The Context and Significance of Arrangement and Description 1
    Its Purpose 1
    A Brief History of Archival Arrangement and Description 5
    Core Archival Concepts 11

2   Principles of Archival Arrangement 16
    Arrangement Options 16
    Respect des Fonds, Provenance, and the Archival Whole 17
    Original Order 22
    Five Fundamental Levels of Control 26
    A Caveat: When Hierarchy and Structure Are Absent 31
    The Granularity of Arrangement 32

3   Principles of Archival Description 35
    The Purpose of Description 35
    Description Is Structured Data, Not Prose 37
    The Relationship of Description to Arrangement 39
    Archival Descriptive Standards 40
    Archival Description Is Multilevel 57
    Describing the Context as Well as the Content 58
    Intellectual Order and Administrative Order: Two Views of One Collection . . . 64

4   Physical Processing and Arrangement 68
    Accessioning: Establishing Initial Controls 68
    The Practice of Arrangement 74
    Arranging the Collection Materials 80

	Dealing with Restricted Materials 88
	Preservation Actions and Processing 89
	Dealing with Accruals 90

5 Describing the Materials 93
    Constructing Descriptions Using DACS Data Elements 94
    Creating Descriptive Metadata 111
    Input Solutions: Creating and Managing Descriptive Metadata 113
    Output Solutions: Publishing and Sharing Descriptive Metadata 122

6 Arranging and Describing Nontextual Formats 129
    Arranging and Describing Sound and Visual Materials 129
    Arrangement and Description in a Digital World 132

7 Emerging Trends and Theoretical Shifts 144
    Challenges to the Concept of Original Order 144
    Revolutionizing Our Models of Description 146
    MPLP and Its Aftermath 148
    Influences from Critical Theory 150

CONCLUSION 156

APPENDIXES

    A Glossary of Arrangement and Description Terminology 159
    B Examples of Institutional Processing Levels 163
    C Finding Aid Examples 165
    D Example of Full Finding Aid Encoded in EAD 176
    E Example of MARC21 Record 182
    F Crosswalks between Descriptive Standards 187
    G Recommended Reading: Archival Arrangement and Description . 192

ACKNOWLEDGMENTS 205

INDEX 207

FOREWORD

The Evolution of a Book Series

The Society of American Archivists (SAA) first conceived the notion of developing and publishing "manuals relating to major and basic archival functions" in the early 1970s. Charles Frederick Williams (popularly known as C. F. W.) Coker (1932–1983), a former US Marine Corps captain and North Carolina state archivist who recently had been appointed to head the Printed Documents Division of the National Archives and Records Services, edited the initial Basic Manual Series. The first five basic manuals, which appeared in 1977, illustrated the ways in which archivists defined and classified their core concepts at that historical moment:

- *Archives & Manuscripts: Appraisal & Accessioning* by Maynard J. Brichford
- *Archives & Manuscripts: Arrangement & Description* by David B. Gracy II
- *Archives & Manuscripts: Reference & Access* by Sue E. Holbert
- *Archives & Manuscripts: Security* by Timothy Walch
- *Archives & Manuscripts: Surveys* by John Fleckner

The entire series accounted for only 163 pages of text, which included numerous illustrations, graphics, sample forms, charts, and bibliographic insertions. Each 8.5" by 11" softbound pamphlet contained three holes, punched down the left side, for easy insertion into a loose-leaf binder that might be handily referenced at an archivist's desk. Individual volumes sold for $4, though SAA members received a $1 discount.

Archivists operated within a far different cultural, legal, and professional framework during the early and middle years of the 1970s. In 1973, the same year that SAA began work on the Basic Manual Series, IBM introduced the Correcting Selectric II typewriter as its major technological breakthrough, thereby eliminating the need for such popular tools as rubber erasers, correction fluid, and cover-up tape. This revolutionary product seemed destined to alter the nature of document creation forever. During this period, a few archivists had begun grappling with the challenges of something known as "machine-readable records," but a bibliographer who surveyed this puzzling development could still confidently conclude in a 1975 *American Archivist* article that "only a few archival establishments" appeared to be "developing programs for accessioning" such materials. Other momentous—and occasionally unsettling—changes appeared on the horizon. A new copyright law, which was enacted by Congress in 1976 and became effective on New Year's Day 1978, contained significant implications for how archivists would manage collections and serve researchers. Richard Nixon's resignation in 1974 prompted the promulgation of new legislation in 1978 that declared for the first time that presidential and vice presidential records are public documents. Professionally, the archival landscape seemed to be shifting as well. The Association of Canadian Archivists launched an exciting new journal, *Archivaria*, in winter 1975/1976, a development destined to deepen the discipline's intellectual discourse. Regional archival associations formed, became fruitful, and multiplied in the United States. In addition, a new era in archival education began as library schools and history departments inaugurated archives-based graduate programs in the late 1970s, ultimately resulting in a highly credentialed and formally trained corps of professional practitioners.

Such transformations, and many others too numerous to mention here, convinced the Society of American Archivists that only an active publications program that regularly refreshed the existing literature could provide its membership with easy access to rapidly changing trends and best practices. SAA accordingly published the Basic Manual Series II—a second set of five volumes—in the early 1980s:

- *Archives & Manuscripts: Exhibits* by Gail Farr Casterline
- *Archives & Manuscripts: Automated Access* by H. Thomas Hickerson
- *Archives & Manuscripts: Maps and Architectural Drawings* by Ralph E. Ehrenberg
- *Archives & Manuscripts: Public Programs* by Ann E. Pederson and Gail Farr Casterline
- *Archives & Manuscripts: Reprography* by Carolyn Hoover Sung

Over the years, SAA published scores of other titles, each illustrating the rich diversity of archival work: administration of photo collections, conservation, machine-readable records, law, management, a basic glossary, collections of readings on archival theory and practice, and books specific to archives in a variety of institutional settings (i.e., colleges and universities, businesses and corporations, religious and scientific institutions, museums, government agencies, historical societies, etc.). Even with the proliferation of publications, the bedrock of archival practice rested on the core knowledge represented in the basic manuals, which were reconceptualized and rechristened between 1990 and 1993 as the Archival Fundamentals Series:

- *Understanding Archives and Manuscripts* by James O'Toole
- *Arranging and Describing Archives and Manuscripts* by Fredric M. Miller
- *Managing Archival and Manuscript Repositories* by Thomas Wilsted and William Nolte
- *Selecting and Appraising Archives and Manuscripts* by F. Gerald Ham
- *Preserving Archives and Manuscripts* by Mary Lynn Ritzenthaler
- *Providing Reference Services for Archives and Manuscripts* by Mary Jo Pugh
- *The Glossary of Archivists, Manuscript Curators, and Records Managers* by Lynn Lady Bellardo and Lewis Bellardo

A second iteration of the seven books in this revamped series appeared roughly fifteen years later as the Archival Fundamentals Series II:

- *Understanding Archives and Manuscripts* by James O'Toole and Richard J. Cox
- *Arranging and Describing Archives and Manuscripts* by Kathleen D. Roe
- *Managing Archival and Manuscript Repositories* by Michael Kurtz
- *Selecting and Appraising Archives and Manuscripts* by Frank Boles
- *Preserving Archives and Manuscripts* by Mary Lynn Ritzenthaler
- *Providing Reference Services for Archives and Manuscripts* by Mary Jo Pugh
- *A Glossary of Archival and Records Terminology* by Richard Pearce-Moses

Mary Jo Pugh and Richard J. Cox edited these multivolume compilations, which almost instantaneously became required texts in archival education courses and necessary additions to archivists' bookshelves. The Archival Fundamentals Series I and II differed in scope and scale from the initial Basic Manual Series. For example, John Fleckner's comprehensive treatment of surveys did not appear in need of revision and dropped out of the series. Security became incorporated into a broader manual on preservation. SAA commissioned an introductory overview of the field, added a new book that focused on managerial issues, and developed a glossary with the goal of defining and historicizing key archival concepts. Beginning in the 1970s, both Archival Fundamentals Series I and II incorporated and delineated the evolving descriptive standards that defined professional practice, dissected the contentious debates surrounding appraisal and deaccessioning that enlivened archival discourse in the 1980s, and reflected the growing emphases on an expanding user base and more complex reference services that revolutionized reading rooms and repositories in the late twentieth century.

This third edition—Archival Fundamentals Series III—contains important continuities and significant departures from its predecessors:

- A new book, *Advocacy and Awareness for Archivists* by Kathleen D. Roe, reflects an increased understanding that these functions undergird all aspects of archival work.
- The management volume, *Leading and Managing Archives and Manuscripts Programs* edited by Peter Gottlieb and David W. Carmicheal, has been reconfigured to focus especially on leadership and to provide readers with opportunities to explore their individual managerial styles.
- *Advancing Preservation for Archives and Manuscripts* by Elizabeth Joffrion and Michèle V. Cloonan addresses digital challenges and focuses on such current issues as risk management, ethical considerations, and sustainability.
- *Arranging and Describing Archives and Manuscripts* by Dennis Meissner, *Reference and Access for Archives and Manuscripts* by Cheryl A. Oestreicher, and *Selecting and Appraising Archives and Manuscripts* by Michelle Light and Margery Sly may appear familiar topics to readers of the previous two series, but each book illustrates the innovations in thought and practice that have transformed these archival functions over the past fifteen years.
- A general overview volume which I am preparing, *Introducing Archives and Manuscripts*, provides a broad introduction to the historical, philosophical, and theoretical foundations of the profession.

One contribution that constituted a cornerstone of the previous series has been reformatted to maximize its currency and usability. Although not part of the Archival Fundamentals Series III, the *Dictionary of Archives Terminology* (dictionary.archivists.org) will replace *A Glossary of Archival and Records Terminology* and will be maintained and updated as a digital resource by SAA's Dictionary Working Group.

We hope that undergraduate and graduate students, new professionals, seasoned archival veterans, and others in the information science and public history fields will find the seven volumes in the Archival Fundamentals Series III helpful, provocative, and essential to both their intellectual life and their daily work. As Richard J. Cox observed in his preface to an earlier edition of the series, the time has long passed "when individuals entering the archival profession could read a few texts, peruse some journals, attend a workshop and institute or two, and walk away with a sense that they grasped the field's knowledge and discipline." This series provides an entry point and a synthetic distillation of a much broader literature that spans an impressive array of academic disciplines. We encourage you, of course, to do a deeper dive into each of the individual topics covered here. But we also remain confident that this series, like its predecessors, provides an honest and accurate snapshot of archival best practices at the end of the second decade of the twenty-first century.

The authors, of course, deserve full credit for their individual contributions. The Archival Fundamentals Series III itself, though, constitutes a collaborative enterprise that benefited from the work of SAA Publications Board members, editors, and interns throughout the past decade. These individuals helped to define the series parameters, reviewed proposals and manuscripts, and shepherded various projects to conclusion. Special shout-outs (in alphabetical order) are owed to: Bethany Anderson, Jessica Ballard, Roland Baumann, Cara Bertram, Mary Caldera, Amy Cooper Cary, Jessica Chapel, Paul Conway, J. Gordon Daines, Todd Daniels-Howell, Sarah Demb, Jody DeRidder, Keara Duggan, Margaret Fraser, Thomas J. Frusciano, Krista Gray, Gregory Hunter, Geoffrey Huth, Petrina Jackson, Joan Krizack, Christopher Lee, Donna McCrea, Jennifer Davis McDaid, Kathryn Michaelis, Nicole Milano, Lisa Mix, Tawny Nelb, Kevin Proffitt, Christopher Prom, Mary Jo Pugh, Aaron Purcell, Colleen Rademaker, Caryn Radick, Dennis Riley, Michael Shallcross, Mark Shelstad, Jennifer Thomas, Ciaran Trace, Anna Trammell, Joseph Turrini, Tywanna Whorley, and Deborah Wythe. Nancy Beaumont has been an inspirational executive director for SAA, as well as a brilliant editor in her own right. Abigail Christian, SAA's editorial and production coordinator, has skillfully shepherded design and layout. Teresa Brinati, keenly insightful and good-humored as always, remains the epitome of competent leadership and has transformed the SAA publications program into a model for professional associations. It has been a privilege and great fun to work with everyone on this project.

PETER J. WOSH
Editor, Archival Fundamentals Series III
Society of American Archivists

1

The Context and Significance of Arrangement and Description

Its Purpose

A summary overview

This book is intended to be a very practical manual. My goal is to explain the principles and mechanics of the work that archivists commonly refer to as arrangement and description—also referred to as processing—so that students and nonarchivists can understand and appreciate this fundamental and ubiquitous work, and so that novice practitioners (and rusty professionals) have a practical guide at hand for actually performing the work. Basic concepts, functions, and history foundational to archives will be introduced briefly when they are particularly important for understanding the function of arrangement and description. Beyond that, I will happily refer the reader to more authoritative sources for that information.

Let's begin with some basic definitions to establish the scope and focus of this manual. What do we mean by the terms *arrangement*, *description*, and *processing* when we apply them to the work performed by archivists? This manual will hew to the standard definitions penned by Richard Pearce-Moses in his authoritative glossary.[1] Leaning on many archival thinkers before him, he characterizes *arrangement* as

> 1. The process of organizing materials with respect to their provenance and original order, to protect their context and to achieve physical or intellectual control over the materials. - 2. The organization and sequence of items within a collection.

In this manual, I will treat the complex function of arrangement as the entire set of activities—some intellectual and some physical—that focus on organizing, structuring, and sequencing the contents of a collection so that the context and circumstances of their creation and management, as well as their intellectual content, are preserved and demonstrated as clearly and fully as reasonably possible.

The *Glossary* defines the function of *archival description* in this way:

> 1. The process of analyzing, organizing, and recording details about the formal elements of a record or collection of records, such as creator, title, dates, extent, and contents, to facilitate the work's identification, management, and understanding. - 2. The product of such a process.

I will stay close to the spirit of this definition, dealing with description as both an intellectual representation for the user of the collection's arrangement, as well as a guide for discovering, identifying, and gaining access to relevant materials in the collection.

Finally, the *Glossary* economically defines *processing* as

> 1. The arrangement, description, and housing of archival materials for storage and use by patrons.

Again, I will stick closely to this usage of the term, emphasizing that, although *arrangement and description* and *processing* are frequently used interchangeably, the term "processing" also pulls in important related activities, such as conservation treatment actions, and housing and storage of collection materials. This manual will always try to maintain that distinction between the two concepts.

Let me also preface what follows by acknowledging a few prejudices that cannot help but influence everything I have to say in this manual. The first of these is my belief that arrangement and description—and especially arrangement—lie at the very heart of the archival endeavor. While all archival functions are crucial and interdependent, it has always seemed to me that the upstream functions like acquisition and those downstream such as reference are enabled and realized through the arrangement and description work that occurs in the middle. In the acts of arranging and describing an archival collection, we archivists perform the most significant value-adding work.

Second, I do believe that in their relationship to each other, arrangement is the hand and description the glove. The most important intellectual work takes place when we arrange materials in the way that optimizes their accessibility to the people who will use them. Description, although it requires technical ability and good judgment, is nevertheless a *reflection* of arrangement and not a thing in and of itself.

Finally, I believe quite strongly that archival units and manuscript collections are more alike than not. So, although most of the principles of our profession derive from the nature of archives, they apply well, or at least can be easily adapted to, the arrangement and description of manuscript collections. For that reason, I will rarely if ever distinguish between the two in any of the advice in this manual. In the same vein, digital archives do not differ intellectually from nondigital archives. The technologies associated with preserving, managing, and affording access to electronic records disrupt many of our traditional approaches to arrangement and description—sometimes constraining us, but more often creating tremendous new opportunities. Nevertheless, this manual is intended to apply equally to digital records.

Having divulged a few prejudices, I would also like to put forward some basic assumptions that underlie my own views about arrangement and description:

- *Serving users is the paramount objective.* Processing is a resource-intensive activity that can only be justified as a user-service function. We therefore need to evaluate our approaches and methods based on their efficacy in serving the requirements of users. Work on collections that does not ultimately benefit our users should be questioned.
- *Users may be machines.* The descriptive metadata that we share online may be discovered and reused by computer systems on its way to reaching expanded audiences of human users. We therefore need to utilize information standards and technologies in our descriptions that make it as simple as possible for machines to process our descriptive metadata.
- *Description is data.* We have a long history of producing our finding aids as prose documents. But such documents are inflexible and difficult to repurpose, and are hard for networked information systems to understand, parse, and share. Archival description is at heart structured metadata, and we should always apply our standards and technologies as vigorously as possible in capturing, managing, and sharing descriptions.
- *Arrangement is an intellectual exercise.* It is more important to establish and express the intellectual structure inherent in a collection—via our descriptions—than to sequence the physical materials themselves. If we can effectively guide the user from the intellectual arrangement, expressed in a finding aid, to the appropriate collection materials, we can often relax our fixation on physical ordering, especially at very granular levels.
- *Economy of effort is beneficial.* We are frequently tempted to expend unnecessary time and effort in arranging and describing materials. Many collection components do not require intensive physical or intellectual work to make them usable. Reducing our efforts, whenever appropriate, allows us to accumulate resources to get more work done. We should target our efforts at achieving the most beneficial outcomes.
- *Archival principles are tools.* Long-honored concepts like provenance, original order, and records hierarchies should be treated as useful tools to guide our work, rather than as sacred verities. Processing is very often an exercise in creative problem solving; we should be sensitive to optimal user outcomes, rather than slavishly adhering to absolutes. Digital archives, especially, will test many long-standing assumptions.

One other thing to note is that this manual may offer less specific and granular treatment of finding aid creation than did its predecessors. Years back, it may have been easier to identify the form that a finding aid should take (a catalog record, a multilevel narrative finding aid), and then to walk through its parts and pieces, advising how to create the information that belongs in each section. But things have grown more complicated over the past ten years or so. The information we are recording is no longer sequentially organized prose, but rather metadata structured and parsed. The functions of data capture (composing, writing) and data transformation (finding aids as products) have been effectively separated. And the varieties of metadata-capture mechanisms, transformation processes, and output artifacts have expanded greatly. Therefore, it makes more sense for this manual to focus on the standards that explain how to form and capture descriptive metadata, and on the platforms and technologies we might use to capture, transform, and publish our descriptions.

In closing this introduction, I wish to emphasize that this manual, although it treats the topic fully, should not be seen as eclipsing previous manuals written on the same topic and, indeed, bearing the same title. The SAA arrangement and description manuals written by Fredric M. Miller[2] and Kathleen D. Roe[3] contain perspectives, insights, approaches, and information that have certainly not all been transferred wholesale into the current volume. I have leaned on them for sound advice, but I have not replicated them. The reader is advised not to disregard them in seeking a fuller understanding of the important work of arrangement and description.

Why do archivists arrange and describe their collections?

Arrangement and description are (or ought to be) a straightforward set of tools and practices that help people use archives effectively and efficiently. In a nutshell, we do this work so that we can connect users with valuable archival resources better and more easily. All the other phases of work in the archival continuum—acquisition and selection, preservation, public services—certainly focus, these days, on serving the needs of researchers. Each of them advances that goal in their own way. Acquisitions archivists ensure that archives retain the most useful collections, that they are unencumbered by nonarchival dross, and that legal custody and access provisions are established through written agreements. Preservation staff work to make sure that collection materials, physical and digital, endure by maintaining a sustainable preservation environment as well as by performing treatment actions on the most vulnerable materials. Reference archivists and other public services staff work closely and directly with users of archives to make certain they find all materials relevant to their work, they understand and can use descriptive metadata effectively, and they can navigate any impediments to access and use of the materials themselves. Every stage in the archival continuum adds value to a collection.

So, what value is added by the archivists who perform arrangement and description? I like to think about this by way of an analogy to electrical energy. Electrical utilities generate energy, transform it into a practical version that we can use in our homes, and then transmit it directly to our homes where we can engage it via access portals like electrical outlets. However, all of that energy that is always available at the outlet is only *potential* energy. It does not become practical and usable until we actually plug an appliance into the physical outlet. At that point, potential energy is transformed into actual energy. Similarly, all the rich materials received in an acquisition only have *potential* value until they are transformed into a product that users are able to discover, to identify and understand, and to access. We can think about arrangement and description as the suite of activities that together transform that potential value into practical, usable value for researchers.

The value added during processing—creating or restoring a helpful arrangement, explaining the nature of the creator(s) and their relationship to the collection materials, explaining the content and location of all the records in the collection—is that a corpus of archival materials is transformed into a resource that can be discovered, appreciated, and used. This is the function of archival processing and the important role played by the archivists who perform this work. The point of this volume is to help them, and others, understand that work and perform it well.

A Brief History of Archival Arrangement and Description

The premodern world through the nineteenth century

In her introduction to the Dutch Manual,[4] Marjorie Barritt offers a two-sentence assessment of what we generally learn about archival arrangement and description prior to developments in Europe during the eighteenth century:

> As archivists we may have been introduced to archival history as part of our archival education. After learning about papyrus and clay tablets and archives in Assyria, the focus probably shifted to the history of archival development in Europe and the chronology was certainly: respect des fonds from the French, Registraturprinzip from the Germans, and the Manual of Muller, Feith, and Fruin from the Dutch.[5]

This almost dismissive encapsulation probably does not do a great disservice. Even though archives and archivists have existed in some shape or form since the foundational civilizations in the eastern Mediterranean and the Far East, their arrangement and description did not rise (at least in the West) as activities meriting significant thought and methodology until perhaps the French Revolution. It is not difficult to see why this would be so. Archives arise in our ancient history as the products and evidence of official, usually government, business. Recordkeeping begins with the growth of literacy married to the conduct of organized affairs, and the impulse to preserve some essential fraction of these records begins shortly after. But even as literacy itself expands slowly, so too do the means of producing and preserving records act as a considerable brake on the accumulation of records. The earliest archives depended upon technologies like carving wood and stone, incising clay tablets, the laborious production of papyrus and, later, parchment and hand-laid paper. As James O'Toole and Richard Cox observe, the efficient and voluminous production of records depends on a long sequence of technological revolutions:

> Successive technical revolutions in storage media and formats—from clay tablets to papyrus scrolls to the parchment and paper codex, from hand literacy to movable type printing and mass production—made writing easier and more widely available.[6]

The point here is that as long as the production of written records was relatively slow and laborious, the small remnant comprising archives accumulated even more slowly. In cultural and administrative environments of slow and incremental accumulation, it remained possible for a small cadre of recordkeepers and proto-archivists to maintain and access the records in their care without recourse to sophisticated or elaborate systems of arrangement and description. Recordkeepers were no doubt quite free to adopt simple and idiosyncratic sequencing and storage schemes just sophisticated enough to permit their collective memories to do the rest—to ensure they could locate and produce documents upon request. And, for the most part, requesters were few in the days before the advent of public archives and bureaucratic organizations.

At any rate, as Theodore Schellenberg reminds us, "[b]efore the nineteenth century no general principles of archival arrangement had been developed in Europe. As records were received by an archival institution, they were usually incorporated into existing collections in accordance with some predetermined scheme of subject matter, much as books are classified in libraries today."[7] This would all change in the wake of the French Revolution, which heralded a dramatic change from the fairly decentralized and informal approach that had characterized the management of archives up to that time. Ernst Posner (1892–1980), a German-born government archivist (Prussian State Archives, 1921–1935) and archival educator (American University, 1940–1961), who wrote and taught extensively on archival theory and history, identifies three contributions to the history of archives stemming from that era. First, there came a marked movement in the direction of archival centralization on a national level with the establishment of the Archives Nationales (1789), which soon developed into a central archives to which all provincial archives were subordinated. Second, the state acknowledged its responsibility for preserving and managing the documentary heritage of its past. And third, the revolutionaries asserted the principle that archives would be accessible to the public. These ideas became core principles that shaped archival development during the nineteenth and twentieth centuries.[8]

In addition to expanding the concept and social roles of archives, the Archives Nationales, in effect, commenced the rapid expansion of archival holdings by mandating the orderly preservation of records determined to possess enduring value. Whereas in ancient and medieval times it could be argued that arrangement (and description) were not essential activities owing to the comparatively tiny magnitude of archival holdings, this was clearly no longer the case. And, in 1841, the Archives Nationales issued a circular that codified a logical scheme for grouping the records of the French regional and local archives. This circular established certain tenets that became the foundation for the modern principles of archival arrangement. Schellenberg relates them as follows:

1. Records were to be grouped into *fonds*,[9] that is, all records that originated with any particular institution, such as an administrative authority, a corporation, or a family, were to be grouped together and were to be considered the *fonds* of that particular institution.
2. Records within the *fonds* were to be arranged by subject-matter groups, and each group was to be assigned a definite place in relation to other groups.
3. Items within the subject-matter groups were to be arranged as circumstances might dictate, either chronologically, geographically, or alphabetically.[10]

So, the 1841 circular is the first articulation of the cornerstone principle of archival arrangement, *respect des fonds*, which basically states that the records created and maintained by a particular entity should be maintained together, neither split apart nor merged with those of a separate entity. This principle was refined somewhat in 1881 in a regulation issued by the State Archives of Prussia, which established the related principles of *provenienzprinzip* and *registraturprinzip*, the former declaring that all records, including the major components of a *fonds*, are to be grouped and maintained according to the administrative units that created them, and the latter holding that the records comprising any given administrative unit should be maintained in the order that they were registered by the agency that created them. This latter was a distinct departure from the French practice of rearranging the materials in a *fonds* according to some arbitrary scheme.[11]

In 1890, a convocation of state archivists from throughout the Netherlands attempted to reach agreement on how archival holdings should be arranged in Dutch repositories. They proceeded to develop classification schemes "based upon the Vermeulen-Muller-Van Riemsdijk principle that each archival group should be kept separate and that all documents from one provenance should be kept together."[12] Muller, Feith, and Fruin then took it a big step farther when, "[t]o the principle of provenance, the Dutch Manual added the principle of *original order*: not only should every document be restored to the archive group to which it originally belonged, but within that archive group to its original place. This was derived from the German Registraturprinzip."[13]

The development of arrangement and description practices in the United States took a somewhat different course than they did in European countries, where public archives and private manuscripts were all subject to the same rules of archival practice. The establishment of two separate national commissions by the American Historical Association—the Historical Manuscripts Commission (1895) and the Public Archives Commission (1899)—created a fork in the road that allowed two separate and distinct traditions to emerge. As a result of this divide, historical manuscript collections that flourished in university and private research libraries were generally treated with arrangement and description practices that evolved from library practices of classification and subject cataloging, along with an inclination to focus on and catalog individual items. Public archives took root in the federal government and, especially, in the several state archival institutions that emerged in the twentieth century following the lead of the Alabama Department of History and Archives (1901). Those governmental institutions largely followed the archival practices of their European peers.[14]

The manuscripts tradition can be traced to the early 1800s, when the aging revolutionary generation incorporated what became hundreds of state, local, and national historical societies and museums, one central purpose of which was to preserve published and unpublished documentation of America's founding and early history. These societies, later joined by college and university libraries, amassed substantial holdings of manuscript materials created by individuals and families, voluntary associations, religious institutions, and—not incidentally—records of local government units. Their purposes and products were basically twofold: to gather together and preserve historically important documents and to organize them into "collections" that were then disseminated widely as published editions.[15]

The archival principles and traditions taking shape in Europe did not influence the historians and antiquarians who dominated these early manuscript repositories. Instead, pursuing historiographical principles and the efficient prosecution of their own publishing projects, they tended to arrange their manuscript materials in arbitrary schemes based around topics, chronological periods, people, and events. So, they ignored principles of provenance and original order in favor of, presumably, facilitating historical research and documentary publications. The meetings and publications of the Historical Manuscripts Commission served to reinforce this approach, which became fairly standard practice throughout historical societies and university special collections well into the twentieth century.

This very nonarchival approach to arrangement and description, known as the *manuscript tradition*, persisted well into the 1970s,[16] most typically resulting in collections in which the individual manuscripts were arranged in long, largely unbroken sequences that were primarily chronological or alphabetical (by correspondent or author). The arrangement tradition practiced in public archives emphasized preserving records according to the units in which they were received and, therefore, as both a practical and philosophical matter, deprecated the rearrangement of the individual items comprising each unit, in the belief that the inherent structure of the record groups, series, and files preserved and explained much of the meaning of the records. Manuscripts practitioners, to the contrary, routinely rearranged items within a collection to achieve the chronological, alphabetical, or other sequencing they desired.

The "registers" or "descriptive inventories" that served as the principal finding aids for these manuscript collections often took the form of extended essays about the contents and creators of the materials, typically bringing in a good deal of additional narrative about the contemporaneous historical context. As you can imagine, the arrangement and description protocols supporting such detailed narratives were extremely time consuming viewed against the comparatively light-handed approach accorded to records units in public archives. These approaches were sustainable if collections in general remained relatively small. However, the twentieth century was about to unleash technologies and recordkeeping practices that would seriously disrupt the traditional approaches taken by manuscript repositories, and this would in turn reshape arrangement and description practices in general beginning around the 1980s.

The impact of explosive growth in the twentieth century

Consider the many (and relatively inexpensive) document recording technologies that came to separate twentieth-century record-making and recordkeeping practices from those of preceding centuries: typewriters, carbon paper, mimeograph machines and photocopiers, snapshot photography, instant commercial printing, and the ubiquitous business and personal computers and printers that allow us to create and easily preserve myriad drafts and variant copies of documents. It takes very little imagination to appreciate the profound effect caused by the enthusiastic uptake of these technologies in all areas of human activity. By midcentury, and multiplied by the exploding size of governments and commercial organizations, the output of official and business records had increased almost exponentially.

The rapid evolution of these technologies, and especially personal computing, had a similar effect on personal and family papers, and the records of nonbusiness organizations, by the close of the twentieth century. Although the impact on public and corporate archives was profound, it was perhaps even greater on manuscript repositories, which clearly lacked arrangement and description approaches and processes that could manage the increasing size of new collections, as well as the rapidly rising tide of new acquisitions. As a result, a large majority of archival repositories reported extensive backlogs of unprocessed manuscript collections around the end of the century.[17]

In the face of this changing reality, archivists in manuscript repositories began to distance themselves from the arrangement and description methodologies of the past and to recommend adopting approaches heretofore associated largely with government archives. And, as a corollary, they began to stress the importance of taking economical approaches to processing as a necessary weapon in the fight against growing archival backlogs.[18]

These archivists argued as well that adopting traditional public archives approaches to arrangement and description not only saves time and effort, but also makes good theoretical sense. This was true because larger units of personal papers and organizational collections began to assume the characteristics of true archival collections and were therefore amenable to similar treatments. As early as 1965, Schellenberg noted that "[r]ecent private papers often have the organic quality of public records. . . . They are often comprised of series pertaining to specific activities or transactions or consisting of specific record types. And recent records produced by economic, religious, cultural, and social institutions and organizations have an archival character."[19]

As this evolution in arrangement and description practices moved along, another important development began to take shape: the adoption of descriptive standards. Archivists, for a variety of reasons, had long resisted the sort of description and cataloging standards that their library peers had been building since the mid-twentieth century. Standards are essential in shaping and developing uniformity and predictability within a community's practice. They allow us to share our descriptive products outside of our own repositories by constructing uniform, rules-based models for such specific things as catalog records and detailed finding aids, as well as for the logical structure of archival descriptive metadata.

These notable benefits seem obvious to us today, so it is somewhat puzzling to realize that we were slow to warm up to the idea of standardization and that it took years of struggle and a fair amount of internecine conflict and resistance before we got on board with our current rich suite of descriptive standards. But archivists have always had, at least at a repository level, an individualistic streak derived in part from beliefs that *our* mission, *our* collections, and *our* users are unique and, therefore, *our* approaches, methods, and finding aids must also be unique. The mantra in any repository was often: this is how *we* do it; this is what *our* users need; this is what works for *us*.

Those assumptions proved to be formidable obstacles, and the effort to overcome them did not gain real traction until the mid-1980s, when the archival profession strove to develop a cataloging standard to parallel and interoperate with the MARC standard that the library community had used since the 1960s.[20] Over some notable resistance, descriptive specialists within the American archives community were able to publish the MARC-AMC standard in 1987 and, over the next few years, to widely demonstrate its utility in providing a standard that would enable archivists to expose their collections and promote their discovery in local online systems and then to share those records in larger bibliographic utilities like OCLC and RLIN.[21] As the benefits in terms of outcomes and efficiencies became obvious, standards aversion began to dissolve. Within ten years, archivists would add new standards aimed at sharing and defining the content of fuller archival descriptive forms. The movement toward identifying needs for standardization, and then developing them, has progressed with increasing energy ever since, and the results are apparent on the rich SAA web pages devoted to sharing archival standards.[22]

The most recognizable of these standards, beyond the MARC-AMC format (*MARC format for Archives and Manuscripts Control*, 1983), are ISAD(G) (*General International Standard for Archival Description*, 1992), EAD (*Encoded Archival Description*, 1995), ISAAR-CPF (*International Standard Archival Authority Record for Corporate Bodies, Persons and Families*, 1996), DACS (*Describing Archives: A Content Standard*, 2004 and under continuous revision thereafter), and EAC-CPF (*Encoded Archival Context: Corporate Bodies, Persons, and Families*, 2011). These standards are differentiated and explained in greater detail later in the manual.

Arrangement and description in the twenty-first century

Not quite two decades into the twenty-first century, archival arrangement and description is already dealing with some profound and escalating changes that both challenge its long-standing assumptions and approaches and provide extraordinary opportunities to serve users better. Not surprisingly, rapidly evolving computer technologies have driven most of these innovations. These technologies are forcing archivists out of their comfort zones and straining their resources but, at the same time, serving up tools and practices that make it correspondingly easier to absorb the changes.

Digital archives

The proliferation of hardware and software that places digitization of collections within the reach of most repositories, as well as the explosion of born-digital records, have created a demand for direct access to digital archives. These have also encouraged a popular misconception that the totality of archives *are* digital already or soon will be. This, in turn, intensifies a drumbeat for greater access to digital materials, a development that brings challenges and opportunities. Repositories are carving out resources to scramble together digitization teams, often as part of their processing units. As a result, an access-focused, web-scale approach to digitizing records has quickly become an adjunct part of the processing workflow in many repositories.[23] Some of these digitization approaches are curatorially driven, while others are driven by user demand. In any case, the rapidly growing digital content on repository websites is quickly shaping arrangement and description practices, producing innovations that help to automate elements of descriptive metadata creation and the delivery of content to end users faster, in more streamlined and innovative ways.

Finding aid creation

Somewhat related to the digital records juggernaut, changes have occurred in archival descriptive metadata and the methodologies for creating and sharing them. The EAD finding aid appeared at the end of the century and has matured through three versions in the past twenty years. Out of attempts to apply descriptive standards in more sophisticated and helpful ways, EAD has become a richer structure for encoding and expressing well-structured descriptive content. While this sometimes made it daunting for archivists to master EAD, a variety of software packages and helper tools has emerged that smooth the process of finding aid creation and publication. They provide archivists with a host of XML (Extensible Markup Language) encoding templates, web forms, macros, and XSLT (Extensible Stylesheet Language Transformations) stylesheets (among other tools), all of which make it easier for archivists to join the finding aid encoding community. They also take much of the drudgery out of metadata entry, making archival description somewhat easier (or at least more standardized) overall and have certainly made processing archivists more productive.

At the same time, the traditional conception of the finding aid as a purpose-built document intended to be carefully read and absorbed by users, is becoming increasingly tenuous. The movement to envision archival description as structured metadata, rather than as simple prose, has encouraged archivists to create and store descriptive information within flexible structures—spreadsheets, databases, collection management systems (CMS), and so forth—that either serve out a finding aid on the fly as a user-requested service, or that bypass the full finding aid entirely by presenting to users only the specific units of descriptive metadata that satisfy their requests.

EAC-CPF and context description

As EAD reached maturity, a related working group developed a companion XML-based encoding standard—*Encoded Archival Context: Corporate Bodies, Persons, and Families*—capable of capturing and publishing rich information about the creators of archival collections, the contexts of their creation and use, and the complex interrelationships that bind creators, other actors, and collection resources together.[24] Still in its infancy in the United States (it is becoming more widely used in Europe) and depending on a few demonstration projects to move it forward, EAC-CPF has great potential for creating powerful aggregations of archival authority records for entities of all sorts. It also has the potential to accomplish a long-standing descriptive goal: to separate the description of *context* from that of *content*.

Records in Contexts (RiC)

At the time of this writing, an International Council on Archives (ICA) Expert Group in Archival Description is working to develop a new structural standard for archival description that marries several existing standards, resulting in a new conceptual model (2016) and an ontology (under development) for a more complex and potentially powerful approach to describing archival resources and agents. Rather than viewing description as essentially a top-down, isolated description of a single collection, RiC aims at comprehending archival description as an expression of the multidimensional web of relationships that exist among diverse records, collections, people, and functions. This almost breathtaking change has the potential to upend many of our current descriptive approaches and practices.

Archival management systems

The past twenty years have also witnessed the growth and maturation of bespoke collection management systems (CMS) for archival holdings. At the time of this writing, the preeminent US project is ArchivesSpace, the result of two merged predecessors: Archivists' Toolkit and Archon. ArchivesSpace, like integrated library systems in the bibliographic world, provides archivists with 1) a form-based back end for entering descriptive metadata in structured ways, 2) a stable environment for storing and managing those data, and 3) a suite of public services that can reformat collection data into a variety of outputs (EAD, HTML, PDF, MARC, and increasingly sophisticated products) to satisfy user requests.

Meanwhile, the ICA has developed its own CMS—AtoM—which also incorporates a powerful public search system capable of exploiting the rich semantics in structured archival description. These systems are proving to be a boon to small and midsize repositories that lack the staffing and resources of their larger peers. CMS packages allow them to start capturing structured descriptive and administrative data about their collections from the point of acquisition, through accessioning, arrangement, description, and finding aid web publication—without redundant effort and without extensive mastery of descriptive standards and complex digital tools. This development should have a significant positive impact on the number of repositories that are able to 1) manage their collection information as structured data and 2) make their descriptive products available to an online audience of users.

It seems likely that we will see extension and maturation in all of these emerging developments. This should bode well for the sophistication and efficiency of our processing endeavors and, especially, for more beneficial outcomes for the users of archival resources.

Core Archival Concepts

Before launching into the necessary work of explaining the foundational principles that undergird arrangement and description, it is first necessary to understand something of the essential nature of archives themselves. Archives are quite different from library and museum holdings, and having a sense of those distinctions helps us understand the requirements for arranging and describing them. Theodore Schellenberg, one of the truly formative American archival theorists,[25] does a typically concise job of presenting those essentials in a compact and accessible way. He identifies several important characteristics of archives and manuscripts, which I have simplified here into a few bullet points:

- *They are primary materials.* Unlike most published information sources, archives are firsthand accounts of events created contemporaneously with those events. There have been no significant intermediaries between the event and its documentation or recording. Furthermore, archives do not *interpret* the event, but simply bear witness to its occurrence. These characteristics lend a singular and powerful credibility to primary sources as forms of documentation. They are presumed to be as close as possible to neutral or unbiased records of events.

- *They are organic materials.* Archives are the natural product of organized activity. Human beings, whether they operate as agents of an organization or as private individuals, create and share records as routine consequences of their many activities. These records flow out of purposeful action—its result and its evidence. As a result, they are born with a certain implicit order and structure already imposed upon them. To one extent or another, they have been grouped and sequenced by their creators to facilitate the performance of the activities from which they result. This has important implications for their subsequent arrangement.

    An important corollary is that, because they result naturally from business transactions, archival materials have not been *intentionally* created to facilitate research. They were instead created to facilitate business, whether the business of some organization or that of an individual. Because of that, much of their meaning emanates from the circumstances and the context of their creation. If records are removed from that context and mixed with records created in a different context, their meaning and significance are likely to be diluted and probably confused.

- *They are heterogeneous in content.* Consider the most ubiquitous of archival artifacts: the letter. While a letter might focus on a single topic, it can just as easily address a number of topics. And those topics may be wide ranging. Think about a letter home from a college student. That epistle might range over a dozen or more topics as the writer attempts to sum up her recent experience and reconnect with family members. Conversely, a publication tends to focus on a particular subject and can therefore be classified according to that subject. Archival collections and subunits, like the individual documents that comprise them, defy classification and tend to confound any arrangement schemes that attempt to group materials topically.

- *They have a collective rather than an individual significance.* Because the materials comprising any archival unit all arise from a particular activity, or some set of related activities, they tend to possess a cohesive, mutually reinforcing character. Unlike a publication, which is a standalone information packet that can be moved from place to place without losing any of its meaning, archives depend upon their situational context—their adjacency—for much of their meaning. It is the natural aggregation of documents that provides their full meaning. When the items comprising an archival unit are dispersed, a collective loss of meaning ensues, perhaps even basic understandability.

- *They are unique.* A published work may be ubiquitous, and the content of an entire library may essentially duplicate that found in other libraries. This is not the case with archives and manuscripts; most of the documents comprising an archives will not exist in any other archives. This imposes burdens on preservation and access.
- *They are not limited by format or medium.* Generally speaking, a publication will have a particular form and medium. But the materials comprising an archives or manuscript collection may include many formats and recording media, none of which is exclusive to archives. These materials derive their status as archives from the fact of their having resulted from the activity(ies) that the archival collection documented or facilitated. This quality has important implications for archival arrangement when it comes to dispersing or removing materials on the basis of their formats or media.
- *Their composition is varied.* Following on from the previous point, any given collection or record unit may contain items in various formats (bound or loose textual materials, images, audio recordings) or recorded on various media (paper, film, magnetic media, wood, digital drives). This creates complications for arrangement, description, and storage of individual archival collections that do not arise in libraries, where the information units (e.g., books) tend to be uniform and self-contained.[26]

Schellenberg also emphasizes that the essential nature of archives and manuscripts makes certain methodological demands in our arrangement and description practices:

- *Archival practices apply equally to the materials comprising manuscript collections.* Since the mid-twentieth century, little reason exists to believe that practices developed for public archival units cannot and should not be applied to the great majority of manuscript collections. The increasing size and complexity of such collections argue strongly for archival approaches. Consider, in this regard, business and nonprofit organizations and their leaders, religious and social institutions, politicians and political organizations, not to mention the exploding ability of typical individuals and families to create records of their activities. Truly, the circumstances under which contemporary manuscript collections are created, and the nature and extent of the records created, are very similar to those created by public entities.
- *Techniques applicable to publications are not applicable without modification to archives.* As we saw in looking at the European antecedents of modern archival practices, trying to make archival materials conform to library practices of arrangement and classification were not sustainable and often produced deleterious results for researchers.
- *Approaches and methods should be standardized.* Standardization of methods yields many positive benefits. Standardizing methods of arrangement and description from collection to collection, as well as from repository to repository, greatly benefits the users of archives. A researcher only needs to figure it out once and is able to work more efficiently thereafter, freed from the need to learn widely differing systems and approaches time and time again. Standardizing practices also benefits the repository and its archivists, as it makes processing more efficient and economical. Standardized processing methods also make it easier to create more uniform and sharable tools, like finding aids or data capture templates, that can reduce drudgery and speed up repetitious work.

- ***Archival methods should be applied to manuscript holdings in libraries.*** Methods and tools that work in traditional archival repositories ought to work for manuscript collections housed in institutions like libraries, museums, businesses, and religious organizations. It is ineffective and confusing to treat archival materials in very different ways across institutions. And it greatly hampers our ability to share collection information with each other, especially in networked environments.

This concludes a whirlwind overview of the purpose, history, and key concepts of archival arrangement and description. I hope that it has brought home a few things: that arrangement and description are functions that lie at the heart of archival practice; that arrangement is essentially an intellectual exercise, rather than a physical one; that description serves to reflect arrangement; that the key principles and approaches are as applicable to manuscript collections as they are to archives proper; that those principles and approaches should be looked at as useful tools, rather than as absolutes. We have also seen that the goal of arrangement and description is to serve users; that those users may increasingly be machines, as well as people; and that to serve all users most effectively and efficiently we must approach description as data, rather than as prose.

In the next chapter we will return to archival principles, this time taking a much deeper look at the fundamental concepts underlying archival arrangement. We will see how those principles emerged to support evolving archival practice and how they have continued to influence and shape our policies and practices through the present day.

NOTES

[1] Richard Pearce-Moses, *A Glossary of Archival and Records Terminology* (Chicago: Society of American Archivists, 2005).

[2] Fredric M. Miller, *Arranging and Describing Archives and Manuscripts* (Chicago: Society of American Archivists, 1990).

[3] Kathleen D. Roe, *Arranging and Describing Archives and Manuscripts* (Chicago: Society of American Archivists, 2005).

[4] S. Muller, J. A. Feith, and R. Fruin, *Manual for the Arrangement and Description of Archives*, translation of the second edition by Arthur H. Leavitt (Chicago: Society of American Archivists, 2003). Systematic arrangement is discussed on pp. 48–59. Generally referred to informally as the "Dutch Manual," it was published in 1898 and authored by a three-member commission of prominent Dutch archivists appointed by the Netherlands Association of Archivists (*Vereniging van Archivarissen in Nederland*) in 1895. VAN was the first professional association for archivists ever formed. Muller was city archivist of Utrecht, Feith the state archivist for Groningen, and Fruin the state archivist of Zeeland.

[5] Marjorie Rabe Barritt, "Coming to America: Dutch *Archivistiek* and American Archival Practice," *Archival Issues* 18, no. 1 (1993): 43.

[6] James M. O'Toole and Richard J. Cox, *Understanding Archives and Manuscripts* (Chicago: Society of American Archivists, 2006), 6.

[7] T. R. Schellenberg, *Modern Archives: Principles and Techniques* (Chicago: University of Chicago Press, 1956; Midway reprint, 1975), 169.

[8] Ernst Posner, "Some Aspects of Archival Development since the French Revolution," *American Archivist* 3 (1940): 161–62.

[9] The term *fonds*, used more widely in archival communities outside of the United States, is explained in the *Glossary* as an intellectual construct encompassing the "entire body of records of an organization, family, or individual that have been created or accumulated as the result of an organic process reflecting the functions of the creator."

[10] Schellenberg, *Modern Archives*, 170.

[11] Schellenberg, *Modern Archives*, 173–75.

[12] Eric Ketelaar, "Muller, Feith and Fruin," *Miscellanea Carlos Wyffels: Archives et Bibliotheques de Belgique* 57 (1986): 256.

[13] Barritt, "Coming to America: Dutch Archivistiek and American Archival Practice," 47.

14. T. R. Schellenberg, *The Management of Archives* (New York: Columbia University Press, 1965), 23–28.
15. O'Toole and Cox, *Understanding Archives and Manuscripts*, 56–58.
16. Roe, *Arranging and Describing Archives and Manuscripts*, 36.
17. Mark A. Greene and Dennis Meissner, "More Product, Less Process: Revamping Traditional Archival Processing," *American Archivist* 68, no. 2 (2005): 210–11.
18. Several good examples of this changing attitude are also excellent sources of sound processing advice in their own rights: Megan Desnoyers, "When Is It Processed?," *Midwestern Archivist* 7 (1982); Helen W. Slotkin and Karen T. Lynch, "An Analysis of Processing Procedures: The Adaptable Approach," *American Archivist* 45, no. 2 (1982); St. Johnsbury Athenaeum Archives, *Archives Processing Manual*, draft 2 (May 2001), http://datadrivenarchives.pbworks.com/f/Processing+Manual+St.+Johnsbury+Athenaeum.pdf, captured at https://perma.cc/LS7F-UGZ7. See the bibliography for additional examples.
19. Schellenberg, *The Management of Archives*, 31.
20. Some of the struggle to develop descriptive standards for archivists is related in Lisa Weber, "Archival Description Standards: Concepts, Principles, and Methodologies," *American Archivist* 52, no. 4 (1989): 504–13. This entire issue is devoted to contemporaneous standards initiatives within SAA and contains other useful articles by David Bearman and Richard Szary.
21. The historical development of these archival description standards is related very succinctly in Roe, *Arranging and Describing Archives and Manuscripts*, 36–44.
22. The descriptive standards currently hosted or promoted by SAA are explained and linked to on the Society's "Standards Portal," https://www2.archivists.org/standards.
23. See for example Jennifer Schaffner, Francine Snyder, and Shannon Supple, *Scan and Deliver: Managing User-initiated Digitization in Special Collections and Archives* (Dublin, OH: OCLC Research, 2011), https://www.oclc.org/content/dam/research/publications/library/2011/2011-05.pdf, captured at https://perma.cc/W4PJ-NS5H.
24. Brief information about EAC-CPF and its development is available on the EAC-CPF official website at http://eac.staatsbibliothek-berlin.de/about, captured at https://perma.cc/2HH9-9G6C. More extensive information is found in Katherine M. Wisser, "Describing Entities and Identities: The Development and Structure of Encoded Archival Context—Corporate Bodies, Persons, and Families," *Journal of Library Metadata* 11 (2011): 166–75.
25. Dr. Theodore Roosevelt Schellenberg (1903–1970), historian and archivist, was one of the pioneers (1935–1963) of the US National Archives and perhaps the preeminent developer of a body of archival writing and practice that adjusted European archival theory to accommodate the unique circumstances that characterized American public records. Schellenberg's initial National Archives appointment threw him into the massive survey of federal executive department records being undertaken by the young agency. That and later assignments concentrated him in pursuing what became the central focus of his career: the development, systemization, and standardization of archival principles and techniques in the United States, based on the understanding that the European records experience had only limited applicability to the arrangement and description of the records comprising American archives, which were exclusively *modern* in scope and character. Their immense volume across the federal agencies forced American archivists to deal with records *en masse* and to develop appraisal and processing approaches appropriately scaled. Over the course of his career, in a variety of leadership positions, Schellenberg promulgated a systematic set of principles for managing archives, wrote manuals of practice to guide work at the National Archives, trained a generation of its archivists, and wrote and spoke widely to professional archivists around the world. His stature at the time of his death resulted in "In Memoriam: Theodore R. Schellenberg, 1903–1970," *American Archivist* 33, no. 2 (1970): 190–202, featuring separate eulogies by seven prominent archival leaders. For more biographical information see Jane Smith, "Theodore R. Schellenberg: Americanizer and Popularizer," *American Archivist* 44, no. 4 (1981): 317.
26. Schellenberg, *The Management of Archives*: 65–74. The nature of archives and archival methods is more fully, and very accessibly, presented in James M. O'Toole and Richard J. Cox, *Understanding Archives and Manuscripts* (Chicago: Society of American Archivists, 2006), esp. chapters 3 and 4.

2

Principles of Archival Arrangement

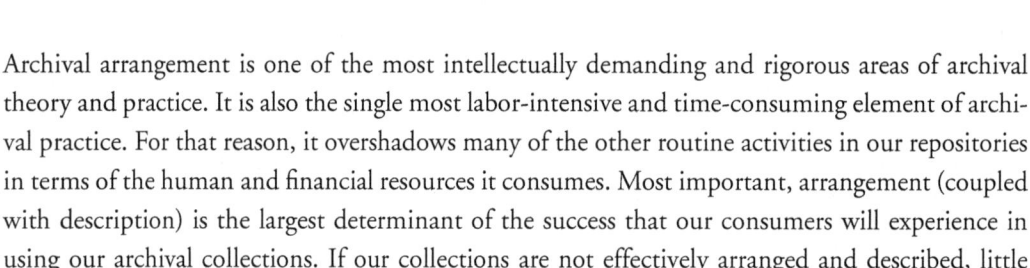

Archival arrangement is one of the most intellectually demanding and rigorous areas of archival theory and practice. It is also the single most labor-intensive and time-consuming element of archival practice. For that reason, it overshadows many of the other routine activities in our repositories in terms of the human and financial resources it consumes. Most important, arrangement (coupled with description) is the largest determinant of the success that our consumers will experience in using our archival collections. If our collections are not effectively arranged and described, little hope exists that researchers will be able to discover, identify, and locate the archival materials relevant to their research.

It is therefore no surprise that such a significant share of archival theory and pedagogy has been devoted to helping archivists arrange their holdings in the most effective and economical ways possible. The bibliography to this work captures much of that theory and practical advice. All of it rests on several fundamental principles foundational to arranging archival materials.

Arrangement Options

A fundamental characteristic of archival collections is their need to be arranged. They may need to be arranged physically; they certainly need to be arranged intellectually, but more on that distinction later on. Whether we are contemplating a "traditional" aggregation of paper-based materials; mixed materials including paper, photographic materials, and sound and moving-image media; or even a collection composed entirely of digital files, the archivist nevertheless faces a large number of items that must be arranged into one or more sequences to be understood and retrieved by their users.

Various options present themselves: sequencing chronologically, arranging by some alphabetical scheme, organizing collection materials by events or subject topics. These have all been tried many times in many places, with generally less than optimal results. In years past, collections of personal papers were frequently arranged in a largely unbroken chronological sequence with the justification that lives are lived chronologically. The chief trouble with this or any other simplistic scheme is that using such a one-dimensional arrangement obliterates the rich structure and dimensionality inherent in archives. One loses a general view in favor of a very particularistic view, which is unhelpful in understanding the papers' creator and the circumstances of their creation. A second weakness in such an arrangement scheme is that it requires a wholesale, item-level dismantling and reassembly of the collection, thus rendering the arrangement process an unconscionably expensive piece of work.

For these reasons, archival thinkers beginning with the Dutch Manual have advised a *systematic* approach[1] to arrangement that is based upon, and takes full advantage of, the essential characteristics of archival materials. Those characteristics, and their utility in shaping approaches to arranging archives, are manifested in the *principles* of archival arrangement presented in the sections that follow.

Respect des Fonds, Provenance, and the Archival Whole

As we saw earlier in considering the history of arrangement and description, arrangement was probably a minor issue in ancient and medieval archives, largely for two reasons. First, accumulations tended to be small, and recordkeepers could control and service the records in their custody with little recourse to formal arrangement regimes. Second, the universe of researchers was similarly small, before the relatively recent expectation of public access, and those researchers were generally insiders who could be presumed to understand the nature and extent of the materials to which they required access. These circumstances changed significantly in Europe after 1789, and formal arrangement increasingly became a requirement for ensuring effective internal management and researcher access.

In the early decades of the nineteenth century, scholars started to dominate administrative practices in European archives, resulting in arrangement schemes that reflected prevailing historical, antiquarian, and publishing interests. Administrators compromised the integrity of archival record groups as they selected and removed materials from diverse administrative units to form topical collections reflecting academic specialties of the day. French archives administrators, trained as librarians or as historians, began to manage the growing accumulation of records under archival control by actively creating research collections based around such themes as historical events, geographic locations, and people. Such research collections were often assembled by removing relevant materials from diverse archives "groups." As a result, the context of the removed and reassembled materials, which illuminated how, when, and by whom they were created and managed, became lost. And with that loss came a degradation in the research value of the materials themselves.

As Posner notes, "A change was bound to come. The principle of *respect pour les fonds*, rising from the conviction that archives bodies correspond to a former or existing administrative unit and should be preserved accordingly, was proclaimed in Belgium and France about 1840 and made its way during the following decades."[2] Although subsequent generations of archivists have enshrined this principle as received wisdom, in reality it was a practical expedient designed to restrain the alarming dismemberment of archival units and the chaos that ensued. The principle was also acknowledged to be clear and simple enough to guide the work of the growing cohort of inexperienced archives employees.[3] *Respect des fonds* declared simply that the overall corpus of records resulting from a single high-level administrative entity—for example, the records of the Foreign Office—should be maintained as an indivisible whole and that no materials from other discrete governmental entities should be added into them. That was the extent of it, its proponents not much concerned with how the many records comprising the *fonds* should themselves be arranged.

Schellenberg points out that the "French principle of *respect des fonds* . . . was made more precise and restrictive in application by Prussian archivists, who formulated the *Provenienzprinzip*, the equivalent of the modern principle of provenance."[4] Provenance basically asserts that the major subunits comprising a *fonds* should also be treated as indivisible organic units. Underlying this principle was the clear recognition that the major administrative units within the *fonds* each had their own specific circumstances of creation and their own administrative history. They had their own leaders and functionaries, their own employees, and their own offices with their own record-keeping systems and use patterns. The principle of provenance therefore asserts that the principal record units within an archival *fonds* or collection should be kept separate and distinct from each other. Furthermore, no records should be removed to add to some other unit and no materials from another separate unit should be added to them.

Schellenberg calls attention to several practical and important reasons for respecting and applying the principle of provenance in arranging archives and manuscripts:

- *The principle helps to protect the evidential value in archives.* The archival collection or series was originally compiled and arranged to facilitate and document the very entities and transactions that created them. Because of that, as a discrete body of materials, they serve as primary and impartial evidence of that history. If they were to be separated and rearranged, that body of evidence would be compromised or lost. This is what we mean when we assert that archives possess evidential value. And the individual items in the archival unit only convey their full meaning through their context as individual parts of a larger whole. To atomize them is to lose that larger meaning.
- *The principle considers the organic nature of the materials to which it is applied.* Unlike works created for publication, archival materials tend to result in a natural and fairly unconscious manner from the business or personal activities that they initially facilitate and thereafter document. A physician drafts a series of case notes to assist with the treatment of her patient, with no intention of their widespread dissemination or general public use. But becoming part of her patient's archives (or her own) transforms those notes into evidence that can be used by a researcher seeking information on some aspect of disease treatment. This "unconsciousness" of creation has been recognized to confer on archives the status of being comparatively free of the bias and premeditation that can compromise documentation. And that quality makes them reliable research sources.
- *The principle encourages archivists to deal with materials collectively.* In the example above, the various documents created or compiled by the physician—they might include textual notes, voice recordings, database query results, printed matter,

and photographs—achieve their full value, indeed their understandability, by virtue of being accumulated together as a patient case file. The individual documents support each other to create a larger, more important, story. If those individual documents were separated and subsequently filed into diverse locations, that story could easily be lost, and the individual documents would contain only limited value. Provenance helps preserve this important collectivity.

- *The principle facilitates the arrangement of the materials.* When the organic groupings of materials are preserved, the mechanics of archival arrangement become straightforward and a great deal of very time-consuming labor can be reduced. Provenance helps suggest a logical structure for arranging the materials comprising almost any collection, freeing the archivist from having to invent one.
- *The principle facilitates the description of the materials.* By the same token, the natural groupings suggested by applying the principle of provenance provide archivists with an intellectual structure they can use to more easily explain the physical arrangement of the materials, as well as their content. This ability helps us guide researchers more effectively and, again, can save a great deal of labor and descriptive verbiage.[5]

So, how do we apply the principle of provenance to arrangement and description? First of all, we should be careful to maintain the integrity of any archives or manuscript collection. We should ensure that all the materials produced and maintained as a collection remain together. As a corollary, we should also ensure that we do not remove any materials from the collection for placement in some other, separate body of materials. Similarly, we should not allow materials from a separate collection or record group to be added into the collection at hand.

We should apply this same practice to the various series that comprise the collection. All the series that form parts of the collection should remain with the collection, and all of the materials that comprise any given series should be maintained together as a discrete series. Materials created and maintained as part of a series should not be removed for addition to some other series within the collection. And items from other series should not be brought into the series at hand. The organic character of each series ought to be preserved. However, the principle of provenance does not require the archivist to maintain any particular sequence of series within a collection. Within the collection that they comprise, the individual series may be arranged into any sequence that facilitates research and the management of the materials.

It is fairly easy to see how provenance works in a traditional setting like the government archives to which it was originally applied. As an example, the National Archives of the United States comprises many record groups (*fonds*) spanning the history and breadth of the federal government. A significant instance of these comprises the Records of the Office of Education (Record Group 12), which divides into the following major administrative units:

- Office of the Commissioner of Education
- Office of the Assistant Commissioner
- Assistant Commissioner for Vocational Education
- Special Projects and Programs 1933–69
- Field Offices

Respect des fonds tells us to keep the records of the Office of Education together, as an organic whole, and to keep them separate from the records of other major departments of government like the Office of the Judiciary and the Department of State, both of which have completely different purposes, mandates, and administrative histories. The principle of provenance simply requires that the records comprising each of the five major administrative units of the Office of Education should likewise, and for very similar reasons, be kept together and not intermingled with records from any of the other four units. Each of these units represents a discrete administrative office within the parent department with a unique function, activities, personnel, and operational history. If we were to combine records from the five units, we would lose those important distinctions. We would lose our sense of the relationships of those units to each other and to the parent agency, and we would likely confuse the meaning of the records themselves, as much of that meaning results from their clustering with other closely related documents.

The principle can also be applied with equal validity to administrative units beneath the major entities described above. For example, three large subsidiary offices report to the Office of the Assistant Commissioner:

- Division of Higher Education
- Division of International Education
- Service Division

Provenance tells us that, for the same reasons, it is equally important to preserve the records of these offices as distinct and separate clusters within the Assistant Commissioner's records. The context of creation is important at *any* administrative level to preserve administrative relationships and clarity, and transmit the full meaning and significance of the documents themselves. Preserving these administrative distinctions within the records produced by the agency helps us understand the history and operations of the agency and its important administrative units, and it also ensures that the purpose, meaning, and value of the individual records comprising the units are preserved.

While we can all probably appreciate the fact that provenance performs an important function in preserving administrative relationships within traditional archives, it can be just as relevant in arranging manuscript collections, whether organizational or personal. It is deceptively easy to see collections of personal papers as one-dimensional aggregations of letters, diaries, photos, emails, and so forth, with little inherent structure that might require a provenance-based arrangement scheme. But people are complicated entities, and nearly all lives represent suites of rather discrete activities, which produce documentation that naturally falls into organic groupings.

Consider a hypothetical, but not atypical, example of such a person. Jane Doe is a lawyer who manages a small family law practice out of her California home. She shares her home with a young son and stays closely engaged with the neighborhood elementary school that he attends. Since her high school days, she has been keenly interested in environmental affairs, especially as they affect her home state. Lately, she has become increasingly involved in racial justice issues—joining a few citizen groups and participating in a couple of California marches. Add to this a genealogy hobby she picked up from her siblings that has resulted in a lot of recordkeeping activity.

If we can assume that Doe naturally creates records in most of these core activities in her life, it becomes apparent that they will possess a rich dimensionality and structure that calls out for applying the provenance principle in their subsequent arrangement. See Figure 1 for a hypothetical collection of documents that might be the organic result of Doe's activities.

> **Jane Doe Papers**
>
> **Law Practice**
> - Client files
> - Tax returns
> - California Bar Association files
>
> **Environmental Issues**
> - Sierra Club membership files
> - Orange County Clean Water Initiative fund-raising files
>
> **Hancock Elementary School**
> - Arts Funding Citizen Awareness Campaign files
> - Parent-Teacher conference files
>
> **Race Equity Activities**
> - Black Lives Matter March files
> - Correspondence with state legislators
> - Letters to the editor
>
> **Doe Family Genealogy**
> - Documents from National Archives
> - African American Genealogical Society of Northern California membership
> - Family history charts and data
>
> **Diaries**
> - College years
> - Trip to France, Belgium, and Germany

FIGURE 1. A representation of the archival materials comprising the Jane Doe Papers, a collection of personal papers

The principle of *respect des fonds* advises us to recognize and preserve as an organic whole all the documents that result from this closely related set of functions and activities, just as we would in a larger and more complex collection of government or business records. In this case, the thing that relates all of these activities is the fact that they, together, comprise and document a human life. The principle of provenance advises us to show the same respect for each of the six series into which Doe's papers divide—not intermixing documents among them. Decades ago, some manuscript curators might have been inclined to disaggregate these materials into separate collections, perhaps removing her Hancock School materials and adding them to a separate collection comprising the business records of that school. If the manuscript repository also owned a collection of papers from a related family member, it may have been inclined to merge the two into a single collection of family papers. In either case, those actions would result in a diminished or compromised understanding of Jane Doe's life. Provenance establishes and preserves the integrity and meaning of any collection that is archival in nature, regardless of the type of entity that created it or the type of repository that owns and administers it. *Respect des fonds* and provenance assert with no equivocation that all of the materials issuing from one corporate or personal creator must be maintained together; they must not be separated into other collections, and materials issuing from separate creators must not be added to them.

It is also worthy of noting that, with the articulation of these two fundamental principles, we begin to see the basis of a *hierarchical presumption* for the arrangement of the documents comprising a *fonds* or a collection. This presumption is baked into the practice of arrangement and description and will be explained more fully in the next few sections.

Original Order

Sitting firmly atop the foundation provided by *respect des fonds* and provenance is the principle of original order, which has a relevance and importance for arrangement and description that is difficult to overstate. The concept of original order, if we approach it correctly, tells us how to devise an arrangement scheme for nearly every collection, helps us explain that arrangement to archival users, eases our decision-making about how to describe collections, and has the power to economize greatly on the resources we plow into the perennially expensive activities of arrangement and description. It is indeed the principle that leverages the power of provenance. Sadly, it is also the archival principle that many of us most often misinterpret, to our great detriment in both the effectiveness and the cost of our arrangement and description endeavors.

Our previously cited *Glossary* defines *original order* as "[t]he organization and sequence of records established by the creator of the records."[6] When we apply this concept to archival arrangement, it urges us to preserve or re-create the basic organizational system used by the people who created and maintained the materials. In practice, this means that we should identify the main groupings into which the records or papers naturally divide themselves. As we have seen in discussing the principle of provenance, these natural groupings generally reflect the main activities and functions of the record creators. The principle of original order advises us to determine and preserve those groupings, and this becomes the most important aspect of arrangement. Assembling the collection into those fundamental groups is the only *essential* sequencing activity involved in arrangement.

Original order has a long tradition in archival theory and goes back at least as far as the Dutch Manual, whose authors treat it at length in four successive rules:

16. The system of arrangement must be based on the original organization of the archival collection, which in the main corresponds to the organization of the administrative body that produced it.
17. In the arrangement of an archival collection, therefore, the original order should first of all be reestablished as far as possible. Only thereafter can one judge whether, and to what extent, it is desirable to deviate from that order.
18. The original arrangement of an archival collection may be modified in order to correct deviations from the original structure of the collection, . . .
19. In the arrangement of an archival collection the interests of historical research should receive only secondary consideration.[7]

Schellenberg points out a few central benefits afforded by preserving the original order of the collection materials:[8]

- *It may show the sequence of actions that occurred during important office transactions.* If we were to destroy the original order during processing and create a new arrangement based, say, on grouping materials by document type, this sequencing of activity would certainly be lost. We could easily lose our sense of how some actions led to other actions, and how transactions across the office might be related to each other. We might lose the larger picture of how a number of discrete actions resulted in the performance of some important activity.

- *It may reveal administrative processes and procedures that are key to understanding the creators and managers of the records during their active life.* Original order tends to cluster records around their creators and internal users, which helps provide a sense of who they were and how they related to each other. It reveals, through the natural creation of records, how agents functioned and collaborated. It can show how different units within an office (or persons within a family) interrelated. It can also make apparent how policies and processes developed to facilitate necessary activities. These sorts of information tend to be revealed when we preserve original order.
- *It may reflect how things were done in an office (or in a household).* Original order can also help provide a clearer picture of office or family *culture*. What norms prevailed in the regular performance of business? Who collaborated with whom? What workarounds developed to keep things going? What was the tone and temper of the human relationships? Preserving original order allows us to interrogate the archival records in ways that we could not do if that organic structure of the archival unit was sundered in a significant way.

To Schellenberg's list I would add another very important practical benefit afforded by original order: *economical processing*. Of all the possible ways in which we might arrange the materials comprising an archival collection, preserving or reestablishing its original order is the only approach that actually saves us time. And it saves us a lot of time. A seminal manual for manuscript librarians noted decades ago the economies that can be realized by employing a processing regimen based upon original order: "Maintaining the original order of a collection as its permanent arrangement makes for quick processing. Frequently the papers can be boxed in order as they are removed from the original file drawers, kept in their original folders, and an inventory prepared which describes the characteristics of the filing system and describes which units are in each box."[9] Because the natural groupings inherent in most archival collections are so helpful in enabling us to comprehend the content of those collections, as well the circumstances of their creation and management, we are generally freed from the most laborious work involved in arranging the individual items that make up a collection. Assuming, of course, that some meaningful original order has persisted in a collection, it is simply unnecessary to laboriously impose a stricter sequencing of its contents.

So, using the principle of original order not only helps us to more fully comprehend the meaning and significance of a collection, it also helps us to arrange and describe that collection much more economically. This all sounds great. But it depends on us having a clear and precise understanding of the real meaning of original order, which archivists frequently misconstrue, thereby misapplying it when arranging collections. Let's look at some of the important, and often underappreciated, aspects that make up the concept of original order, including

- Real order versus accidental order
- Intellectual order versus physical order
- Necessary order versus unnecessary order

Real order versus accidental order

A rather common mistake made by collection processors is to assume that original order refers to the order that the collection happened to be in at the time they received it. This belief influences them to do one of two things: either to slavishly perpetuate that order, or to declare that no apparent order exists and to rearrange the materials into some entirely new scheme of their own devising. Neither of these alternatives is likely to produce a good outcome. Original order, to the contrary, should be thought of as the *meaningful* order that naturally resulted from the activities through which their owners created and then maintained the materials. That order is a largely intellectual structure that directly embodies the structure of a person's life or the administrative history of an organization.

But many things can and do happen to a collection in the long interval between creation and transfer to an archival repository. Materials get packed haphazardly into containers that, in turn, get reshuffled multiple times before they are reunited again in a repository. The author has dealt with instances in which the once orderly contents of entire file cabinets were unceremoniously upended into transfer boxes with no care for maintaining their arrangement. Many other filing mishaps routinely occur over the lifespan of collection materials. The result is that collections arrive in something better characterized as "loading dock order" rather than anything resembling *original* order. The person arranging the collection must recognize the difference and must then use knowledge about the creation and business use of the materials to return them to the organic groupings that originally existed. Accidents of storage and shipping should never be preserved or treated as meaningful conditions. An original, and meaningful, order is almost always present, and the preeminent task of the archivist is to reestablish it in the course of processing the materials.

Intellectual order versus physical order

As the foregoing discussion suggests, the original order we are striving to re-create in processing is an arrangement that conveys essential meaning. It reflects the administration and history of the entities that created it. As such, it should be thought of as an intellectual structure, and that intellectual arrangement is much more important than the literal physical arrangement of the collection materials.

If we look back at the example of the Jane Doe Papers depicted in Figure 1, we can see that the arrangement of the materials forms an intellectual construct that reflects key activities and the overall structure of Doe's life. That intellectual arrangement will often represent the literal arrangement of the collection materials filed in an archives' physical containers—but not always. Practical exigencies may require us to physically arrange and store collection materials in a sequence that deviates from the more important intellectual arrangement. Fragile magnetic media, digital files, and oversize materials may all need to be stored in separate containers from the rest of the materials with which they naturally interfile. We should not let such practical necessities deter us from preferencing, and focusing on, the intellectual arrangement of the collection as the true arrangement that we present to users.

We maintain our focus on the intellectual arrangement, while simultaneously disarranging the materials in a purely physical sense, through our finding aids. Finding aids, our chief descriptive constructs, allow us to simultaneously view the intellectual structure of a collection *and* its literal physical arrangement. We will examine this thoroughly later on when we consider description. The important message here is that we need not let physical arrangement deflect our focus on original order as the heart of our processing approach.

Necessary order versus unnecessary order

Original order advises us to respect the structure imposed by the creators of collections and to preserve or reestablish that organic order to the greatest extent possible. The principle, however, does not really speak to the degrees of labor that archivists must expend in replicating that order. Many processing archivists assume that the principle demands that we attempt a very literal arranging of all the individual items in the collection to re-create the exact order in which the materials must have originally been created or maintained in the locus of origin. This would suggest that if all of the items comprising a given set of files had probably been filed chronologically, then it would be incumbent on us to make sure that all the items in each of those files are indeed arranged in a true chronological sequence.

This interpretation of the requirements of original order greatly inflates the costs—financial and psychic—of archival processing and contributes to the notable explosion of unprocessed backlogs in the majority of archival repositories in recent decades. But is this intensive level of processing labor really necessary? We might justify this level of work on a number of grounds, but not in terms of fulfilling the requirements of original order. That principle does not really apply to the arrangement of the myriad items within folders, files, and other low-level groupings of records. Rather, it focuses on identifying the major groupings within a collection and keeping them intact and organized in relation to each other. The Dutch Manual draws an analogy to the work of a paleontologist who, in assembling the fossil remains of some animal, is careful to bring the principal bones into proper relation to each other to achieve an accurate representation of the whole.

None of the traditional archival theorists worried much about sequencing items and focused most of their attention on understanding and arranging materials at something like the *series* level. Arrangement work below that level is usually treated as less important. Schellenberg makes a very important point in this regard:

> Usually the order given items in an archival series does not reveal any significant facts about activity, administrative processes and the like. It does not, ordinarily, show how an activity was begun, the manner in which it was carried out, or the results obtained from it. Such facts are revealed because the series as such was kept intact, not because of the order given items within it.[10]

In sharing advice from the venerable and highly regarded Massachusetts Institute of Technology archival processing manual, Helen Slotkin and Karen Lynch emphasize that the "[a]rrangement of individual items is time-consuming and we have learned to avoid it unless there is a compelling benefit to be derived from such detailed work."[11] One very thoughtful and well-written repository processing manual offers the following advice:

> When arranging a collection, the ultimate goal is to make the materials available expediently and efficiently. Respect the organization imposed by the person who created the records. Not only is this sound archival practice, but it will save you from having to devise an elaborate and time consuming alternate arrangement scheme. Strive for simplicity. There is no need to create complicated hierarchies of series and subseries if you don't need to.[12]

So, we should conclude from all of this that the truly necessary activity in re-creating original order is to maintain the arrangement of the series, and perhaps the files or other major units within them. Maintaining the order of items ought to be seen, in most cases, to be unnecessary to the preservation of original order. To visualize this better, we can turn again to the example of the Jane Doe Papers in Figure 1. The structure of series (e.g., Law practice) and files (e.g., Client files) depicted there represents the essential original order that needs to be maintained or reconstructed. The many, many items that doubtless comprise the files are less important to meticulously arrange. The researcher's ability to understand and access the collection materials is unlikely to be materially affected by the precise sequencing of those items.

Five Fundamental Levels of Control

Our foray into arrangement principles has thus far emphasized that an archival collection, as a whole, has integrity and carries meaning that requires it to be kept together as a single body of materials and that its principal constituent parts should be similarly treated. They, under normal circumstances, should be neither sundered nor added to. On top of this, original order insists that the collection materials that comprise this indivisible whole should themselves be arranged in the basic structure and sequence devised by the entities that created and maintained them.

The next fundamental principle, posited most forcefully by American archival theorist Oliver Wendell Holmes,[13] asserts that the original order of archival collection materials—that intellectual arrangement—tends to be *hierarchical* in nature. This is true about traditional mixed paper materials, sound and moving image collections, digital records, or any conceivable aggregation of archival materials. Furthermore, any sufficiently complex body of archival materials includes five distinguishable levels. These are intellectual levels, and they will be identifiable and relevant in the collection's original order. The work of arranging archival materials must be carried out conscious of, and informed by, these five levels, and each level requires a different sort of activity. In preparing to explain levels of arrangement, Holmes importantly says:

> Archives are already arranged—supposedly. That is to say, an arrangement was given them by the agency of origin while it built them up day after day, year after year, as a systematic record of its activities and as part of its operations. This arrangement the archivist is expected to respect and maintain. Arrangement is built into archives; it is one of the inherent characteristics of "archives," differentiating them from nonarchival material.[14]

Holmes goes on to say that the hierarchy of information baked into archives tends to manifest itself in identifiable levels that always appear from collection to collection, regardless of who created them. These five levels are

1. The repository
2. The record group or collection
3. The series
4. The file
5. The item

These levels have important implications for arrangement work because, first, they provide a navigational guide to help the archivist perceive and implement the original order inherent in the collection, and, second, they help determine the type and intensity of arrangement work that will be performed on the various documentary units constituting the collection. Let's examine each of them.

Repository level

Arrangement at this level does not actually involve any physical work in any of the repository's collections. Instead, this is really an administrative tool that an institution will probably use, especially when it holds a large number of archival collections, to categorize its holdings into separate large divisions. Doing so can make it easier to manage the physical collections (e.g., organizing storage space to group similar or related collections together) or to clarify the nature and extent of the archival holdings to researchers. For example, the Minnesota Historical Society traditionally divided its archival holdings administratively into its 1) manuscript collections and 2) the Minnesota State Archives; it less formally divided its manuscript collections into personal papers, business collections, and public affairs collections.

Record group, or collection, level

This second level, which refers to the whole group or collection, also involves no direct physical arrangement activity. Although defining this level has proved to be challenging in some contexts, we should generally understand it to refer to the full body of organically related records or papers established on the basis of provenance. In governmental or other organizational settings, it may be referred to as the "record group" (United States) or "*fonds*" (Canada, continental Europe), while in manuscript repositories it is generally referred to as a "collection." For the sake of convenience in this work, I will generally use the term "collection" to apply to all archives and manuscript groupings at this level. Regardless of terminology, the persistent concept is that these are the whole of the materials created and maintained by an organization, a person, or a family in the course of carrying out their affairs. The important notion here is that each one of these collections needs to be preserved, maintained, arranged, and described separately from every other collection in the same repository.

Series level

At this third level we first begin to physically manipulate the records themselves. In the first two levels, we really just establish intellectual boundaries between entities. At the series level, we organize and sequence the physical or digital materials that comprise the collection. The series has proven to be a challenging concept for the archival theorist to explain and for the novice or user to understand. The *Glossary* provides a rather crisp definition in referring to it as a "group of similar records that are arranged according to a filing system and that are related as the result of being created, received, or used in the same activity."[15] The crucial concept is "activity." The documents in a series may share a common form or format (diaries, photographs, ledgers) or may be heterogeneous in form, but they all share a common identity as archival materials documenting some purposeful and discrete activity in which their creator(s) was engaged for some period of time. If we look at the example of the Jane

Doe Papers in Figure 1, the headings in boldface represent the six series into which the collection is arranged. All of the series represent discrete activities in which Doe was engaged. While most of the series contain a mixture of document types, the "Diaries" series consists of a single record format. An important takeaway is that the diaries are not treated as a series simply because of their common format, but because, in the case of Doe's papers, they represent a distinct activity—the act of creating and maintaining a daily chronicle to document various phases of her life.

Two fundamental arrangement activities happen at the series level: segregating the materials in one series from those in any other and then sequencing the series in relation to each other. The latter work requires the most thought and planning because, as Holmes points out,

> Although through classification schemes and filing practices an agency may have given a definitive arrangement to documents and filing units within each series, it almost never established a sequential arrangement for the many different series it created. It never dictated that a certain series was to come first, a certain other series last, and that each of the others was to have its place at some definite point in between. This larger classification sequence is what the archivist must establish for each record group. It is an operation that requires a full knowledge of the principles of archival arrangement and a knowledge of the administrative history of the agency or agencies whose records are involved. In many ways this is the heart of archival work, because the inventory and all other finding aids merely reflect this level of arrangement and are keyed into it.[16]

As Holmes emphasizes, the archivist must sequence the various series because the creators of the collection will not have done so. The archivist must sequence the series in a manner that helps the user to understand the nature and interrelationships of the activities represented in the collection materials. Generally, similar or mutually dependent activities ought to be grouped together rather than scattered. If no such meaningful grouping of series is apparent, then the archivist is free to sequence the series in any way that facilitates their retrieval and use.

The arrangement work that takes place at the series level may also be the most important portion of the overall work. Arguably, the arrangement value added at that level is more helpful to researchers than the work performed at the two lower levels, which generally requires more intensive labor. Therefore, significant economies may be achieved by focusing more attention on the series level and then addressing the lower levels with a lighter touch. Schellenberg, for example, asserts that "[u]sually the order in which individual record items within a series are arranged does not significantly reveal how things were done. The order seldom has a presumptive value and usually must be judged strictly on its merits."[17] By organizing collection materials into series, we help to create an understandable picture of a person's life or an organization's history. Those series are the significant pieces in the larger documentary puzzle. Having them in place, regardless of how much additional arrangement work we perform, allows the users of the collection to understand the inherent structure of the organization or the lived life and then to make reasonable decisions about the portions of the collection that will be relevant for their research.

File level

Files are typically the chief building blocks within a series and, in the great majority of situations, most of the labor involved in arrangement will be expended on identifying the files that comprise a series and then sequencing them within the series. Holmes characterizes files succinctly in saying that "[a]lthough filing units within series may be single documents or single documents with enclosures and annexes, they are more likely to be assemblages of documents relating to some transaction, person, case, or subject . . ."[18] These assemblages document some particular entity or transaction that relates directly to the activity that concerns their parent series. They may consist of a single document type or a heterogeneous combination of formats.

If we turn once again to the Jane Doe Papers (Figure 1), we can see these characteristics in the three files comprising the "Law Practice" series. The "Client files" document individuals and organizations that Doe represented and the many transactions that defined their business relationships. Although the documents in the file may represent a single sequence, it is much more likely that they are segregated in folders by client or case and that the entire file consists of many of these folders. Doe's "Tax return" files are more likely to be a chronological sequence of tax returns with appended correspondence, invoices, and related supporting documentation. The "California Bar Association files" might very well contain a number of folders or other aggregate units organized by meetings, by committees, by issues or subjects, or by people with whom she collaborated. Files are very flexible units; they may consist of a single file or a number of related subfiles, as in the client files.

Item level

The fifth and final level is the item or document itself. Defining an item is a bit ambiguous in the archival context, because what is considered to be an item can range widely in size and scope. The *Glossary* characterizes it as a "thing that can be distinguished from a group and that is complete in itself."[19] By this reckoning, items would include the following documents: a 1-page letter, a 200-page diary or ledger, a long report with cover document and appendixes, and a moving image film on several reels. Whatever the form or scale, the work of arrangement at the item level involves manipulating the sequence of documents within their parent file or, if no file level exists, series.

More than at any other level, archivists have a wide range of acceptable alternatives available to them in sequencing collection items within their parent unit.

- They can elect to do nothing, especially if the collection is tiny or if, as is typical, items tend to exist within well-ordered files. In such cases, rigorously sequencing the items may add little value for either researchers or administrators, as any user will be able to quickly ascertain the scope and content of the materials without carefully ordered constituent items.
- They can partially arrange the items, for example, roughly grouping materials together by year, rather than in an exact chronology. Such a light-handed approach can help to improve the usability of documents in a relatively large file, while at the same time saving a great deal of processing time and expense.
- They can arrange—usually, rearrange—all the items in some formal and consistent scheme. Depending upon the nature of the materials, that scheme might be chronological, alphabetical, geographical, or topical. Often, it will be a more complicated combination of these variables. No matter the scheme, item-level sequencing requires the processor to handle and make a judgment about every item. Obviously, taking such an intensive approach to arrangement reduces processing speed to a crawl. While taking

such an approach is never *wrong*, it should always be taken with a clear understanding of the economies involved and the overall access value it will create.

"Artificial" levels: subgroup and subseries

Although repository, record group/collection, series, file, and item comprise the canonical levels of archival arrangement and description, they are not always sufficient to express the hierarchical complexity of archival collections. In these situations, archival theory makes provision for inserting intermediate levels to expand the hierarchy.

The *subgroup* can be applied between collection and series when necessary and can be used multiple times in the same collection. Subgroups come into play most often when a large and complex organization has many administrative subdivisions, each of which produces record series. Think of a governmental body or corporation with, for example, geographical divisions subdivided into functional operating departments. That level of hierarchical complexity could not be expressed without dividing the collection into subgroups.

The *subseries* performs a similar role between the series and file levels. Again, in large or complex collections, a given series may need to be broken into parts that become the immediate parents of the various files produced. For example, a series of "employee records" may divide naturally into two subseries: "hiring files" and "performance files." All the files produced in that series pertain to one or the other subseries, rather than to the parent series itself.

To make this a bit less abstract, let's look at an example taken from a collection of organizational records that utilizes both subgroups and subseries to effectively deal with the administrative complexity of its archives (see Figure 2).

FIGURE 2. Levels of arrangement in a collection of organizational records. Andersen Corporation Records. Minnesota Historical Society.

In this example, the records of a large corporation divide naturally into a number of functional departments, in this case Human Resources, which can only be accurately expressed at a subgroup level. The Human Resources Department itself produces many record series, one being its files relating to former employees. Its "Historical" Employee Records is a complex series that naturally divides into several subseries, such as the Quarter Century Club, and those subseries are the originators of all the records produced at the file level. Therefore, the subseries level must be employed to represent this administrative complexity and to provide a home for those files. As is true with subgroups, multiple levels of subseries can exist in a collection—as many as necessary to accurately reflect the complexity of the records.

Now, it is certainly most common to see subgroups and subseries applied in a collection of organizational records. However, these levels are just as applicable to collections of family and personal papers when those collections are sufficiently complex to warrant it. This will tend to be more the case in which a family collection divides into large subgroups for different individuals, or when the papers of a single individual document a life characterized by many significant roles and activities (e.g., papers of a congressperson). Here is an example of such a complex collection of family papers:

FIGURE 3. Levels of arrangement in a collection of family papers. Donald Wandrei and Family Papers. Minnesota Historical Society.

Briefly, in this collection of family papers (see Figure 3), there are groups of papers for several different family members, requiring subgroups to represent this complexity. One of the individuals, science fantasy writer and publisher Donald Wandrei, produced documentation of several activities, the most prominent of which was his writing and publishing career. The series relating to this activity subdivides into units documenting various writing projects and publishing activities, one of which was his Arkham House publishing company. That business obtained the rights to the book *Conan the Barbarian*, the subsequent management of which produced a large set of files.

A Caveat: When Hierarchy and Structure Are Absent

I have made a strong case in the preceding sections for respecting original order and hierarchy in arranging archival materials. And in nearly all collections that will prove to be good advice, which will instruct and usually simplify the work of arrangement. But it would be false to suggest that *every* collection exhibits an organic order, or presents some internal hierarchy of groupings, or reflects anything that could even remotely be called *structure*.

It will be pointless to attempt applying those arrangement principles to that small fraction of collections. These exhibit no identifiable structure and, in extreme cases, no discernable relationship among the collection items apart from reflecting a shared acquisition. Such collections are usually tiny, often comprising just a few random items from an individual's or an organization's disparate activities that have no meaningful relationship to each other. For example, a collection of family papers might consist of the following:

- a letter written by the creator of the papers
- a postcard sent to his great grandmother
- two photographs of someone whose relationship to the family is unknown

- a title abstract to a property parcel
- a report card for a student whose family connection is unclear
- newspaper articles on diverse topics from various time periods

So, although the most important question may be "why do we want this collection in the first place?," it may nevertheless be our lot to arrange and describe this puzzling set of documents. Obviously, no hierarchical structure exists; nor any organic relationship—original order—that can be discerned. In cases like this, the archivist lacks the wherewithal to create an arrangement that could be seen as meaningful. So, all we can do is punt: arrange the items in any helpful sequence (perhaps chronologically) and list them individually, since making a more general characterization is hopeless. They are just strangers on a train, and there is no point in tying ourselves in knots by attempting to present them as something else.

Other, less extreme, examples will occur in which the relationships among the collection materials are stronger and more amenable to explanation. Yet, they may still be so diverse in nature and purpose as to exhibit no useful hierarchy. So, we end up with what is frequently referred to as a "flat" collection: a group of items that comprise a collection with no series, files, or other subsidiary semantic units. Arrangement becomes a single sequence of items with no attempt to suggest more faceted relationships.

The Granularity of Arrangement

When it comes to the actual mechanics of arrangement, one of the most crucial concepts—and decision points—for the archivist is the level of granularity to apply. As noted throughout the prior section, collections may be arranged at any number of levels: record group/collection, subgroup, series, subseries, file, and document/item. But the important thing to remember is that archival theory or principle does not require us to perform arrangement work at all of these levels. We can choose to perform arrangement at the series level, but to refrain from doing so at the lower file or item levels. Our preeminent goal in arranging archives is to make them available to researchers in a usable form that facilitates their research, but to do so as efficiently as possible.

Why stress efficiency? Arranging and describing collections is one of the most expensive aspects of administering an archives program, and the decisions we make about the granularity of processing result in substantial differentials in the cost of processing any given collection. If we think of Holmes's five levels of arrangement, we can imagine each level as representing a different magnitude of processing intensity or granularity. As we move down that hierarchy from collection to item, each arrangement level increases the time expenditure by something like a factor, rather than by a mere increment. When we perform arrangement at the subgroup level, we are manipulating large chunks of the collection that requires little hands-on work. When we perform arrangement at the series level, we are manipulating a larger number of smaller chunks, requiring somewhat larger labor input. When we arrange the files that encompass a typical series, we are manipulating a much greater number of more granular chunks. And when we arrange the items in a series or file, we are performing some sort of manipulation of every single document. If we look at these levels of granularity in terms of overall processing productivity, we can see stark differences. Arranging a traditional, largely paper-based collection at a series level can generally yield productivity of around 4 to 6 hours per cubic foot of documents. Arranging that same collection at an item level might result in productivity as small as 40 hours of labor per foot.

So, the performance implications are clear. We can reduce the costs of arrangement work significantly by deciding to process collections at some less granular level. Furthermore, we are in no way bound to make granularity decisions in a crude way; we can do so with considerable flexibility. We can decide to arrange the materials in one collection to a file level, those in another to a series level, and the documents in a third to an item level. Furthermore, we need not arrange every component part of a single collection to some uniform level of granularity. Some series or files, for example, may be perfectly understandable and usable in more or less their received state, while other units may need very intensive rearrangement to be usable. The important lesson here is that archivists have a great degree of latitude when deciding how intensively they will arrange collection materials. Arrangement decisions, as one archivist sensibly advised a number of years ago, are choices along a continuum, rather than absolute requirements:

> . . . instead of trying to maintain an ideal standard level of processing, we [should] look at processing as a range of choices along a continuum for each of the four essential processing activities: arrangement, preservation, description, and screening. The continuum runs from the found, or original, state of the material up to the highest possible level of each activity. . . ."[20]

Some repositories approach the question of "how much granularity" by establishing defined *levels of processing* that can be established to guide archivists. Each level in such a protocol will define certain threshold and ceiling efforts for the work that will be performed in a project defined at that level: how much arrangement, preservation, and description effort will be permitted. Appendix B examines the processing levels concept as applied at one such repository.

The deciding factors in each case should be ease of use and institutional resources. Archivists should make such decisions to facilitate research in a satisfactory way and to expend institutional resources (people and dollars) sustainably. Archivists do themselves no favor by choosing to process one collection in an impeccable manner if doing so leaves them with insufficient resources to process the other collections in their repository. That misguided logic has been a big factor in the growth of unprocessed backlogs in many repositories.

We can end this section with some sound practical advice from one of the better institutional processing manuals:

> Avoid devoting too much time to arranging items within file units. In some cases you will need to do this to make the materials accessible and in others you will not, so use your best judgement. When arranging a collection, the ultimate goal is to make the materials available expediently and efficiently. Respect the organization imposed by the person who created the records.[21]

These, then, are the essential principles that undergird the arrangement of archives and manuscripts. Taken together, they suggest a systematic approach designed to facilitate use, while still preserving scarce processing resources. *Respect des fonds*, provenance, original order, and the natural hierarchy into which records tend to organize themselves are the tools that help us to arrange collection materials effectively and sustainably. But having arranged the collection, we need some additional tools to guide us in expressing that arrangement to potential users of the collection. In the next chapter we will move ahead to consider the principles underlying description, the other key processing activity. We will examine the relationship of description to arrangement, and we will explore the concepts and standards that shape and govern how we describe archives.

NOTES

1. S. Muller, J. A. Feith, and R. Fruin, *Manual for the Arrangement and Description of Archives*, translation of the second edition by Arthur H. Leavitt (Chicago: Society of American Archivists, 2003). Systematic arrangement is discussed on pp. 48–59.
2. Ernst Posner, "Some Aspects of Archival Development since the French Revolution," *American Archivist* 3, no. 3 (1940): 166–67.
3. The pragmatic development of early arrangement principles is summarized in the introductory portion of Jefferson Bailey, "Disrespect Des Fonds: Rethinking Arrangement and Description in Born-Digital Archives," *Archive Journal*, no. 3 (June 2013).
4. T. R. Schellenberg, *The Management of Archives* (New York: Columbia University Press, 1965), 90.
5. Schellenberg, *The Management of Archives*, 91–95.
6. Richard Pearce-Moses, s.v. "original order," *A Glossary of Archival and Records Terminology* (Chicago: Society of American Archivists, 2005), 280–81.
7. Muller, Feith, and Fruin, *Manual for the Arrangement and Description of Archives*, 52–66.
8. Adapted from Schellenberg, *The Management of Archives*, 100–102.
9. Ruth B. Bordin and Robert M. Warner, *The Modern Manuscript Library* (New York and London: The Scarecrow Press, 1966), 44.
10. T. R. Schellenberg, *The Management of Archives*, 102.
11. Helen W. Slotkin and Karen T. Lynch, "An Analysis of Processing Procedures: The Adaptable Approach," *American Archivist* 45, no. 2 (1982): 157.
12. St. Johnsbury Athenaeum Archives, *Archives Processing Manual*, draft 2 (May 2001), http://www.vermont-archives.org/boards/vhrab/processing.doc.
13. Dr. Oliver Wendell Holmes (1902–1981) joined the National Archives in 1935, part of that initial cohort that would transform archival thinking in the United States. He became a founding member of the Society of American Archivists (1936), as well as director (1961–1972) of the National Historical Publications Commission. Holmes's publications include many that became foundational texts on archival theory and history. But he remains most widely remarked for his seminal article on archival arrangement, "Archival Arrangement—Five Different Options at Five Different Levels," cited elsewhere, which has ever since influenced archival thinking about original order and the organic hierarchies into which units of archival records fall.
14. Oliver W. Holmes, "Archival Arrangement—Five Different Options at Five Different Levels," *American Archivist* 27, no. 1 (1964): 21.
15. Pearce-Moses, s.v. "series level," *A Glossary of Archival and Records Terminology*, 358.
16. Holmes, "Archival Arrangement," 28–29.
17. T. R. Schellenberg, "Archival Principles of Arrangement," in *A Modern Archives Reader*, ed. Maygene F. Daniels and Timothy Walch (Washington, DC: National Archives Trust Fund Board, 1984), 158. Further discussion can be found in Greene and Meissner, "More Product, Less Process," 240–45.
18. Holmes, "Archival Arrangement," 33.
19. Pearce-Moses, *A Glossary of Archival and Records Terminology*, 220.
20. Megan Desnoyers, "When Is It Processed?," *Midwestern Archivist* 7 (1982): 311. Also, see the "Arrangement Continuum" depicted on p. 315 of the article.
21. St. Johnsbury Athenaeum Archives, *Archives Processing Manual*, 9.

3

Principles of Archival Description

The Purpose of Description

Description is the other side of the processing coin. Arrangement lends an intellectual and physical structure to the collection materials, which is essential if users of the collection are going to be able to locate any of the materials, let alone make sense of the collection. But all of that careful structuring is of no avail if we do not also provide some sort of explanatory guide that allows users to understand that structure and the informational content of the records, as well as the context of their creation and administration. That is the purpose of description.

Actually, description has two rather different purposes. The first is simply to provide physical control over the collection materials for administrative purposes. What materials do we hold, and where are they located? This is a basic and essential need accommodated by a description that lists (but does not itemize) the materials that comprise the collection. The second, and more complex, purpose is to provide rich intellectual control over the collection. What is the informational structure of the collection? How do the parts relate to each other? What is the informational content of each collection unit? How and when were these materials created, by whom, and for what purpose? Good archival description makes a collection and its contents discoverable by researchers and answers these and other important questions.

What is a finding aid?

The descriptive tools that archivists have traditionally created to perform the functions of administrative and intellectual control are broadly referred to as *finding aids*. Throughout this manual, I try to use the term in its most generic sense, adhering to the canonical definition found in the *Glossary*: "1. A tool that facilitates discovery of information within a collection of records." While popular understanding of the term, and our historical practice, call to mind a standalone document that describes all the parts and pieces of an archival collection, the term is used here in a more comprehensive sense to refer to any and all of the descriptive metadata forms that we might employ to help researchers discover, understand, and use archival materials.

This suite of tools grows ever larger and more complex. It includes not only the catalog records, inventories, registers, and other detailed textual documents commonplace in most repositories. It also encompasses structured data that produce textual descriptions only as service outputs in response to user queries. As we go forward, we will create and manage more and more of our descriptive information as structured data because it is more flexible and responsive to user demands.[1] Although structured data can certainly be stored as EAD-encoded documents, for example, it is increasingly likely to be housed and managed within some sort of complex, fielded data set from which it can be shared with diverse information systems, many of them external (and perhaps foreign) to archives and archivists. The point here is to treat archival description as "shareable metadata"—carefully constructed data points expressed in formal ontologies—that are readable by both humans and machines depending upon the information exchange taking place.[2] Structured archival description can live in spreadsheets and home-grown databases, in collection management systems like ArchivesSpace, and in institutional repositories. The array of approaches and mechanisms for managing and sharing archival description will be considered more fully in chapter 6.

We ought to begin by taking a general look at the whole concept of archival finding aids.[3] In fact, why do we have finding aids in the first place? Why has the archival community invested so much thought and effort in designing and creating these descriptive tools? Archival repositories have formed and grown as the result of a two-pronged impetus: preservation of historically and administratively valuable documents, and providing public access to those preserved materials. But more and more, the latter impetus, the use of these materials by researchers, has really come to be seen as the only acceptable justification for the high costs associated with their preservation. And, if these collections are to be used effectively, they must be described—both to publicize their existence and to provide a guide for using them. Archival finding aids play these roles.

In their very helpful SAA description module, *Standards for Archival Description*, Sibyl Shaefer and Janet Bunde give further thought to the crucial outcomes afforded by well-crafted archival finding aids. They assert that robust description provides four types of information about the collection:

- *Context*. Archival description must explain the circumstances under which the collection was created and used prior to its becoming part of an archives, and it must describe the creators themselves, as well as other important entities and actors represented in the records.
- *Content*. Of course, finding aids will delineate and explain the information content of the significant intellectual components making up the collection.
- *Structure*. Unlike bibliographic catalogers, archivists are required to explain the innate hierarchical structure of the collection materials—their intellectual arrangement—so that the users can understand the often complex relationships that exist among the

collection components. Understanding this structure in itself conveys a certain level of meaning and helps researchers know where to look for particular sorts of information.
- *Function.* Archivists need to explain the functions that the record creators were responsible for, and the activities that they were performing, in the course of producing and using the collection materials. Knowing these things helps to explain the purposes behind the collection, and *why* it has been acquired and preserved in the archives.[4]

Description Is Structured Data, Not Prose

What is structured data? Structured data simply refers to any data that reside in fixed fields within a record or file. This certainly includes data contained in relational databases and spreadsheets, the data structures with which we are probably most familiar. But it also includes the data contained within an EAD-encoded document or in a MARC catalog record.[5] Structured data, first and foremost, comprises organized information recorded within some formal structure, which has several salient characteristics:

- *It is highly **organized** information.* It is typically organized into data elements or fields, the fields representing different types of information (name, title, inclusive dates, quantity, and so forth).
- *Its organizational structure is based on a **data model**.* The model, which in the cases of EAD and HTML are XML schemas, defines the data elements and expresses the relationships among them, which are often hierarchical.
- *Its underlying data model imbues it with **semantic value**.* This means that all the data contained within a particular field share common characteristics or meaning. For example, all of the information in a field called "extent" might relate to the quantity of the archival collection or one of its units; it would not refer to the creator of the materials. The semantic value is achieved through a precise definition of the field's data, including properties, attributes, and normalized forms.
- *The semantic value of the data can be **understood by machines**, as well as by humans.* Computers processing the information in the preceding bullet would understand that the information in the field relates to quantity and would be able to separate it from other data not pertaining to quantity. The machine could also understand how that information could be made to interoperate with analogous data from some other domain.
- *It is commonly **encoded** in a programming language that allows it to be easily manipulated and to be shared in networked environments.* EAD instances, for example, are encoded in a particular vocabulary built in XML schema language.

When we treat archival description as structured data, we confer huge advantages on our descriptions that greatly enrich outcomes for users and that also create efficiencies for archivists:

- *Structured data is easier to store and reuse.* It can be transformed in many ways: the same data could be rendered as an HTML or PDF document, as a data table, as braille text, or as an audio output file. It is truly *output-neutral*, which greatly increases its flexibility and its overall value.

- *The data can be migrated relatively easily to new storage and retrieval systems, or to new software versions, as technology evolves.*
- *Archival descriptions can interoperate with other information systems without any loss of meaning.* For example, biographical information from archival descriptions can be imported into shared online authority files like OCLC's Virtual International Authority File (VIAF).
- *Users could conceivably create their own finding aids by pulling together descriptive pieces from multiple separate archival (or nonarchival) descriptions as they develop their own research plans.*

When we create our descriptive information as structured data, we greatly expand the domain in which our collections are available for discovery. We make them as accessible on the open Web as they are within our repository domains, which most of our consumers expect as a matter of course. Jen Schaffner makes the case well in an OCLC Research white paper:

> These days we are writing finding aids and cataloging collections largely to be discovered by search engines. People expect to find archives and special collections on the open Web using the same techniques they use to find other things, and they expect comprehensive results. Invisibility of archives, manuscripts and special collections may well have more to do with the metadata we create than with the interfaces we build. Now that we no longer control discovery, the metadata that we contribute is critical. In so many ways, the metadata is the interface.[6]

Unstructured data, on the other hand, tends to be free-form, nontabular, dispersed, and not easily retrievable; such data requires deliberate intervention to make sense of it. Unstructured data is usually created in a single form for a single purpose, and it cannot be easily transformed into something else or otherwise manipulated; nor can it be easily shared on networks, at least in any way that preserves and exploits its semantic value. Computer systems cannot make sense of unstructured data, and most of the considerable advantages that accrue to structured data are lost as a result.

Archival descriptions created with word processors are classic examples of unstructured data. Such unstructured descriptive metadata, even in a digital document like a PDF file, is largely opaque to any web appliance trying to process its content. The best result that can be achieved is a simple text string search, which is a far cry from being able, for example, to understand that a particular text string—"Jane Doe"—identifies an entity that is the creator of certain archival records, that is related to certain other organizations and persons, and that functioned in a certain geographic place during a certain time period. Structured data makes possible web searches of archival information that are capable of returning not only instances of the searched term, but also the archival context in which the term appears. This is the power that structured data can give to archivists and users. Our descriptive efforts should *always* position us to harness that power, rather than thwarting it.

We need to envision the content of archival description as *metadata*, rather than as prose. It is simply information that identifies and characterizes the information contained within the materials comprising the collection. We should think about our description activities—how we go about doing it—in those data-centric terms. We should refrain from thinking about description as prose. In creating descriptive information about a collection, we are not seeking to write an expository narrative, a work of prose that describes the collection. Instead, we are creating and recording data in a structured way so that those data can be manipulated in diverse environments, by humans and machines alike, to create particular and wide-ranging descriptive outputs.

Certain of those outputs might take a narrative form. They may also take the form of a structured list of results satisfying a search engine query. They might satisfy an open web search or a more constrained search within an integrated library system, an institutional repository, or an archival database. In such cases, the user might never be presented with a full finding aid, but only with descriptions of the specific collection unit(s) satisfying the search parameters. The important thing is that we are recording the various units of descriptive information as data, and we are utilizing the rules and guidelines found in our descriptive standards to form those data so that they can be effectively shared across many systems for many purposes at many different times.

Thinking of description as structured data also frees us to uncouple metadata capture (back-end work) from metadata sharing (public service). Separating those two activities introduces a great deal of flexibility into our work and also positions us to achieve more powerful outcomes for users. When we approach our work in recording descriptive documentation as metadata capture, we can simply utilize any tool for capturing structured data that is reliable and efficient, that is affordable to us, and that we have the skill to master. These tools—spreadsheets, databases, collection management systems—change comparatively slowly.

The tools aimed at sharing our metadata, however, are changing very rapidly and are becoming increasingly powerful. It therefore makes a great deal of sense to uncouple the two so that our tool for capturing metadata does not lock us into some particular tool(s) for sharing it in the widest and most meaningful ways possible. In the parlance of web programmers, any product created to serve out descriptive metadata to users is a *serialization* of that data. An EAD document, a PDF, an HTML page, or a result set from an Apache SOLR search could all be serializations of the same underlying set of structured descriptive metadata. Separating serialization from data capture ensures that we are not imprisoning our data in a way that holds them hostage to what may soon become bygone technologies.[7]

The Relationship of Description to Arrangement

Simply put, description reflects arrangement. The arrangement of the collection, as we discussed in the preceding section, is an intellectual construct that re-creates the original order of the records. The essential purpose of archival description is then to represent that arrangement to users in such a way that they can visualize and understand that original order. It may be helpful to use a cartographic analogy. The arranged collection represents the landscape that researchers need to traverse, or at least to understand and appreciate. Description—the archival finding aid—can then be seen as the *map* that provides a visual and semantic representation of the arrangement.

The purpose of description is to facilitate access to and use of the collection. It needs to help users understand the nature of the records, the context in which they were created and administered, the informational content of the records, their physical location, and how to gain access to them. This is a large task, and it needs to be done as sparingly as possible in terms of verbiage, because researchers rarely want to spend their time reading finding aids. A map is preferable to an essay, so efficient archival description is a roadmap to the collection.

The descriptive function can be facilitated using a variety of different output tools:

- *Container lists* provide the simplest rudimentary control over a collection by merely listing the essential contents of each of the containers comprising the collection. The level of control might be at the subgroup, series, or file level, but whatever the level, it provides the most basic administrative and intellectual control over the materials in the collection. Container lists are often prepared during the course of accessioning the collection and suffice until such time as the collection is formally processed. But in some repositories with limited resources, container lists may become the normal finding aid, perhaps accompanied by a catalog record or a brief collection-level summary of content and context.
- *Catalog records* provide a very brief overview of the collection as a whole. Catalog records are most often encoded as MARC records in local or shared public access catalogs (OPACs) and often coexist with similarly encoded records for books and other bibliographic holdings. Like bibliographic records, their main purpose is to facilitate the discovery and basic identification of relevant collections, rather than to provide detailed information about the content of the collection.
- *Detailed finding aids* may be referred to as inventories, registers, or simply finding aids. These highly organized documents carry the burden of description in current descriptive practice at most repositories. They fully represent the intellectual arrangement of the collection so that users can understand and navigate its parts and, eventually, determine which files or other subunits are most relevant for the research at hand. Typically, the finding aid also describes the creator(s) of the collection to provide a deeper understanding of the collection's context and the significance and meaning of the various collection materials. They may be hand-constructed, or they may be machine-generated as an output from some database structure. At present—whether presented as HTML, PDF, or other textual forms—detailed finding aids derive from rich and detailed descriptive information encoded into EAD (Encoded Archival Description), a markup standard that permits the easy communication and sharing of archival descriptions.
- *Guides* to collections are often prepared by repositories to provide users with brief inventories of all of their collections that can be perused to get a picture of the overall holdings in a repository. Rather than providing a single guide, a repository might break its holdings into several guides, each of them listing a portion of their holdings, organized by research topic (social welfare collections, mining industry), holding area (personal papers, business records, government records), era, geographic region, or some other meaningful category.

Archival Descriptive Standards

Archival description is based on standards. These standards have developed over the past forty years and are owned and maintained by professional associations like the Society of American Archivists and the International Council on Archives, among others. Although broad areas of consensus have always existed regarding the composition and structure of archival description, recent decades have witnessed increasing energy and focus within the archival community both in developing new standards and in asserting their authority in guiding descriptive practice.

Why are standards so important? I shave with a double-edge razor, and I know that international standards for the physical specifications of razor blades allow me to purchase blades made anywhere in the world with confidence that they will fit my razor. Similarly, I can buy a new razor from any manufacturer knowing that it will accept any of my razor blades without a hitch (though, occasionally, with a nick). Standards permit us to move with that same level of confidence in preparing archival descriptions. Standards help ensure that 1) users can become familiar with the conventions and forms of archival description because they are standardized; 2) metadata input appliances are all built to accommodate the defined elements of archival description; and 3) output appliances know how to assemble finding aids because the metadata elements and their relationships are the same for all collections being described.

Archivists over many years have come to believe that the application of descriptive standards will afford the most effective access to the greatest number of users. We have come to see the enforcement of descriptive standards as key to researcher success in several areas. First, it reinforces *predictability* in that users will, after a few attempts, become adept at navigating and understanding the finding aids because of the common elements in each. Second, it will enable *interoperability* in the sense that finding aids can coexist intelligibly in a union or interdisciplinary environment if they share a common structure and presentation. Third, it creates *efficiency* for archivists by permitting them to develop templates and automation tools not possible in an idiosyncratic environment. And, finally, because standards make use of recognized best practices, they help elevate the *quality* of description throughout the archival community.

When we adhere to descriptive standards, we know that we are following current *best practices*, which assures us that we are producing finding aids of high quality, that conform to community expectations in terms of content and structure, that are efficiently produced, that are reasonably consistent in look and feel from finding aid to finding aid, and that are as straightforward as possible for researchers to navigate and understand.

The standards that apply to archival description break down into several distinct types, each of which serves a different purpose and all of which are interdependent in unleashing the power and effectiveness that we expect from standards. Different writers categorize the standards differently. For me, the categorization provided by Fox and Wilkerson in their brief manual is the most helpful. They break down descriptive standards into four types based on function:

- Data structure standards
- Data content standards
- Data interchange standards
- Data value standards[8]

Data structure standards

In a sense, the bedrock of descriptive standards, data structure standards provide the elemental framework for creating descriptive metadata. Structural standards define the suite of data elements required for robust description and then define a structure of relationships existing among those elements. We can visualize that structure as a set of related boxes or bins, each of which is specified to accept a certain category of data (name, title, quantity, and so forth). They do not, however, tell us how to format the information that goes into those boxes nor how much information to include. Other standards guide those decisions.

Figure 4 depicts the set of data elements defined by the *General International Standard for Archival Description* (ISAD(G)), which is the profession's accepted structural standard for controlling information primarily about the *content* of archival collections, although it also accommodates information about *context*.[9] This reflects the predominant practice today, in which all descriptive information tends to be expressed in a single finding aid, rather than being dispersed between separate collection and creator descriptions.

The International Council on Archives (ICA), an international organization whose mission is to support the archival profession in nations across the globe, maintains the standard, adopted in 1999 by its Committee on Descriptive Standards. As a standard adopted by an international body,

3.1. Identity Statement Area
    3.1.1. Reference code
    3.1.2. Title
    3.1.3. Dates
    3.1.4. Level of description
    3.1.5. Extent and medium of the unit of description

3.2. Context Area
    3.2.1. Name of creator
    3.2.2. Administrative/biographical history
    3.2.3. Archival history
    3.2.4. Immediate source of acquisition or transfer

3.3. Content and Structure Area
    3.3.1. Scope and content
    3.3.2. Appraisal, destruction and scheduling information
    3.3.3. Accruals
    3.3.4. System of arrangement

3.4. Conditions of Access and Use Area
    3.4.1. Conditions governing access
    3.4.2. Conditions governing reproduction
    3.4.3. Language/scripts of material
    3.4.4. Physical characteristics and technical requirements
    3.4.5. Finding aids

3.5. Allied Materials Area
    3.5.1. Existence and location of originals
    3.5.2. Existence and location of copies
    3.5.3. Related units of description
    3.5.4. Publication note

3.6. Notes Area
    3.6.1. Note

3.7. Description control area
    3.7.1. Archivist's note
    3.7.2. Rules or conventions
    3.7.3. Date of description

FIGURE 4. ISAD(G) data elements

it is intended to influence the development of national standards and to be used in concert with them. In the two decades since its publication, it has become the recognized structural standard in the United States and many other countries and is the base upon which our content and interchange standards rest.

ISAD(G) establishes twenty-six data elements relevant for describing content and requires that six of them (Reference code, Title, Creator, Dates, Extent of the unit of description, Level of description) be used in every description. So, the standard gives us very important guidance for creating finding aids that contain all the information that our descriptive principles and our knowledge of use and users suggest will create sufficient and consistent descriptions of the content of our collections. It also gives us a basic structure for grouping and presenting that information in a finding aid.

ISAD(G) organizes and structures the essential elements of archival description into several basic functional areas:

1. *Identity.* This small set of elements provides the essential pieces of information needed to identify a unit of collection materials at *any* hierarchical level. These elements are just as important in describing an item or a file as they are in describing the collection in its entirety.
2. *Context.* These elements describe the creator, the creation, and the administrative history of the collection unit being described. Again, they are valid at any level.
3. *Content.* These elements describe the informational content and the internal arrangement of the materials, at any appropriate level, as well as information about their acquisition.
4. *Conditions of access and use.* These elements specify *how* the materials may be accessed and then used by researchers. They deal with both the legal requirements involved, as well as potential physical (form, media) or intellectual (language) barriers to use.
5. *Allied materials.* These elements make the user aware of related information resources that share a common provenance with the collection being described. They may reference variant forms of the same materials or other materials separated at some point.
6. *Notes.* This simply provides a convenient place to record other descriptive narrative that cannot be accommodated intellectually into any of the other elements.
7. *Descriptive control.* These elements provide a place to record information about the finding aid itself, rather than about the collection materials.

Taken together, these twenty-six elements accommodate all of the information categories generally accepted to be necessary for robust description of archival holdings. And the standard organizes them in a system that helps promote effective understanding and navigation when preparing findings aids.

Shaefer and Bunde also call out the important role ISAD(G) plays in establishing a framework for multilevel description, and they emphasize the four principles for multilevel description bound into its assumptions and requirements:

1. Description proceeds from the general to the specific.
2. Only information relevant to the level of the unit being described should be provided.
3. Levels of description should be linked.

4. To avoid redundancy, information should be listed only at the highest applicable unit of description.[10]

So, ISAD(G) provides archivists with three important things as a structural standard: it specifies and defines information elements necessary for describing the content of archival collections; it provides a structure for organizing those elements in a lucid manner that facilitates use; and it ensures that multilevel description is accommodated throughout.

But it is not the only structural standard used by archivists. While ISAD(G) provides a framework for describing content, a second structural standard—the *International Standard Archival Authority Record for Corporate Bodies, Persons, and Families* (ISAAR(CPF))—serves as our companion structural standard for describing collection *creators* and the other agents and actors reflected in a collection, rather than collection content.

Like ISAD(G), ICA maintains the standard, developed (beginning in 1993) and adopted by its Committee on Descriptive Standards (CDS); the current second version was published in 2003. The CDS realized during the development of ISAD(G) that it, by itself, was insufficient to guide complete archival description. A companion standard was needed to define the structure and data elements necessary to describe creators and prepare robust archival authority records. As they described their objectives in the preface to the publication:

> The primary purpose, therefore, of this standard is to provide general rules for the standardization of archival descriptions of records creators and the context of records creation, thus enabling:
> - access to archives and records based on the provision of descriptions of the context of records creation that are linked to descriptions of the often diverse and physically dispersed records themselves;
> - understanding by users of the context underlying the creation and use of archives and records so that they can better interpret their meaning and significance;
> - precise identification of records creators incorporating descriptions of relationships between different entities, especially documentation of administrative change within corporate bodies or personal change of circumstances in individuals and families; and
> - the exchange of these descriptions between institutions, systems and/or networks.[11]

So, ISAAR(CPF) has ambitious goals beyond those embraced in the Context area of ISAD(G):
- To enable archivists to describe creating entities in a much fuller way than the rules of bibliographic authority records permitted
- To enable richer and fuller authority records able to express all of the contextual information relevant to robust archival description
- To enable the description of relationships—between all the entities who were creators and subjects of archival resources—in ways that content description alone could not accommodate

To accomplish these objectives, ISAAR(CPF) defines twenty-seven data elements relevant to describing the creators and the subjects of archival collections, as well as a basic structure for grouping all of that information. Figure 5 depicts the information elements that comprise the standard, which fall into four essential areas:

1. *Identity.* A set of subelements defines and uniquely identifies the entity being described. They include establishing whether it is a person, corporate body, or family, and then expressing the authorized form of the name, as well as variations.
2. *Description.* This semantically rich area is intended to describe the history, roles, context, and activities of the corporate body, person, or family. It specifies dates of existence of the entity, a brief historical or biographical sketch, the places where the entity was based, as well as denoting the functions, roles, and activities central to the entity. It also provides a place to record a family genealogy and the legal status and mandates associated with a corporate body.
3. *Relationships.* This area is used to describe the entity's relationships with other corporate bodies, persons, and families that may be described in other authority records. This is an important inclusion in the standard because it allows the archivist to link entities together and provide rich descriptions of relationships themselves. The relationships between entities convey much of the meaning in archival description.

5.1 Identity Area
    5.1.1 Type of entity
    5.1.2 Authorized form(s) of name
    5.1.3 Parallel forms of name
    5.1.4 Standardized forms of name according to other rules
    5.1.5 Other forms of name
    5.1.6 Identifiers for corporate bodies

5.2 Description Area
    5.2.1 Dates of existence
    5.2.2 History
    5.2.3 Places
    5.2.4 Legal status
    5.2.5 Functions, occupations and activities
    5.2.6 Mandates/Sources of authority
    5.2.7 Internal structures/Genealogy
    5.2.8 General context

5.3 Relationships Area
    5.3.1 Names/Identifiers of related corporate bodies, persons or families
    5.3.2 Category of relationship
    5.3.3 Description of relationship
    5.3.4 Dates of the relationship

5.4 Control Area
    5.4.1 Authority record identifier
    5.4.2 Institution identifiers
    5.4.3 Rules and/or conventions
    5.4.4 Status
    5.4.5 Level of detail
    5.4.6 Dates of creation, revision or deletion
    5.4.7 Languages and scripts
    5.4.8 Sources
    5.4.9 Maintenance notes

FIGURE 5. ISAAR(CPF) data elements

4. *Control.* This area may contain technical and administrative information about the authority record itself.

The standard specifies all the information elements necessary for a standalone authority record, or for all the contextual information that might be incorporated into a typical integrated finding aid. Together, ISAD(G) and ISAAR(CPF) comprise the structural standards necessary for uniformly and completely describing archival collections.

Data content standards

Data content standards tell us how to express the information that goes into each of the data elements that forms the structural standard. Whereas the structural standard tells us what *type* of information is required, optional, or not acceptable for each type of data, the content standard explains the purpose and scope of that content, the sources within the collection or other resources from which the information should be drawn, how to form and punctuate the information, and examples of how it should look. If our structural standard is the skeleton of the body of description, the content standard provides the flesh and blood.

Data content standards were the first category of standards explored and adopted by the archival description community. As archivists moved toward adopting some version of the MARC format for creating catalog records, they attempted to apply the library community's content standard—*The Anglo-American Cataloging Rules, Second Edition* (AACR2)—but found it wanting in several respects. Chapter 4 of AACR2 provides explicit rules for cataloging manuscripts, but those rules are clearly tailored for individual manuscript items in rare books and manuscripts environments. The rules posed several serious problems:

- *They were not developed to accommodate collection-level cataloging.* As Steve Hensen notes, they "invariably made the mistake of assuming that, for cataloging purposes, the analog to the book was the individual manuscript, often treasured if for nothing more than its autograph value."[12] This disregards the archival principles emphasizing the unity and primary significance of the whole of the collection and, in purely practical terms, results in an explosion of catalog records for collection items that can only confuse users.
- *The "source of information" in archival description is profoundly different from that in bibliographic cataloging.* While library catalogers can depend upon the work's title page and its verso, archivists almost always lack a clear expression of necessary descriptive information in some prescribed place. Instead, they must rely on information they themselves compile in the course of producing other finding aids beyond the catalog record—administrative and biographical notes, container lists, content notes, and so forth—as well as information recorded in the collection materials themselves. Asserting the legitimacy of those sorts of information for descriptive purposes empowered archivists to hew to their fundamental principles and to avoid the draconian punctuation requirements for identifying "supplied" (as opposed to title page) information.
- *The catalog record is typically only one of multiple devices employed in archival cataloging.* Archivists generally use a catalog record for one specific purpose: to discover and identify a particular collection within some larger universe of archival collections,

whether a single repository or multiple repositories sharing a union catalog. Fuller descriptive data that describe in greater detail the hierarchically arranged components of the collection generally bear the greater descriptive weight. An archival content standard needs to address all such descriptive surrogates within the same general set of rules.

- *Bibliographic rules for forming names and other access points are unhelpful for archivists.* The authors of published works are known (if not widely known) entities, whose identities are typically controlled in authority records. The creators and other named entities in most archival collections are generally not so lucky and therefore need to be fully identified within archival descriptions, not simply to distinguish them from similarly named entities, but also to explain their relevance or importance to the collection at hand. Library conventions, which tend to preference the sparest form of identifier, are inadequate to serve archival needs. Therefore, archival content standards need a more robust set of rules and guidelines for naming persons, corporate bodies, families, and other entities.

These important needs compelled the first (1983) archival content standard, *Archives, Personal Papers, and Manuscripts* (APPM), which carefully trod a middle ground that respected archival principles, provided functionality that archivists required, and still aligned closely enough with AACR2 rules to ensure that archival catalog records might coexist peacefully with bibliographic records in a shared catalog. While APPM was neutral enough to provide basic rules that worked for all forms of archival finding aids, it was nevertheless obvious that it was optimized for creating archival catalog records. As such, it was perfectly suited to constructing brief records describing entire collections and less so for describing the component parts of archival collections, especially their hierarchical complexity. Although a number of repositories experimented with workarounds, such as creating separate catalog records for each series (or even file) and then linking them together into a hierarchical structure, such approaches proved unwieldy to create and confusing for researchers to use.

So, in the early 1990s, SAA placed APPM on a formal revision schedule with the understanding that it needed to be replaced with a new content standard that could accommodate all finding aid types and the full complexity of archival description. With the added incentive provided by the initial launch of EAD (1996) and the publication of ISAD(G) (1999), an international team of US and Canadian archivists (Canadian-US Task Force on Archival Description, aka CUSTARD) began discussions to develop a joint standard that could supersede both APPM and the existing Canadian *Rules for Archival Description* (RAD).[13] Those deliberations ceased in 2003 with mutual acknowledgment that significant differences in approach and requirements existed between the description communities in the two nations. As a result, the Canadian members worked to revise RAD, and the US team members proceeded to adapt the existing CUSTARD project draft into a new content standard; SAA adopted it in 2004 as *Describing Archives: A Content Standard* (DACS).[14]

Describing Archives: A Content Standard

DACS provides an output-neutral set of rules to create a variety of archival descriptions, including detailed finding aids and catalog records. It is divided into two parts: Part I provides rules for forming the information content that goes into the twenty-six data elements defined in the structural standard ISAD(G); Part II provides rules for forming names and creating archival authority records in keeping with the twenty-seven data elements defined in the structural standard ISAAR(CPF). For each data element in Part 1, DACS organizes its prescriptions as follows:

1. Naming the data element
2. Explaining its purpose and scope
3. Identifying the recommended sources of content information
4. Providing general rules, with examples
5. Providing examples of full encoding of that element as it might be expressed in both an EAD finding aid and a MARC catalog record

For the Part II elements, DACS provides general rules, variations for particular situations, and examples. As a result, DACS, in a very comprehensive and explicit manner, explains how to source and then express in written form the content that goes into each ISAD(G) or ISAAR-CPF data element.

Because an important goal of DACS is to facilitate multilevel description, its opening chapter is devoted to explaining multilevel description as an approach necessary in many cases, but unnecessary in others depending upon the archivist's objectives (Am I pursuing full control or only preliminary control?); her resource constraints (Do I lack the time or staff to perform detailed description?); and the nature of the collection (Does this collection simply require multilevel description to be usable?). It goes on to define the data elements required, and those that are optional, in both single-level description and in multilevel description. As the authors emphasize, "[n]ot all of the DACS elements are required in every archival description. Combinations of descriptive elements will vary, depending on whether the archivist considers a specific description to be preliminary or complete and whether it describes archival materials at a single level (e.g., collection level or item level) or at multiple levels that have a whole-to-part relationship."[15]

The DACS authors also ground the rules in a "Statement of Principles" that establishes their *bona fides* in long-standing archival theory and usage, and seeks to further move the descriptive community toward best practices. They assert the following:

> **Principle 1:** Records in archives possess unique characteristics.
> **Principle 2:** The principle of *respect des fonds* is the basis of archival arrangement and description.
> **Principle 3:** Arrangement involves the identification of groupings within the material.
> **Principle 4:** Description reflects arrangement.
> **Principle 5:** The rules of description apply to all archival materials, regardless of form or medium.
> **Principle 6:** The principles of archival description apply equally to records created by corporate bodies, individuals, or families.
> **Principle 7:** Archival descriptions may be presented at varying levels of detail to produce a variety of outputs.
> **Principle 7.1:** Levels of description correspond to levels of arrangement.
> **Principle 7.2:** Relationships between levels of description must be clearly indicated.
> **Principle 7.3:** Information provided at each level of description must be appropriate to that level.
> **Principle 8:** The creators of archival materials, as well as the materials themselves, must be described.[16]

DACS therefore emphasizes that archives are unique resources with important characteristics and needs that must be respected and leveraged in their descriptive surrogates. The standard is built intentionally for the archival community, is sufficient to their needs, and can produce effective results.[17]

Data interchange standards

While our structural standards provide frameworks for defining and organizing the information elements essential for documenting archival holdings, and content standards guide us in choosing and expressing the information that populates those frameworks, our data interchange standards provide the technical structure and specifications that enable archivists to publish and share that documentation locally and over global networks. They provide the encoding structure and semantics required so that archival finding aids can interoperate successfully and meaningfully with similarly encoded documents in supporting networks anywhere in the world.

These standards can go by various names. Sometimes they are referred to as *encoding standards* because they provide technical syntaxes for encoding archival description in specific programming languages. They are also called *communication standards* to reflect their role in allowing archival description serializations to talk to specific automated systems capable of hosting finding aids and to interoperate with other resource description instances within those systems. They have also been called *transmission standards* to emphasize their functional ability to turn finding aids into stable technical packages that can be transmitted over networks to various destinations.

These variant names all suggest the role and power of these standards in transforming archival finding aids into efficient, mobile, and semantically rich documents that can be structured, repurposed, and shared to be as useful as possible. And, at their most powerful level—something still emerging—they can transform archival documentation from *documents* to *data*. In doing so, archival descriptive tools have metamorphosed from fixed semantic structures with limited manipulability into extremely parsible data with no fixed form that can be repurposed into many forms and interrogated in unlimited ways, with the ultimate goal of providing the greatest value to users of the collection and its description. These interchange standards are leading us into these exciting and professionally empowering new directions.

At the time of this writing, archivists have formally adopted three interchange standards: the MARC21 format (MARC is the acronym for MAchine-Readable Cataloging) for encoding collection-level (usually) catalog records, *Encoded Archival Description* (EAD) for encoding full, multilevel (typically) finding aids, and *Encoded Archival Context–Corporate Bodies, Persons, and Families* (EAC-CPF) for encoding information about creators, agents, and subjects of collections and, more important, comprehensive and semantically rich archival authority records. Of the three formal standards, the Library of Congress maintains MARC21, while SAA maintains EAD and EAC-CPF, inherently archival standards.

MARC21

The earliest of the three to be adopted by archivists is MARC21, the current version of the format for exchanging bibliographic and other information maintained by the Library of Congress. Its adoption proved to be a crucial tipping point in getting the archival descriptive community to envisage both standardization of practice and the automated exchange of descriptions as positive goods. As Kathleen Roe explains it:

> The introduction of the MARC AMC format in 1983 and the possibility for exchange of information, participation of library systems, and national utilities were major catalysts for organizations to develop standardized practices. MARC AMC was instrumental in putting to rest the former notion that archival descriptive practices in the United States could not be codified into any common guidelines or standards applicable to a wide variety of institutions, and particularly to both archives and manuscripts. While it was and remains an imperfect solution to the multidimensional, multilevel needs of archival description, the dissemination and adoption of MARC AMC was critical in bringing about a transformation in the standardization of archival description. The archival profession finally was developing common terminology, common practices, and common retrieval alternatives to support the needs of users.[18]

MARC21, which is the result of the 1998 integration of the multiple MARC formats (including MARC AMC), has since become the accepted standard for exchanging encoded archival description at the collection level. All of the essential DACS content elements can be mapped (see Appendix F) to data fields comprising the MARC21 format. But, because MARC21 records are unsuited to multilevel description, the format has become constrained in archival practice to creating brief collection-level records that can be shared in local online public access catalogs and in larger union catalogs and databases. The purpose of archival MARC21 records is therefore not to describe the content of collections in any meaningful detail but, instead, to facilitate their discovery and basic identification by researchers within some larger catalog or search system. The library world is at this time moving away from MARC21 as a cataloging platform and is moving haltingly toward a new encoding platform based upon the emerging *Resource Description and Access*, a new content standard intended to replace AACR2. Nevertheless, MARC21 is likely to play a role among archival interchange standards for the next several years.

It is important to note here that MARC21 is a data interchange mechanism used by many archival repositories, but certainly not by all. As the library community originally developed it, MARC21 tends to be employed most widely in academic archives, which depend at least in part upon online public access catalogs (OPACs) for the initial discovery of their resources. Other types of repositories—these include government units, businesses, religious institutions, museums, and other cultural institutions—only rarely depend upon MARC21 records as descriptive tools. Because nearly two-thirds of US archivists work in academic library environments, MARC21 remains an important descriptive tool. The importance of the standard is no doubt waning, however, as academic repositories make increasingly greater use of institutional repositories and the open Web as platforms for basic discovery.

EAD

The second interchange standard, *Encoded Archival Description*, serves the descriptive community as its bespoke vehicle for encoding and sharing full archival finding aids. As such, it is the flagship (or at least the workhorse) of the three interchange standards. Its encoding architecture realizes the structural framework expressed in ISAD(G), so it enables the creation of finding aids that conform fully to the international structural standard at the base of descriptive standards. It also fully complies with the DACS content standard and provides a large set of elements and modifying attributes able to fully express and conform to the principles, rules, and semantics that make up DACS.

The long and arduous process to develop a data encoding and interchange standard simultaneously complex enough, flexible enough, and practicable enough to accommodate robust archival description requirements, as well as the wide-ranging practices of diverse archival repositories, commenced in 1993 with the Berkeley Finding Aid Project. That effort brought together a small community of US descriptive and technical experts to develop an encoding structure that could meet these difficult, sometimes conflicting, requirements. Developed initially in Standard Generalized Markup Language (SGML,) the prototype migrated to the emergent Extensible Markup Language (XML) platform prior to its alpha release in 1996. The release was followed by a period of testing at a number of institutions, which widened to include European and Canadian repositories. The first stable release finally appeared in 1997.[19]

Although its use within descriptive communities began immediately, its uptake remains a work in progress, and a significant plurality of repositories remain outside of the large and growing EAD community.[20] SAA supports that community through the work of its Standards Committee and through rich information and implementation resources on its Standards Portal.[21]

Through the nearly continuous work of SAA's EAD Working Group and, later, its Technical Subcommittee on Encoded Archival Description, EAD has matured and sharpened its focus through three maintenance and revision cycles culminating in the 2015 release of the current stable version, EAD3. The TS-EAD cochairs sum up the standard's breadth and importance succinctly in the preface to the EAD3 Tag Library:

> Encoded Archival Description (EAD) is the international metadata transmission standard for hierarchical descriptions of archival records. Developed by the EAD Working Group of the Society of American Archivists and first published in 1998, EAD is an Extensible Markup Language (XML) format used by archivists around the globe. The development of EAD made it possible to create electronic finding aids within a specifically archival data structure compliant with General International Standard Archival Description (ISAD(G)). This innovation was a crucial impetus behind the swift migration of archival description to the internet, the acceptance of national archival descriptive content standards like Describing Archives: A Content Standard (DACS), and the emergence of a professional consensus that archival description existed to be shared widely and shared well.[22]

EAD3 comprises 165 data elements that together encompass all of the pieces of information that archivists have determined to be useful for describing archival materials. EAD easily accommodates all of the functionality and nuance suggested within ISAD(G) and DACS. To many archivists, such a large set of elements seems to overcomplicate the work of creating finding aids and to create too many possibilities to choose from. Some incorrectly believe that most or all of the EAD elements are required in a given finding aid; they are not. Others worry that the EAD element structure forces them to forsake the look and feel of their finding aids; it generally does not. What EAD does do is create a common language for encoding finding aids—identifying and "marking up" all their pieces and parts—so that those finding aids can be widely shared across the Web and can be expected to interoperate effectively with the EAD-encoded finding aids of any other repository, all to the ultimate benefit of users who always benefit from standardized approaches to conveying information about collections.

Fears about EAD being unsustainable in terms of laborious encoding requirements are exaggerated. Assuming that a repository has typical desktop workstations that can support the usual suite of office applications, only a relatively inexpensive piece of XML editing software is required to create EAD finding aids. Many tools, templates, and instruction manuals are available on the aforementioned SAA Standards Portal, as well as on the extremely helpful official EAD website.[23] It is also possible to create EAD documents without doing the encoding work directly. Collection management systems aimed at archival repositories, especially ArchivesSpace, allow archivists to enter collection descriptions into convenient fill-in forms, which then transform the input data into EAD documents, if necessary,[24] on the public service end.

More important, EAD, like DACS, does not require any particular level of detail or complexity in a finding aid. As long as the basic DACS rules for single-level or multilevel descriptions are adhered to, valid and satisfactory finding aids can be created by using a relatively small number of data elements.

At its heart, an EAD document has only two basic parts. A top element called <eadheader> contains information about the finding aid itself and the repository that produced it, expressed in a few separate subelements. The second part, <archdesc>, contains all of the subelements necessary to describe the collection materials themselves. The first section of <archdesc> contains the subelements necessary to describe the collection as a whole, as would be the case in a simple collection-level description or in a MARC record. It generally contains the following subelements, although it may include others, if necessary:

- <origination>, the creator's name
- <unittitle>, the title of the collection
- <physdesc>, the physical extent (quantity) of the collection materials
- , a brief scope and content summary
- <accessrestrict> <userestrict>, restrictions governing access and/or use
- <arrangement>, the arrangement scheme of the collection
- <bioghist>, a biographical or historical note (or notes)
- <processinfo>, information about the processing of the collection
- <scopecontent>, one or more notes about the scope and content of the collection materials
- <controlaccess>, one or more subject or name access points for the collection

Then, in multilevel descriptions, a repetition of these same elements follows for each hierarchical unit of the collection being described. Each of these descriptions of specific component parts of the collection is contained within a <c> (for component) element. The <c> instances are numbered to express the hierarchical levels within the arrangement of the materials. They might go something like this:

<c01> Series 1
    <c02> File 1
    <c02> File 2
<c01> Series 2
    <c02> File a
    <c02> File b

Within each of these nested <c> elements, all of the content descriptors previously noted (and many more) are available to be used. But, at any hierarchical level, only those elements *required* by DACS must be used. All other elements are optional, to be used at the discretion of the repository. So, although the 165 EAD elements offer almost endless descriptive possibilities and alternatives, EAD is a helpful servant, not a master, and we are free to make our description as lean or as verbose as we choose. The utility and sustainability of EAD lie in understanding that important spirit of the standard, which the large community of archivists who have developed it over the years carefully baked into it.

EAC-CPF

The third data interchange standard is also the most recent and, as a result, has yet to be implemented in any consequential way, at least in the United States. *Encoded Archival Context—Corporate Bodies, Persons, and Families* (EAC-CPF) represents the 2011 culmination of efforts that began in 1998 with meetings of a small group of archivists from several countries who were interested in applying the technologies and objectives of EAD to the description of archival creators and context.[25] They were following on the heels of the ICA's adoption in 1996 of ISAAR(CPF), which provided a structural standard for producing descriptions of creating entities and the context of archival collections. The archivists were also motivated by complementary advice in DACS:

> [I]nformation about creators of archival materials can be captured and maintained in a separate system of archival authority records that are linked to the archival descriptions rather than being embedded within them. This approach reflects the model created by the International Council on Archives where the General International Standard for Archival Description (ISAD[G]) provides rules on description and the International Standard Archival Authority Record for Corporate Bodies, Persons and Families (ISAAR[CPF]) governs the creation of information about creators.[26]

The resulting EAC-CPF standard, maintained by SAA, provides an XML-encoded platform for creating archival authority records that utilize the structure defined in ISAAR(CPF) and embraces the rules for expressing content found in DACS, Part II. Although EAC-CPF at this date has been applied largely on a project basis rather than as a part of normal repository procedures, it provides a clear way forward to separate archival finding aids into those describing collection materials and those describing the entities who create collections or are the subjects of them (aka CPF entities). This separation could have several advantages:

- Description of content via EAD may become, somewhat counterintuitively, *leaner* and *richer* at the same time. EAD finding aids could be relieved of the burden of describing the many creators and other significant entities that populate collections. Finding aids could simply link out from their names to freestanding authority records using open linked data functionality.
- EAD records may require fewer remedial actions in future, as entity descriptions would no longer become dated or inaccurate over time.
- Description of entities can become much more robust because an archival authority record is able to contain much more granular information about the CPF entity than an EAD finding aid could ever sustainably include. And every finding aid, in any repository, that links to a given authority record benefits from this same richness.

- The finding aid information about CPF entities perforce becomes more trustworthy, as all of the information concerning the entity is compiled in a single authenticated space. And that information would presumably be amenable to continual improvement because of its transparency to a larger description community. Our contextual description is thus more accountable.

An EAC-CPF record is an XML instance describing a single entity, and it may draw on a vocabulary of eighty-eight defined data elements to create a very robust and granular description. The record contains two parts, a <control> element that contains identifying and administrative data about the record itself, and its maintenance over time, and a <cpfDescription> element that contains all of the content information about the entity. The latter element includes several basic sections, each with its suite of subelements:

- *<identity>* (required). This is a complex structure containing the name or names used by the CPF entity over the course of the entity's existence.
- *<description>* (optional). This is a container for all of the formal description elements parallel to those in ISAAR(CPF) for the description of the CPF entity. These include such data points as dates of existence, history, places, legal status, functions, occupations, and activities and provide the rich description of the entity.
- *<relations>* (optional). This section includes one or more references to, or descriptions of, related corporate bodies, persons, or families <cpfRelation>; related functions <functionRelation>; or related resources <resourceRelation>. It is this set of elements that enables the powerful linking of one authority record to another, of an authority record to an EAD finding aid, and from an authority record to any external information resource (e.g., a publication, a database). EAD3 was subsequently developed, in part, to take advantage of the relational functionality built into EAC-CPF.
- *<alternativeSet>* (optional). This section allows the inclusion of two or more descriptions for the *same* CPF entity derived from two or more separate systems, expressed within a single EAC-CPF instance.[27]

In some future archival description environment, EAD and EAC records are intended to interoperate very flexibly with the assistance of their interdependent metadata elements, perhaps to deliver custom finding aids to end users that each draw information out of multiple EAD and EAC instances. Needless to say, that day remains some time off, but a number of promising experiments are proving the viability of the concept.

Data value standards

The final category of descriptive standards consists of those that, rather than providing frameworks or rules to guide our finding aid creation, provide us with controlled vocabularies—sets of preselected, authorized terms that we can use to populate various data elements in our descriptions. What value do controlled terminologies offer? The benefits are basically twofold: 1) providing consistency for users who benefit from employing standardized search terms for a given concept, topic, or name; and 2) facilitating discovery and retrieval by helping to collocate all existing resources documenting a particular concept, topic, or name in response to a search.

Controlled vocabularies may appear in simple dictionary form (*Library of Congress Subject Headings*) or in hierarchical thesauri (*Art and Architecture Thesaurus*). They may be rigidly constructed authority files, or they may be de facto standards that accommodate some flexibility in application by practitioners. At this time, none of these vocabularies have been specifically created by archivists for the use of archivists. While some particular agency or community supports each, they all tend to be widely used by resource description practitioners in many information communities.

Archivists can, and do, utilize controlled vocabularies when expressing names (especially), places, events, occupations, topics, and concepts within the title elements and the unstructured narrative notes throughout their finding aids. Doing so can offer a great assist in expediting user success, as it tends to gather together all relevant sources. It can be very helpful, for example, to always refer to one particular Native American people as *Ojibwa*, rather than using variant forms like *Chippewa, Otchipwe, Ojibwe*, and so forth. In practical terms, however, controlled terminology is most frequently used to populate data elements specifically intended for searchable access points (like the *subject* field in a MARC record). This tends to be a more manageable approach in terms of processing labor and leverages some of the value of machine searchability.

Archivists routinely use several data value standards:[28]

- **Library of Congress Name Authority File (LCNAF).** LCNAF is a steadily expanding list of authorized name forms that comprises eight million names of individuals, events, corporate bodies, places, and titles. Authorized bibliographic catalogers who belong to the Program for Cooperative Cataloging Name Authority Cooperative (NACO) contribute records to the widely shared resource. Because a chief objective of the file is to disambiguate names, the amount of information included for any given name may range from the very brief (*Smith, Bob*) to the very full (*Smith, Robert Gerald, 1832–1912*), even including occupation and place information.[29]
- **Union List of Artists' Names (ULAN).** ULAN is maintained by the Getty Research Institute and is an authoritative source for standardized names of individuals and corporate bodies associated with the production, administration, and use of visual art and architecture. A structured thesaurus rather than a simple list, it contains hierarchical, equivalence, and associative relationships among terms and entities.[30]
- **Library of Congress Subject Headings (LCSH).** A dictionary of terms rather than a carefully structured thesaurus, LCSH may include topical terms, geographic terms, historical events, and form and genre terms. Rules permit the user to expand core LCSH terms by adding subheadings, places, and dates drawn from controlled lists and/or rules. LCSH terms, often not current usage or natural language terms, are best applied in controlled access point data elements in MARC records and EAD finding aids.[31]
- **Art and Architecture Thesaurus (AAT).** Because of the profusion of document types found in our collections, it has always been important for us to identify those document types in our descriptions as part of our effort to explain the content of the materials. To accomplish this, it benefits us to have precise, agreed-upon terminology to reference document *genre* (e.g., architectural drawings), as well as document *form* (e.g., blueprints). The AAT,[32] which is another project of the Getty Research Institute, provides

a very rich compendium of terminology organized in faceted hierarchies, which take users from an abstract concept down a decision tree that ends with a preferred term. In the case of the genre/form examples above, users enter the hierarchy at the "visual and verbal communication" concept and end up at the form term "blueprints," including a definition and related terms and objects.

AAT, in addition to terms for collection objects and document types, contains separate hierarchies for *functions* and for *agents*. Both of these are, of course, germane to archival description, which requires us to identify the functions and activities documented within a collection, as well as the types of agents who perform those functions.

Companion standards

While EAD and DACS are purpose-built to manage archival materials in any form or medium, including digital collections, in some cases, digital objects made available directly online may require additional descriptive metadata, either to enhance their discovery and retrieval, to ensure they are rendered properly to be directly accessible and understandable, or to communicate and manage important rights associated with them. In such situations, companion standards developed by other information-sharing communities are important resources for descriptive metadata. A large number of these companion standards have relevance for archival description under certain conditions; the SAA Standards Portal (from which the following descriptions are paraphrased) notes and links to them. A few are particularly notable for archivists:

- **Dublin Core Metadata Element Set *(DCMES)*.** The DCMES[33] is a basic fifteen-element set designed to represent core features of resources across all formats. The *Dublin Core Usage Guidelines* sometimes suggest (but do not require) specific content guidelines or controlled vocabularies. Simple Dublin Core (DC) is widely known as the baseline metadata format required for all resources shared via Open Archives Initiative Protocol for Metadata Harvesting (OAI-PMH). It has also been used to encode individual photo images and similar item-level resources for basic online discovery. The ability to map DCMES to EAD elements creates a powerful tool for allowing EAD data to interoperate with nonarchival data in external systems that do not recognize native EAD instances.
- **Metadata Object Description Schema *(MODS)*.** MODS[34] was developed by the Library of Congress Network Development and MARC Standards Office as a MARC-compatible metadata format expressed in XML and using language-based element names. It utilizes a reduced set of MARC fields in a way that allows a MARC-like record to be enclosed within some other metadata structure (e.g., METS).
- **Metadata Encoding and Transmission Standard *(METS)*.** METS[35] is an XML metadata standard maintained by the Library of Congress intended to package all the information needed to represent a complex digital object, including both the content files and the metadata that describe them. METS interprets the nature and structure of complex digital objects (multiple pages, multiple files) so that they are rendered properly for users.

Archival Description Is Multilevel

A distinctive feature of archival description that separates it from resource description in other environments is the notion that description is multilevel in nature. This idea proceeds directly from the hierarchical nature of arrangement discussed earlier. If a collection breaks down into natural intellectual groupings that can be presented hierarchically, and if a goal of description is to represent that arrangement, then a full description of the collection and its essential parts will be multilevel in nature. In any collection complex enough to express multiple levels of intellectual arrangement, a full detailed description will first describe the collection as a whole and will then move on to describe each of its important parts, paralleling the intellectual order reflected in its arrangement.

In the case of the Jane Doe Papers represented in Figure 1, a multilevel approach would provide an overall description of the collection as a whole. It would then describe each of the parts, as warranted by their importance, in an order reflecting their arrangement. So, we would first describe the Law Practice series, followed by descriptions of the Client files, the Tax files, and the California Bar Association files that comprise the series. Then we would describe the Environmental Issues series and its component files, and so forth until all of the essential components had been described.

DACS and ISAD(G) emphasize several important principles for creating multilevel description:

- *Multilevel description is an option, not a requirement.* It is completely appropriate to describe a collection as a whole without describing its parts. This is especially true for small collections that exhibit no real intellectual hierarchy in their arrangement. Even with regard to a collection that has a complex hierarchical arrangement, a repository may elect not to perform multilevel description, or to defer doing so, for reasons of economy and practicality.
- *The levels of description correspond to the levels of arrangement.* Because description reflects arrangement, the components being described in a multilevel description should match those intellectual components preserved in the physical arrangement of the materials.
- *Description flows from the general to the specific.* In arranging the materials, we performed our work first at a subgroup or series level, and then proceeded to subseries or file levels, and so forth. Description should follow the same path so that the resulting description, when complete, reflects the intellectual arrangement of the collection.
- *Information provided at each level should be appropriate to that level.* When we describe a particular series, we should not lose our focus and introduce information about the contents of a file or some particular items within the series. We should provide information that describes the series as a whole. If we introduce biographical or administrative information in a series description, it should be relevant to the subject of the series and not to the collection as a whole. Furthermore, if we applied our greatest

arrangement effort at the series level, rather than at the file level, we should probably provide richer description at the series level than at the file level.

- *Information should not be repeated.* If, for example, in describing the contents of a file, we repeat the same information that we provided in describing its parent series, we are likely to create confusion, waste our own time, and produce unnecessarily long-winded finding aids. Restricting information to the level at which it applies, and only to that level, accommodates crispness and clarity.

- *Relationships between levels should be clearly indicated.* A primary objective in constructing our finding aids is to enable clear and effective navigation for researchers. To accomplish this, it is important to describe the nested levels of the collection to clearly express the parent-child relationships that exist throughout the collection. In other words, we need to represent the intellectual arrangement of the collection clearly and accurately.

Describing the Context as Well as the Content

Perhaps the most profound difference between describing archives and describing other cultural resources abides in the requirement that archivists must describe the creators of the resources, and the circumstances surrounding their creation and use, in addition to describing the resources themselves. This creates a stark contrast with bibliographic description wherein creator description is limited to simply assuring that the names of the resource creators are sufficiently differentiated from all other names so as to facilitate clear identification. Daniel Pitti, who has written authoritatively for years on creator description, notes that the library community "traditionally has concentrated on controlling names, and not on detailed description of the people and organizations bearing the names."[36] Even the description of cultural objects in the museum world devotes limited attention to creators and owners beyond establishing names, dates, events, and places associated with a resource to clarify the chain of provenance.

The archivist's description of creator and context goes well beyond controlling names and relating the simple facts of custody. We are required to describe creator and context with the same care and intensity that we describe the records themselves. Again, Pitti makes the case succinctly:

> In order to evaluate, understand, and interpret records, users need to know the circumstances that surrounded their creation and use. Recording information about individuals, families, and organizations responsible for the creation of records is essential in the documentation of context. In particular, such creator description needs to document the name or names used, biographical or historical information about the creator, and information concerning activities and responsibilities.[37]

So, describing the records' creator(s), as well as the activities, functions, and events associated with their creation and management, helps us understand *why* the records were created and maintained. It probably also helps us understand *how* their creators managed and used them. Why is this so important?

- *It suggests the overall meaning and significance of the collection and the records that comprise it.* As we saw in discussing the importance of provenance, understanding who created the collection, for what purpose the records were created, and how they were used over time helps us to appreciate the nature, value, and significance of the collection materials. By the same token, when we describe the collection's creators and the context of that creation and use, we are able to directly convey a sense of that meaning, value, and significance to the researcher. For example, almost every collection will contain one or more files of correspondence. The knowledge that correspondence exists tells us nothing about what the correspondence reveals—who the correspondents are, the significance of the communications, and the topical contents. But gaining some understanding of the entities and the business or personal activities that generated the correspondence arms us with some foreknowledge of their likely content and significance. It has important explanatory value in and of itself, and it helps us make the basic determination about whether the collection, or some particular parts of the collection, is likely to contain information helpful to us in our research.

- *It helps us intuit the topical content of the various record series and, often, the depth or importance of that information.* Let's look at Figure 6 for an illustration of this in action. The Administrative History of the Nine Mile Creek Watershed District describes the creators of the documents in this group of records and their management of the materials during their tenure. Although this contextual description is quite brief (probably reflecting the significance and quantity of the records), it nevertheless provides some important clues into the likely content of the twenty-five folders of District Correspondence. Despite the fact that we are given no information specifically about the contents of the folders, we can still infer enough to tell us whether we want to examine these materials. We can assume that the correspondence files will probably document discussions, decisions, and transactions that directly affected the management of the rivers, streams, lakes, ponds, and marshes that fell within the jurisdictional boundaries of this agency during the 1969–1982 period. By the same token, we can reasonably assume that the series of Minutes, especially if they are verbose and not pro forma, will shed further light on the board's decision-making, the selection and service of its directors, and perhaps the political pressures that it faced. The documentary value for our research may turn out to be rich, or it may be thin, but the description of creator and context has arguably provided sufficient information for us to decide whether we want to look at the files in the first place. This suggests the power and importance of contextual description.

- *It simplifies users' searches by pointing them to the particular units of the collection most likely to contain materials of interest.* When we provide contextual description that is full and accurate, we can immediately begin to answer researcher questions about which series or files might contain relevant information, as well as how rich or authoritative that information might be. Looking again at the example in Figure 6, let's say that the historical sketch also explained that the agency had, during a certain period, been under the political lens for allegedly mishandling its funds and for making misguided decisions about where to prioritize its spending projects. That information in the administrative history, though it did not make reference to any of the collection materials, would still be sufficient to guide an interested researcher to the Financial Statements and the Minutes, and perhaps to the correspondence for the time period in question.

- *It greatly reduces our need to describe the content of records units at length and in great detail.* The preceding research scenarios bear witness to this truth. In those cases, we saw how satisfactory description of creator and context was sufficient to guide researchers to particular files, even in the absence of any specific information about the content of those files. If we devote ourselves to creating comprehensive and accurate contextual information, we can greatly reduce the amount of effort we put into writing descriptions of the content of the series and files that comprise the collection, as users will already be able to infer much of that information from the historical and biographical notes. In approaching our finding aids this way, we also eliminate a lot of the narrative superfluity that makes finding aids unwieldy in online environments and that forces users to wade through excessive descriptive information.

So, contextual description serves an important purpose in describing archival collections. How do we accomplish this purpose? Describing creator and context is certainly no simpler than describing content; it has multiple parts. These parts must all be present in some fashion to ensure robust contextual description in finding aids:

- *Names of entities and identities.* As in the case of a bibliographic authority record, an archival description needs to express the names of all the people, organizations, and other entities crucial to the records. Those names are important to understand responsibility for creating and maintaining the materials and relationships with other resources apart from this collection, and to suggest the content of the various collection units. To perform these functions, names must be accurate, complete, and disambiguated or normalized to the greatest extent possible.
- *Functions and activities.* The entities and identities considered above, whether or not they created the collection, are all *actors* in the web of experiences and transactions that the archival collection documents. An important element of contextual description is therefore describing the essential actions that drive the dynamic of the collection over time. To accomplish this, we must provide information on several elements. In carrying out their business and personal actions, organizations and individuals perform a variety of *functions*. The performance of these functions lies at the heart of our archival purpose in acquiring and sharing collections. Functions might include providing legal services, raising children, and participating in environmental activism in the case of our Jane Doe Papers, or perhaps managing water resources in the case of the government records we considered in Figure 6.

  It is therefore essential to identify and explain those functions in relation to the collection. Our entities carry out those functions by performing a continuous stream of *activities*, some or all of which will be documented in the collection. Our lawyer keeps client records, attends school and committee meetings, prepares legal documents, makes conference speeches, and engages in lobbying activities. Those activities may be legion; the important thing is to summarize the subset of activities reflected in the collection materials. Activities usually play out in individual events. Again, events occur every day in dizzying number, but the important thing for descriptive purposes is to identify the relatively small group of such events that have real significance for understanding the documents in the collection and then ensuring that they get treated

NINE MILE CREEK WATERSHED DISTRICT
An Inventory of Its Records

OVERVIEW OF THE RECORDS

Agency: Nine Mile Creek Watershed District (Minn.).

Series Title: Records.

Dates: 1959–1989.

Quantity: 3.5 cu. ft. (4 boxes).

Location: See Detailed Description section for box locations.

ADMINISTRATIVE HISTORY OF THE NINE MILE CREEK WATERSHED DISTRICT

The district was established by order of the Minnesota Water Resources Board on June 23, 1959, pursuant to the Watershed Act [Laws 1955 c799 s1]. Its function is to protect and manage the water resources within the district, which is approximately 50 square miles in surface area and encompasses the land area tributary to Nine Mile Creek in southern Hennepin County. Portions of the cities of Hopkins, Bloomington, Edina, Richfield, Eden Prairie, and Minnetonka are located in the district.

The activities of the district are managed by the five member Board of Managers, who are appointed by the Hennepin County Board of Commissioners. Managers serve staggered three-year terms and must live within the legal boundaries of the district.

The record set of minutes came from the district office; all other materials in this series were assembled and maintained by James A. Jones as district director and officer.

SCOPE AND CONTENTS OF THE RECORDS

Minutes, correspondence, annual reports, engineers' reports, project files, and miscellany documenting all aspects of the watershed's organization and administration.

DETAILED DESCRIPTION OF THE COLLECTION

Box 1 Minutes, 1959–1989.
       Official record set of the district's Board of Managers' meetings; they include financial and project data.

Box 2 Annual reports, 1968–1977, 1979–1981.
       Non-District correspondence regarding conservation activities, 1963–1969. 2 folders.
       District correspondence:
           1969–1977. 16 folders.

Box 3 1978–1982. 9 folders.
       Over-all plan, 1961. 1 volume. (By Douglas W. Barr)
       Rules and regulations, 1973. 2 volumes.
       Engineers' annual reports, 1969–1976, 1978–1979, 1980–1981. 13 volumes.
       Financial statements, 1971–1975, 1980–1981.

FIGURE 6. Contextual information in a finding aid. Adapted from a finding aid in the Minnesota State Archives.

in the finding aid. By ensuring that we deal in some brief but adequate way with the functions, activities, and events key to the documentary significance of the collection, we are making an important contribution to helping collection users understand the materials and their research utility.

- *Relationships.* An essential part of contextual description is describing important relationships that exist among the entities featured in the collection. While the most obvious relationships exist between the collection creator and other individuals, a host of different relationships generally exist and are often important:

    - *Person↔person.* Multiple individuals may be significant actors and subjects within a collection. Each will have a relationship with the collection creator, but some may have significant relationships with other individuals documented in the records.
    - *Person↔organization.* The creator and other people that figure prominently will often interact with organizations important to the content of the collection.
    - *Organization↔organization.* A collection of organizational records is certainly likely to evidence important relationships with other organizations that may be related to it hierarchically or may be completely separate entities. However, those relationships may be present and important in personal papers, as well.
    - *Persons and organizations↔resources.* The creating entities of a collection are obviously related to some or all of the materials that comprise the collection. In addition, any of them may also be related to relevant resources that exist outside of the collection, whether archival or nonarchival.
    - *Resources↔resources.* Some of the collection materials may be related in some important and relevant way to other resources in some external archival, bibliographic, or informational resource. This is especially true when archives related by provenance have been divided into separate collections, perhaps in different repositories.

Any or all of these relationships can exist in any collection. When those relationships are important to understanding the collection, they need to be explained as part of the description of context. Typically, this is accomplished through text in the historical or biographical narrative. Such was the case in Figure 6 in which the administrative history notes the Nine Mile Creek Watershed District's relationships with the Hennepin County Board of Commissioners, as well as with James A. Jones who assembled the files. In these narratives, such relationships have been noted very briefly and not evaluated at any length in the interest of keeping the description economical.

However, with the advent of the ISAAR(CPF) structural standard and the EAC-CPF encoding standard, which facilitates encoding and sharing such archival authority records, the intensity with which we record all of these relationships within and among archival collections is changing. In a descriptive world in which archivists share very

- *Historical and biographical information.* In typical finding aids, the bulk of contextual description is expressed most saliently in some narrative sketch that is either the administrative history of an organization or the biography of a person. Those entities are usually the creator(s) of the collection, but they may also be other individuals or corporate bodies that are predominantly represented in the collection materials or are otherwise key to the history of the collection. A number of information elements are typical and generally necessary to convey this information; Michael Fox and Peter Wilkinson, in their basic guide to archival description, offer these up: "For persons and families, information such as dates of birth and death, place of birth and domicile, variant names, ethnicity, gender, occupations, and significant accomplishments is needed. For corporate bodies, information about the functions, purpose, and history of the body, geographical location and jurisdiction of its activities, its administrative hierarchy, and earlier, variant, and successor names is needed."[38] As a general rule, such narratives should strive to summarize the entities, the activities, the places, and the events relevant and significant for understanding the collection materials.[39]

It has generally been true that the description of context is built into the same finding aids that describe the content of the collection. Muller, Feith, and Fruin advised archivists at the turn of the twentieth century to place at the "head of each main division of the inventory . . . notes describing the history and functions of the board or official from whom this division is derived."[40] This advice has been heeded over the years, and full finding aids generally begin with one or more brief biographical or historical narratives that treat all of the contextual elements previously described. A description of the content of the materials usually follows that section of contextual description. This practice has, by and large, served researchers well and was really the only practical alternative in pre-internet (and especially precomputer) times when it would have been almost impossible to create separate descriptions of creators and records and then somehow link them together.

However, that goal of separate finding aid systems for describing creators and describing collection materials has always been a holy grail of archival description. Bibliographic systems, for example, do not embed author information within catalog records. Instead, they rely on a separate system of authority records to carry that information. This is more efficient because multiple catalog records for different works by the same author can all link to a single authority record about that author. In addition to creating efficiency, such a two-pronged system also ensures greater accuracy. As information about an author changes over time, it only requires updating in one record rather than multiple catalog records, which would be practically impossible, especially because all of those catalog records for a given work will be multiplied across the universe of libraries owning copies of that work.

These same problems of efficiency and accuracy have always existed for archives, as well, as a single person or corporate body may be responsible for creating multiple archival collections (unrelated by provenance), may exist as an author or topic in many other collections, or may be related in some meaningful way to yet other collections. In our current dominant finding aid model, we find ourselves having to create new biographical or historical sketches for the same entity in the separate finding aids for multiple collections. Furthermore, these context descriptions get created in multiple repositories, some of which may only have limited access to authoritative information about that entity. An inefficient system rife with inaccuracy across repositories ensues.

So, it would make a great deal of sense to follow the bibliographic community's approach and create separate authority records for each entity responsible for the content of some archival collection. In such a system, a unique record would exist for each entity and all repositories could link their content records to that entity record, saving them the need to create historical narratives on their own. Each repository could simply update the existing authority record with additional information unique to the collection in their custody. In that way, archival authority records grow richer, more complete, and more accurate over time.

The principles and tools for doing so exist in ISAAR(CPF), which provides rules for structuring authority records and populating them with content, and EAC-CPF, which provides a technical tool for encoding and sharing them. A fully stable version of EAC-CPF has existed since 2010, but it is still early days for archivists in terms of implementation. Creating a local description regime for authority records introduces training, retooling, and other costs, as well as questions about the treatment of existing legacy finding aids. These questions are similar to those archivists faced with the implementation of EAD twenty years ago, so we can probably expect a similarly lengthy implementation curve. In the meantime, most archivists will continue to express the duality of archival description within single EAD finding aids.

Intellectual Order and Administrative Order: Two Views of One Collection

A frequently unstated presumption holds that any multilevel finding aid gets presented in one way and one way only. This expectation likely has its roots in the precomputer age when longish finding aids were produced on typewriters. It would have been understandably profligate to turn around and present that document in some alternative way, even if a second representation of the collection may have added a useful, different perspective on it. And, because description represents arrangement, we have come to organize the information in our finding aids to faithfully represent either the intellectual arrangement of the materials, or else their physical arrangement. But not both.

But, today, with our descriptive metadata captured in digital form, we no longer need to restrict ourselves (and our users) to a single presentation of collection information. It is relatively easy, though not perfectly so, to draft a finding aid that represents the intellectual order of the collection and then rearrange some of the information in the file to represent the true physical arrangement of the collection, at least in the form of a separate container list. Thus, we can, and we should, be doing this as a matter of routine. Why would we want to invest some effort in producing two finding aids for a collection? We do because an intellectual representation and an administrative (or "physical") representation can serve two different and equally useful purposes. The finding aid presented in intellectual order benefits researchers seeking information about the content of the collection. The finding aid presented in physical order benefits the repository by helping it simplify and maintain its administrative control over the collection itself (what materials are in each box?), as well as shelf control.

Although these are the two most common forms of control, others may appear in particular situations. There may be many ways in which we might seek to reorder finding aid information to clarify its meaning for certain users, or to enable some particular administrative purpose for the repository. We should start thinking about the semantically rich information in our finding aids as data, pure and simple. And, we should therefore start thinking of our finding aids simply as expressions of that data, which can take many forms over time to achieve many purposes, and to stop conceiving of them as static documents created once and once only to serve the best immediate purpose.

This long chapter has covered a lot of ground. It has considered the purpose of description (user access and administrative control), the relationship of description to arrangement (description reflects arrangement), and the wide range of devices that might be called finding aids. It has emphasized that, in this day and age, effective description should be based on structured data, not on unstructured prose. It has devoted a lot of space to descriptive standards—structural, content, interchange, and vocabularies—stressing their crucial importance in enabling user success, encouraging efficient description, and facilitating interoperability in networked environments. Those standards, taken together, specify the data elements relevant to archival description and condition when and how they should be used to achieve their greatest effects. The chapter has also emphasized that archival description is multilevel in nature. For most collections, we must describe the whole of the materials, and then the component parts, in a systematic way that reflects the arrangement hierarchy. Finally, it remains crucial to remember that describing the context of archival records is just as important as elucidating their content.

Chapters two and three have explored the principles, concepts, and tools that shape and support arrangement and description. Chapter four will take us from theory to practice—exploring the hands-on activities that constitute arrangement work and determining the sequence in which they ought to occur.

NOTES

[1] For a good overview of the possibilities afforded by a structured data approach to description, see Daniel A. Santamaria, "Designing Descriptive and Access Systems," in *Trends in Archival Practice: Archival Arrangement and Description*, ed. and with an introduction by Christopher J. Prom and Thomas J. Frusciano (Chicago: Society of American Archivists, 2013), 173–90.

[2] Archival description as sharable metadata is described and promoted in Jenn Riley and Kelcy Shepherd, "A Brave New World: Archivists and Shareable Descriptive Metadata," *American Archivist* 72, no. 1 (2009): 91–112; and in Jennifer Schaffner, *The Metadata Is the Interface: Better Description for Better Discovery of Archives and Special Collections, Synthesized from User Studies*, report produced by OCLC Research, 2009 and available online at http://www.oclc.org/research/publications/library/2009/2009-06.pdf, captured at https://perma.cc/G48C-QXF8.

[3] Parts of this section originally appeared as the author's contribution to Kate Cruikshank, Caroline Daniels, Dennis Meissner, Naomi L. Nelson, and Mark Shelstad, "How Do We Show You What We've Got?: Access to Archival Collections in the Digital Age," *Journal of the Association for History and Computing* 3, no. 2 (2005).

[4] Sibyl Schaefer and Janet M. Bunde, "Standards for Archival Description," in *Trends in Archival Practice: Archival Arrangement and Description*, 17–19.

[5] Structured data and their utility in archival description is explained in a number of works. Three helpful sources are Daniel A. Santamaria, *Extensible Processing for Archives and Special Collections: Reducing Processing Backlogs* (Chicago: Neal-Schuman, an imprint of the American Library Association, 2015), esp. 77–82, 93–94; Schaffner, *The Metadata Is the Interface*; and most recently Aaron Rubenstein, "Sharing Archival Metadata," in *Trends in Archival Practice: Putting Descriptive Standards to Work*, 308–12.

[6] Schaffner, *The Metadata Is the Interface*, 1.

[7] See especially Rubenstein, "Sharing Archival Metadata," 309–24.

[8] Michael J. Fox and Peter L. Wilkerson, *Introduction to Archival Organization and Description* (Getty Information Institute, 1998), 26, http://www.getty.edu/publications/virtuallibrary/0892365455.html, captured at https://perma.cc/ZZK9-UGYL.

[9] International Council on Archives, Committee on Descriptive Standards, *ISAD(G): General International Standard Archival Description*, 2nd ed., adopted by the Committee on Descriptive Standards, Stockholm, Sweden, September 19–22, 1999, https://www.ica.org/en/isadg-general-international-standard-archival-description-second-edition, captured at https://perma.cc/RT86-RAQE.

[10] Schaefer and Bunde, "Standards for Archival Description," 37.

[11] International Council on Archives, Committee on Descriptive Standards, *International Standard Archival Authority Record for Corporate Bodies, Persons and Families*, adopted Canberra, Australia, October 27–30, 2003, 2nd ed., https://www.ica.org/en/isaar-cpf-international-standard-archival-authority-record-corporate-bodies-persons-and-families-2nd, captured at perma.cc/2UQ4-SDCC.

[12] Steven L. Hensen, *Archives, Personal Papers, and Manuscripts: A Cataloging Manual for Archival Repositories, Historical Societies, and Manuscript Libraries* (Washington, DC: Library of Congress, 1983), 35.

[13] *Rules for Archival Description* (Ottawa: Bureau of Canadian Archivists, 1990), http://www.cdncouncilarchives.ca/archdesrules.html, captured at https://perma.cc/3LVX-462V.

[14] *Describing Archives: A Content Standard*, 2nd ed. (Chicago: Society of American Archivists, 2013), https://www2.archivists.org/standards/DACS.

[15] *Describing Archives: A Content Standard*, 7.

[16] *Describing Archives: A Content Standard*, xv–xix.

[17] In March 2017, a group of twelve archivists representing the SAA DACS Technical Subcommittee and the wider archival description community met at the Walpole Library to consider revising the DACS principles, both to update them and to broaden them in the hope that they might come to serve as foundational principles, not just for DACS, but for the entire archival description enterprise. The revision process is underway at this time, but a report describing the working group's meeting and its tentative outcomes is available at https://www2.archivists.org/sites/all/files/0517-VI-I-DACS-PrinciplesDevelop.pdf, captured at https://perma.cc/YP6V-MPQ9.

[18] Kathleen D. Roe, *Arranging and Describing Archives and Manuscripts* (Chicago: Society of American Archivists, 2005), 38–39. Roe offers a helpful synopsis of the early efforts to adopt MARC and other archival standards in the United States and Canada on pp. 36–44.

[19] Daniel Pitti, "Encoded Archival Description: The Development of an Encoding Standard for Archival Finding Aids," *American Archivist* 60, no. 3 (1997): 279–83.

[20] "[I]n a 2008 study, nearly 50 percent of respondents reported that they had not adopted the standard." As quoted in Schaefer and Bunde, "Standards for Archival Description," 30.

[21] The SAA Standards Portal is maintained by the association's Standards Committee and includes SAA-approved standards, guidelines, and best practice documents. It is available at https://www2.archivists.org/standards.

22. Technical Subcommittee for Encoded Archival Description of the Society of American Archivists, *Encoded Archival Description Tag Library, Version EAD3* (Chicago: Society of American Archivists, 2015), p. iv, https://www2.archivists.org/sites/all/files/TagLibrary-VersionEAD3.pdf, captured at https://perma.cc/GD5D-XRDB.
23. Library of Congress, "Encoded Archival Description Official Site," http://www.loc.gov/ead.
24. When EAD-encoded data is maintained within a database structure, a repository may never need to transform the data into a standalone finding aid of the traditional sort. It may only need to serve out contextualized snippets of information adequate to satisfy search requests. Regardless, the EAD encoding syntax is very useful in preserving semantic control over the descriptive metadata about the collection. Its value as an encoding and transmission package does not depend upon its ability to generate a collection guide.
25. The history and development of EAC-CPF is related in Katherine Wisser, "Describing Entities and Identities: The Development and Structure of Encoded Archival Context—Corporate Bodies, Persons, and Families," *Journal of Library Metadata* 11 (2011): 166–75.
26. *Describing Archives: A Content Standard*, 87–88.
27. This information is drawn from the preface of the *EAC-CPF Tag Library* (2010), which is available on the official EAC-CPF website at https://eac.staatsbibliothek-berlin.de/schemata-and-tag-library/, captured at https://perma.cc/9NZM-579P.
28. Much of the information in the "Standards" section is based upon Schaefer and Bunde, "Standards for Archival Description," 45–54.
29. Library of Congress, "Library of Congress Names," http://id.loc.gov/authorities/names.html, captured at https://perma.cc/8EF8-8EE8.
30. Getty Research Institute, "Union List of Artists' Names Online," http://www.getty.edu/research/tools/vocabularies/ulan.
31. Library of Congress, "Library of Congress Authorities," http://authorities.loc.gov/cgi-bin/Pwebrecon.cgi?DB=local&PAGE=First, captured at https://perma.cc/LPE8-8Q4L.
32. Getty Research Institute, "Art and Architecture Thesaurus Online, http://www.getty.edu/research/tools/vocabularies/aat.
33. Dublin Core Metadata Initiative, "Dublin Core Metadata Element Set, Version 1.1: Reference Description," http://www.dublincore.org/documents/dces, captured at https://perma.cc/AK5F-Z5D8.
34. Library of Congress, "MODS," http://www.loc.gov/standards/mods.
35. Library of Congress, "METS," http://www.loc.gov/standards/mets.
36. Daniel V. Pitti, "Creator Description: Encoded Archival Context," *Cataloging & Classification Quarterly* 38 (2004): 203.
37. Pitti, "Creator Description: Encoded Archival Context," 203.
38. Fox and Wilkerson, *Introduction to Archival Organization and Description*, 13.
39. DACS Chapter 11 enumerates the information elements that should be considered for inclusion in a biographical sketch or administrative history and provides examples for recording the information. See *Describing Archives: A Content Standard*, 2nd. ed., 101–9.
40. Muller, Feith, and Fruin, *Manual for the Arrangement and Description of Archives*, translation of the second edition by Arthur H. Leavitt (Chicago: Society of American Archivists, 2003), 147.

4

Physical Processing and Arrangement

Physical processing and arrangement embrace all of the work that we perform to organize the collection materials in a physical sense and then to ensure the viability of the physical materials by performing preservation actions on those whose continued physical existence is in some jeopardy. I should perhaps make it clear that the activities and the recommendations that follow pertain to *all the materials regardless of form or medium*. I will explain separately exceptions specific to materials in a particular format or recorded on a particular carrier or medium. In general, they also apply to digital records, although those materials lack true physicality. Considerations and recommendations that apply exclusively to digital materials are found in a separate chapter.

Accessioning: Establishing Initial Controls

Accessioning is either the final step in the process of appraising and acquiring a collection or the first step in the process of arranging and describing it. Where it falls on the archival continuum depends largely on the administrative structure and practices of the repository. The first Archival Fundamentals Series published by SAA addressed accessioning within both the *Selecting and Appraising Manuscripts* and the *Arranging and Describing Manuscripts* titles. As a result, the essential steps involved in accessioning centered around issues of legal custody and physical transfer in the former and focused more on bibliographic controls within the repository in the latter.[1] The Archival Fundamental Series II more definitely placed accessioning as the initial step in the long chain of processing actions. Regardless of where we pin it in terms of staffing and workflows, the function of accessioning is always concerned with establishing three types of control—physical, administrative, and intellectual—over some new acquisition. Individual actions in each of those three areas generally do not occur in a neat sequence, but are instead intermixed and sometimes concurrent.

Accessioning really encompasses a small but crucial set of activities that occupy a transition from the acquisition phase to the processing phase in archival administration. Accessioning accomplishes several things:

- It ensures that ownership is documented;
- It ensures that papers are physically accessible by staff;
- It ensures that content is generally known and accessible;
- It starts to make an acquisition look and behave like an archival collection.

That said, a couple of things should be noted. First, there may be no one-to-one correlation between an accession and a collection. An accession may divide into multiple whole or partial collections, and any given collection may eventually comprise multiple accessions over the course of its custody. So, one objective of accessioning is to break the acquisition into its provenance-related parts, as necessary. Second, although accessioning tasks are concerned with the arrangement and content of the materials, it is *traditionally* not a stage when serious processing work takes place. (See "Accessioning as Processing" for a divergent approach.) As Fredric Miller states succinctly, "[a]ccessioning is not the time to process, but it is the time to identify appropriate sets of records for processing in the future."[2] In most cases, we should resist the temptation to dig into processing, thus preventing premature and unsubstantiated decisions about the final state of the materials.

Let's identify the actions that comprise accessioning as they break down into those three areas, bearing in mind that they won't fall into a straight sequence. As is true with a lot of arrangement and description work, repositories are wise to create an *accessioning checklist* based around their own organizational structure and staffing, to ensure that tasks are performed in an efficient sequence and that none are missed.

Physical control

Several elements concerning the control of the physical materials themselves are important objectives of accessioning:

- *Location.* It should be clear to all relevant staff where the accession, and each of its containers, is located. This seems obvious, but it can get complicated when odd-sized containers or diverse media end up requiring storage separate from the rest of the acquisition. Container-level control becomes important. Because collection materials can be received in every sort of container imaginable, it is also important at this stage to determine whether the materials will be transferred into standard archival containers. Doing so can make them more secure and easier to manage until they are processed.
- *Extent.* How much is there, in which forms and media? Understanding the physical scope and breakdown of the collection materials is an important element in establishing effective control and planning for their processing.
- *Condition.* Are there materials whose condition is so fragile or otherwise problematic as to warrant concern? Can they wait patiently until processing, or must they be dealt with now? Are some materials impossible to access until they are processed? These questions

help determine our processing timeline, how we store them in the meantime, and whether preservation interventions need to be started. If staff are available to perform treatments or to reformat materials, this might be the optimal time to do so, rather than waiting until processing or afterward. A useful practice is to record notes on the condition of materials either in the *accession report*, in the *preliminary container list*, or in some special *condition of collection form*, so that these conditions don't pass out of memory. Some common conditions might include:

- Nitrate and acetate prints and negatives
- Deteriorating or rolled photoprints and drawings
- Analog magnetic media—audio and video
- Digital disks, tapes, and removable media
- Dampness and mold
- Pest infestations—insects and rodents
- 3-D objects requiring special storage or handling

- *Preservation assessment.* Following on directly from the last point, accessioning is the right phase of processing to perform a formal, thorough *preservation assessment.* In establishing the overall physical controls noted, the accessioner will have noted preservation conditions and will have taken steps to ensure that anything requiring immediate attention is dealt with promptly and that other conditions and issues are noted for attention during arrangement or at some other time, perhaps as a special project. The best practice is to take a bit more time and prepare a formal assessment of the preservation status of the collection. This does not need to be a lengthy process and can be expedited with a brief form to which a longer narrative could be attached, as necessary. Such a form—ideally, created and maintained online—will accommodate checkoffs and/or notes for the most typical situations:

    - Moisture
    - Mold infestations: active/inactive
    - Pest infestations: active/inactive
    - Film stock: nitrate or acetate media
    - Physical damage: torn, crumpled, soiled, burned materials
    - Unstable paper
    - Presence of food and chemicals
    - Analog magnetic media
    - Digital media

    The assessment, in whatever form it takes, should bring together all the information necessary to create an overall treatment plan and to define the conservation actions to be undertaken as part of the collection processing project at some later date. The assessment report should become part of the permanent accession file that guides future work.[3]

Intellectual control

Once the physical condition of the materials is understood, recorded, and worked into processing planning, the next step is to ascertain and describe, in a general and perfunctory way, the intellectual content of the materials. As noted already, the object is not to rearrange the materials or to describe them in any detail. Rather, it is to characterize them broadly, probably at the container level, so that we have enough information to understand the provenance of the materials, persons and corporate bodies represented, the types of materials present, their current arrangement, and the basic set of activities, functions, and broad topics documented within them. This is as far as we need to go during accessioning, and it is almost always accomplished sufficiently via a *preliminary container list* (perhaps with a few inserted content and condition notes) and a thorough *accession report*. The staff who acquired and transferred the accession and the accessioning staff frequently share these responsibilities.

Administrative control

These controls concern the repository's overall ability to know, with regard to the accession, what it legally owns, what those owned materials consist of, what rights it has to provide access to and use of the materials, and the current physical availability and processing status of the records. The work involved in gaining physical and intellectual control, as described, facilitates much of this understanding. The administrative control piece largely involves assembling that documentation into an *accession file* comprising a number of standard forms and documents that will serve as a central file for all staff on the nature and status of the acquisition:

- *Accession register.* While not in universal use, this internal document is a concise and useful chronological record of all accessions received by the repository. It may exist as a bound or loose-leaf volume or in electronic form as a spreadsheet or database. It might be an output report from data in a collection management system. It typically logs in the accession number, name of creator, title of collection, name and address of donor/source, date of receipt, date accessioned, and provisional location of the materials. Utilizing a register can also simplify the process of assigning accession numbers to new acquisitions, as it supplies a running record.
- *Accession report.* An essential document, it synopsizes the acquisition and the materials in a brief standard form, often a single page. Typically, this report is generated as a standard output from some database, often the repository's collection management system. Lacking such a comprehensive system, it can be easily handled through a flat-file database documenting the sequence of acquisition and accessioning actions, or even from a word-processing template. In its most robust form, it ought to include the following information:
    - ***Donation information***
        - donor name
        - mailing address
        - contact phone number, email, etc.

- provenance (at least, immediate source of acquisition)
- contract summary

- ***Collection information***
  - accession number
  - creator name
  - collection title
  - inclusive dates
  - extent
  - scope and content note
  - restrictions

- ***Processing and preservation information***
  - whether an addition to an existing collection
  - appraisal note
  - arrangement note
  - physical condition note
  - processing notes: suggestions for processing, background information
  - disposition of unwanted items

- *Copies of key documents.* The deed of gift or transfer agreement, other legal agreements, field notes and memos from acquisitions staff, and notes and file lists from the donor are all valuable source materials for the person(s) processing the collection, as well as for other staff who may need information about the acquisition and its subsequent management.

- *Preliminary container list.* The various actions involved with assessing the physical condition and extent of the accession, its current arrangement, and its basic intellectual groups and content will provide the information necessary to develop a rough container list. As the name suggests, it identifies the basic content of each container. If intellectual groupings are apparent at this stage, they are usually not described below a series level. Containers are assigned numbers and, ideally, a provisional shelf location. When the container list is appended to the acquisition report, a brief but sufficient finding aid exists—a basic package describing the legal and access status, provenance, location, overall scope and content, and current arrangement of the accession.

When accessioning is complete, the acquired materials are in a known location, are available to appropriate staff, and have had any immediate physical and access conditions dealt with or at least acknowledged. They are fully under the repository's control and ready to be arranged and described.

Accessioning as processing

In the first decade of the twenty-first century, many archivists, especially those working in repositories with frustrating backlogs, began pursuing innovations aimed at processing collections rapidly. These new approaches often focused on transforming policies and workflows to remove barriers to efficient processing.

One of the common barriers so identified was the traditional practice of treating accessioning as a discrete activity disconnected from the larger arrangement and description workflow. This thinking encouraged archivists to perform their accessioning routine on each collection and then, in effect, add it directly to their unprocessed backlog. The innovators asked: would it not be more efficient, in certain cases, to simply complete all essential processing work at the point of accessioning, rather than consigning the collection to an unprocessed (and thereby unavailable) interregnum? In the cases of small and uncomplicated collections, especially, often very few additional tasks are essential to completing basic processing work. It makes sense to complete that work in the course of accessioning—taking such a collection out of the backlog and putting it into the hands of researchers. The Manuscripts and Archives unit at Yale University Library pioneered this approach, cementing it into its processing regimen early on.[4]

This excerpt from the Technical Services processing manual of Harvard's Houghton Library summarizes the mechanics of this approach:

> The goal is to provide baseline level access to collections as they are accessioned. Accessioning archivists are in an advantageous position to capture important documentation related to a collection's arrangement, condition, and content. While accessioning, and with a minimum of additional effort, a collection can receive collection level description, basic rehousing, and even some preliminary intellectual arrangement and description at the series or file level. In this way, collections never enter into a backlog or processing queue. Future user needs may then dictate whether more description is warranted.[5]

Processing at the point of accessioning helps to reduce backlogs and makes collections available much sooner, because they don't have to wait their turn in the processing queue. The approach also adds considerable efficiency, as immediate knowledge about the collection gained during accessioning is not lost during the months or years that might go by before processing occurs. However, to be a likely candidate for this approach, a collection should manifest certain characteristics:

- It should require little, if any, additional physical arrangement or, if digital, any further file manipulation or analysis to be usable.
- It should already possess a serviceable container list if it comprises multiple containers.
- It should not require immediate conservation actions before making it available to users. Existing folders and other subcontainers should be in acceptable condition.
- Access and use conditions should be clear and easily explained. No further rights analysis or negotiations should be necessary.
- It should be fairly quick and easy to create minimal but sufficient descriptive tools, whether catalog record, EAD finding aid, database entries, and so forth. The collection does not require further analysis.

If these conditions prevail, a few additional processing steps will quickly produce a collection that is arranged and described sufficient to accommodate research use:

1. Placing materials in archival containers
2. Labeling containers
3. Producing descriptions
4. Shelving collections
5. Producing and filing repository paperwork and electronic forms

Establishing this convention can make a significant contribution toward keeping processing backlogs manageable and making more holdings available to researchers as expeditiously as possible.

The Practice of Arrangement

Our friend Schellenberg likens arrangement to the process that a paleontologist uses in reconstructing the skeletal remains of a vertebrate fossil. Understanding the function of each bone, how it relates to all the other bones, and where it fits into the whole organic structure is, in a nutshell, what the work of arrangement entails. He identifies the essential steps as follows:

1. Analyze the structure and functions of the entity that produced the records.
2. Analyze the records, as a whole, before proceeding to arrange any of the parts.
3. Identify or establish series if at all possible.
4. Organize the materials intellectually before attempting any physical arrangement.
5. Then follow archivally accepted arrangement principles.[6]

The arrangement practices that follow honor this broad approach.

Prepare to process the collection

Workspace and materials

We, of course, think about arrangement and description as primarily intellectual endeavors, but all of that thinking and analysis rests upon a very physical bedrock of space, equipment, and tools. If we underprepare in those areas, we are very likely to make our work more arduous, more time-consuming, and less effective overall. These considerations, because they affect every processing project, are best implemented as part of a repository's sustainable processing infrastructure so that we do not have to re-create these resources with each new project. Ideally, we have created and maintained an adequate space devoted to processing work, which is outfitted with a flexible mix of furniture, equipment, and basic supplies that can serve as the backbone for any and all projects.

Workspace. This is the most elemental factor for processing collections that are largely non-digital in nature. Space needs vary widely from project to project, but a robust processing area can support a wide variety of projects in a flexible way and, as is often the case, multiple projects at any given time. Different archivists work in different ways, and no two collections of a given size lend themselves to exactly the same processing mechanics. Some collections will require processing archivists to spread out a greater proportion of their contents at any time. Other collections, because they are simpler or were received in better order, require very little processing real estate relative to their size.

This makes it hard to dictate basic space requirements. That said, I'll take a stab at it. Any archival collection up to about 10 cubic feet in volume will probably require about 25 square feet of table-height working surface augmented with some surrounding floor space. Floor space allows containers to be shuffled around on the floor and the contents of some containers to be worked with on table surfaces. This provides a fairly flexible and adequate space to review, compare, and rearrange all the various intellectual and physical units that constitute the collection. Then, with each *doubling* in volume of the collection, the combined table and floor space also needs to double. This maintains a pretty satisfactory working area to carry out processing work as efficiently as possible.

Obviously, this repeated doubling will burn through unused processing space at some point, and then we must simply accept less efficient conditions and adapt our procedures to suit that fact. At some point, it becomes judicious to sacrifice table space for greater floor space, which can make it easier to shift materials among a number of containers at once. Experience is the best teacher in understanding how much space we need and how best to use it. The important point is that we should avoid painting ourselves into a corner at the start by underthinking the work we will have to do and the space necessary to accommodate it.

By the same token, there is no optimal standard size for table surfaces. The best preparation may be to make a variety of table sizes available so that work areas can be reconfigured from project to project. A real benefit is to mount larger tables (other furniture too) on wheels or casters to make such reconfigurations as simple and painless as possible.

Supplies and equipment. Keeping the most commonly used supplies and materials within easy reach makes a processing regimen more efficient and convenient. These certainly include a small inventory of archival supplies like boxes, subboxes and spacers, file folders and envelopes in various sizes, fasteners, soft pencils and brushes, Band-Aids (not kidding!), and so forth. Technology like laptops and desktop workstations, scanners (if records will be digitized in the course of processing), and the attendant software makes for a robust operation. These days, it is almost senseless to take notes by hand and then enter descriptive information into computers as a second step. We should have the technology at hand that enables us to capture descriptive metadata, and even construct finding aids in their final form, as we proceed along the processing path. Such pedestrian equipment as carts, book trucks, pallets, and the equipment to move them should also be provided. It is a misery to haul boxes around one at a time.

Research creator, context, and content

Before removing the lid from any of the collection boxes, the very first thing to do is to review any and all documentation that accompanied the acquisition. In a top-notch repository, much of this will have already been compiled into an accession file (described earlier). An acquisition report, preliminary contents list, legal agreement(s), donor correspondence, field notes, memoranda, and other useful documents should convey a good understanding about what the collection is, why the repository acquired it, access and preservation concerns, and perhaps suggestions for arranging and describing it. Accession documentation should also tell us if the acquisition breaks down into multiple separate collections or gets parceled out among several existing collections. Remember the "gotcha" class quiz that first cautioned you to read every question before answering any questions and then informed you, in the very last question, that you were not really required to answer any of the questions after all? Well, it is like that; studying existing documentation carefully before undertaking any other work avoids a lot of pain.

Understanding the collection's creating entity is crucial, and sufficient information may not appear in the accession documents. It may be necessary to consult readily available sources—historical and biographical encyclopedias, websites, annual reports, news outlets, and so forth—to fully understand the context of the collection. When the collection's creators are not prominent entities, the collection materials themselves may turn out to be the best source; but we should turn there *after* we have reviewed authoritative external sources.

Review the collection

Only at this juncture do we turn our attention to the records themselves and start to think about arranging them. I use the word *review* very intentionally here. This is not the time to begin actively arranging and rearranging the collection materials. This, instead, is the time to give the contents of each container a cursory look with an eye toward understanding a number of things: Is the preliminary container list (if any) accurate? Do there appear to be materials not previously accounted for? Where within the containers are the major units (series, files) located? Are there preservation issues to note or correct (dampness, mold, deteriorating paper, fragile magnetic media)? The point is simply to understand the collection in its received state. As that understanding emerges, we start to piece together a plan for arranging the materials.

The temptation is huge to launch immediately into arranging materials as we start looking in the containers. But this is the wrong time to do so! Consider the problem of the buffet table. At any meal function jam-packed with attractive foods, my own predilection is to start grabbing savories right and left as I move around the groaning tables. Bad move. No sooner is my plate full than I start seeing other items that I like even better than things already on my plate. Had I instead been smart (for a change) and reviewed *all* the dishes available to me, I could have made a superior—and sustainable!—selection. This lesson applies to processing. If we start arranging and, inevitably, reboxing materials during our initial pass through the collection, we will miss parts of series that lie scattered throughout later boxes; we will prematurely begin to develop an arrangement scheme that does not consider the full range of the collection; and we may paint ourselves into any number of corners simply by being ignorant of the full scope and condition of the collection. Processing needs to be done *planfully*, making decisions based upon a clear understanding of the collection and its real and full processing needs.

In reviewing the collection, we are accomplishing a number of particular objectives:

- *Getting a feel for the collection.* What do the materials we are only so briefly handling tell us about their creators and the circumstances of their creation and use? What is their informational content and significance? What is their organizational structure? What surprises jump out at us—physical condition, unexpected record units or record types, access problems, clues to their original order? Through these insights, a processing plan often starts to emerge: How long is this going to take? In what order should I do things? Which parts need the most attention? Do I need to turn to specialists to complete some of the tasks?
- *Identifying the creator's principal activities.* Even this perfunctory glimpse of the contents should provide a pretty good sense of the significant activities in which the creators of the materials were engaged, whether individuals or corporate bodies. This awareness starts to shape our sense of intellectual hierarchy (subgroups, series, files) that will be necessary to express the original order we are seeking to reestablish throughout our arrangement work.

- *Identifying major series and their physical dispersion.* As was emphasized in considering arrangement principles, the series into which the collection divides form its intellectual structure. This high-level review of the collection is crucial to identifying those series (though perhaps not exhaustively). It is also essential for noting their locations throughout the unprocessed collection. Series, which may be extensive, are frequently dispersed as a result of use, storage, and shipping actions over the course of their active life. In the current recordkeeping environment, it is increasingly common for materials comprising a series to be segregated by form and media, with digital and analog magnetic media housed apart from more traditional formats. In any event, this initial pass-through affords the opportunity to pull these related intellectual pieces together in advance of making any important arrangement decisions.
- *Formulating the arrangement structure.* All of this knowledge gained through the collection overview puts us in a position to experiment with the eventual arrangement structure and, usually by the time we're done, settle in on a final arrangement scheme. And we have accomplished this without shuffling (and unshuffling) any collection materials.
- *Identifying preservation and physical access issues.* The optimal time to become aware of such potential problems is during the initial review. Doing so gives us the opportunity to identify and initiate parallel projects, like conservation treatments, digital preservation actions, and media reformatting, so that such work does not slow us down while we are carrying out the rest of the processing activities. Otherwise, they can become stumbling blocks or speed bumps later on in the project workflow.

Although we don't want to initiate any real arrangement work during the overview, we want to record information about our discoveries. As we move container-by-container through the collection, we should be taking notes on content and structure (perhaps using the preliminary container list as a starting point), physical condition, access and formatting problems, and rearrangement ideas. We should also be fleshing out the contextual information that will later become biographical and administrative history narratives. Needless to say, we should be entering this data electronically so that the notes we take can evolve over the course of our work into the collection finding aid, as well as into such other items as condition of collection reports, disposition reports, and other administrative documents. And, we should be as thorough and accurate in our note-taking as possible, because we really don't want to have to go back through containers a second (or third) time to refresh our memory.

Appraisal during the collection review

The most appropriate and effective time to conduct appraisal work on a collection is, of course, during the fieldwork that occurs prior to its acquisition. But, even fairly rigorous appraisal in the field, or during accessioning, does not guarantee that low-value materials will not be found among the accessioned records. So, appraisal should be considered a normal activity during arrangement. This is, of course, equally true whether the records are analog or electronic.

The most effective and least disruptive time to identify and remove undesirable materials is during, or on the heels of, the initial collection review. At this stage, the archivist has developed a comprehensive sense of the collection and its component parts and is therefore equipped to recognize materials that do not appear to belong in the collection. Those materials may duplicate information in other, higher-value materials; they may be unrelated to the creator or to the other records; they may be inappropriate to retain for legal reasons or because they contain especially sensitive materials; they may simply lack research value. Regardless of the reason, this is the right time to remove them.

The most important consideration here is that the appraisal actions performed during arrangement not become an impediment to the efficient processing of the records. This can easily happen if the archivist launches a search-and-destroy mission to find and remove undesirable materials, especially during the later stages of arrangement when the contents of individual files are being examined. If we fall into the trap of assessing records at an item level to see whether disposition is warranted, then we almost inevitably slow the pace of arrangement to a crawl, thereby creating severe performance problems (and backlogs).

How can we avoid this? The most effective way to conduct our appraisal is to focus on the series and file levels, *not* on the item level. We should be looking for opportunities to streamline and focus the collection by eliminating sizable units truly worth the time investment in removing them. Generally speaking, we do not significantly reduce a collection's size or improve its usability by weeding out items or small clusters of items. But we *can* accomplish both bulk reduction and improved usability by removing irrelevant, redundant, and inappropriate records at a file level and above. Our desire to achieve our repository's objectives in acquiring the records should guide our appraisal efforts. Why did we want them in the first place? What researcher interests or documentary goals will they satisfy? We should only undertake appraisal in the course of processing if we improve the collection in relation to those concerns. And, at this stage in processing when we have reviewed the significant collection components, we are in the best position to remove unwanted materials at a nontrivial level.

Defining the project and creating a workplan

A common and costly mistake is to launch into a processing project without first developing a very intentional workplan. Planning is an essential activity for any enterprise, and a failure to do so typically results in wasted effort, misspent resources, and undesired outcomes. This is no less true in managing an archival repository or, on a more granular level, arranging and describing a single archival collection. If we don't plan the work beforehand, we are likely to experience frustrating results. Our research for the More Product, Less Process (MPLP) project demonstrated forcefully that archivists routinely and unnecessarily extend the timeframe for a typical processing project by their failure to develop, and then follow, a careful plan for the work. An effective project workplan should encompass processing goals, mechanics, and performance. It helps ensure that we follow the critical path, and it helps the processing archivist to proceed in a surefooted and systematic manner.[7]

Processing project workplans can be developed in various ways, especially these two:

- *The supervisor can develop the plan prior to assigning the project.* Such a plan is probably preliminary and suggests hoped-for outcomes based on what is known about the collection following its accessioning. Such a plan needs to be reviewed—perhaps renegotiated—after the processor has completed the thorough initial review of the records. A collaboratively produced plan has perhaps the best chance of being realizable,

as it marries administrative objectives with the processor's informed understanding of the collection itself.
- *The processing archivist can develop the plan following the collection review.* Such a plan will be grounded in the processor's knowledge of the collection. It needs to be brought to the supervisor to ensure that its recommendations align with the repository's resources and expectations.

Goals and outcomes

An arrangement and description project, whether it encompasses a few cubic feet of materials or many hundred feet, should have an overall purpose. What is the collection's research value, and who are its anticipated users? How will their research experience be well served? An understanding of these things can influence how intensively we process the collection. It could tell us where we might take shortcuts and where we should avoid them.

Methods and mechanics

An effective workplan ought to give the processing archivist useful guidance on *how* to arrange and describe the collection materials, thereby avoiding unnecessary confusion and generally speeding up the work. To accomplish this, the archivist preparing the workplan must acquire a baseline understanding of the collection, usually from communications with the acquisition archivist and/or donor, existing inventories and content notes, and, especially, a preliminary and superficial survey of the collection materials. This awareness puts the planner in a position to make at least preliminary recommendations in several important areas.

Arrangement. The workplan can identify the probable series or other major units into which the collection divides. It might also suggest an optimal sequencing of these units. It should also indicate, if possible, what level of labor ought to be invested in each unit of the collection. Should a given series be left entirely as is—warts and all? Should the files that comprise it receive extraordinary attention, such as individual scope and content notes? Should the items comprising it be carefully sequenced (chronologically, alphabetically, and so forth), or should they simply be left as they are? Are there fragile materials or other conservation issues that the processor should deal with, or instead ignore? Are there materials of a particularly sensitive nature that ought to be sought out and removed or redacted? Providing this sort of guidance, to the extent possible, can go a long way toward achieving successful outcomes, including reducing processing costs.

Performance expectations. Perhaps most important of all, a workplan should be explicit about performance objectives. What is the time budget for the collection? What deadline dates for critical milestones should be observed? Experience and research have both taught me that a project (especially a large one) without a deadline will drag on longer than it should and have a greater chance of actually running off the rails. Many repositories fail to prevent accumulating backlogs of unprocessed collections and also fail to meet their own annual processing objectives. Reasonable, informed project deadlines are key to maintaining a sustainable processing regimen. An important role for supervisors in achieving these deadlines is establishing a routine communication loop with archivists processing collections. Assessing performance milestones at regular intervals is the only way to ensure that overall project deadlines are met and deliverables achieved.

Processing management. Workplans also make an important contribution to sound management of the processing function at the repository level. Repositories with active collecting programs need to manage the arrangement and description of many collections of varying sizes over the course of an annual administrative cycle. Creating a workplan for each processing project allows the manager to define the resources—personnel and otherwise—that will be applied to any given collection. Doing this helps ensure that the manager can make a repository-level plan for processing all of the collections that need to be addressed during the planning cycle. Results not planned for do not often occur, so workplans become important tools in helping to achieve overall goals by controlling individual projects.

Arranging the Collection Materials

At this point, we have reviewed the entire collection so that we know in general what's there and what notable issues may lurk within the materials. Based on that general knowledge, we have prepared a workplan that establishes our processing objectives, manages our expectations regarding which actions we will take and which we won't take, and establishes an overall project budget that constrains and shapes the time and resources to be expended in carrying out all of this work. Only at this point are we ready to begin the actual arrangement work.

We can proceed in two ways with the physical work of arrangement. One way is to perform all the steps simultaneously. We identify a starting point—our initial high-level intellectual group (a subgroup or series)—and then begin pulling together all of its component parts (subseries, files, and so forth) and arranging them each in turn. So, by the time we have finished with the initial series of records, we will have arranged all of its subsidiary units and the contents of all of those units, and the work on the series will be complete. Then we move on to the next high-level unit and perform the same steps on all of its parts and pieces. By this method, we will have moved through the entire contents of the collection in one sequential pass and, when we have finished, all of the arrangement work on every subunit of every series will have been completed. Or so we hope.

What might be wrong with this approach? One serious flaw, in my estimation, is that by digging sequentially into a single subgroup or series at a time, we risk losing our sense of the whole of the collection. Arranging everything intensively in a given series, to the exclusion of all the other series, can leave us lacking an overall vision of the collection and the relationships between its major components. In a sense, we are only seeing one of the creator's activities or functions at a time and are somewhat blind to the others. We risk missing relationships among records, and archives are all about the relationships among the parts that give meaning to and define the whole. A second problem is that, in simultaneously performing all of the processing actions on a single series at all levels of granularity, we can easily lose our perspective regarding the work that must be performed on all of the *other* series before the project is finished. If we end up lavishing attention on one part of the collection without keeping in mind the work needed on other parts, we often end up going way over budget. We lose our budgetary roadmap.

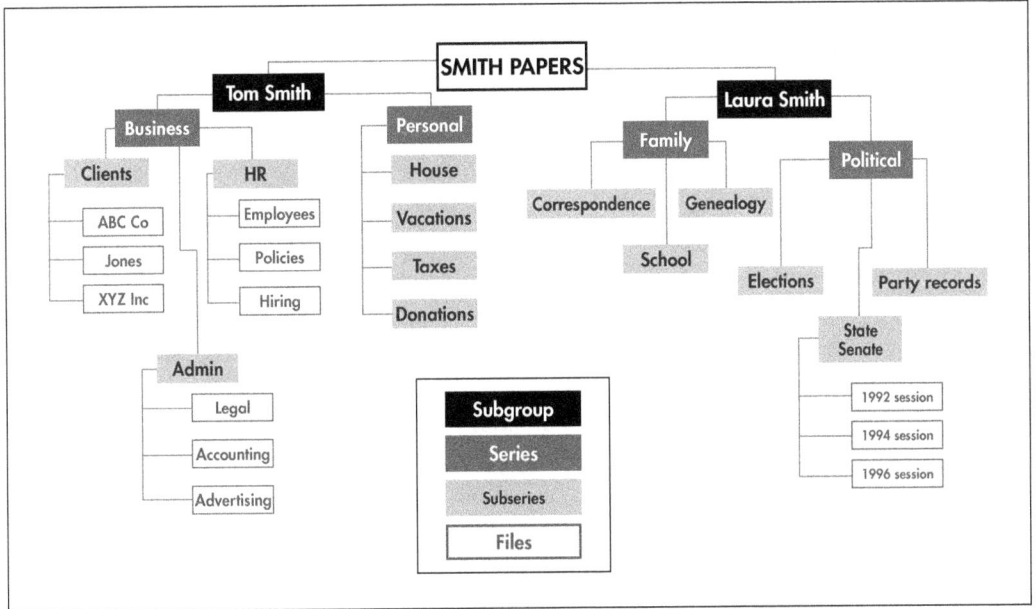

FIGURE 7. A depiction of intellectual structure in a hypothetical collection of family papers

The other way to proceed is to process the collection hierarchically. Figure 7 depicts a graphic of the intellectual structure of a moderately complex collection with several levels of hierarchy: subgroups, series, subseries, and files. To avoid the problems with the other approach, we can arrange the collection materials one level at a time, rather than drill all the way to the bottom of each subgroup or series before doing any real arrangement work on any of the others. Let's look at how we might proceed with such an approach.

Arrange the subgroups

Our first objective, utilizing what we know from the notes made during our collection overview, is to arrange the two subgroups of the Smith Family Papers: Tom's papers and Laura's papers. Our actions are limited and simple: we are simply dividing the collection materials into those two large parts by their creators. We are not attempting to separate and organize the series, let alone the files, that make up either subgroup. At this juncture, we are usually just moving boxes and other containers around so that we end up with two self-contained piles. But we have also accomplished something important in an intellectual sense. In the course of examining the collection materials *just enough* to create the subgroups, we have gained a clearer understanding of both the context and the content of the records comprising the collection. We can also be fairly confident that we have not missed anything that might qualify as a third subgroup and that no substantial groups of papers actually belong in the other subgroup.

Arrange the series

Having satisfied ourselves that we have successfully divided the materials, we can pull together the series within each subgroup. Tom's papers appear to divide into two series: papers documenting his business activities and papers documenting his personal life. Similarly, Laura's papers break into series documenting her political activities and documenting family activities. At this stage, *all* we are doing is subdividing the collection into those four series. Each of them consists of multiple files, but we are not going to make any effort to arrange any of those file groupings in any of the four series. We are only gathering together the materials that belong to any particular series, thereby separating them from all the rest.

By separating the collection into its component series, we have achieved the important intellectual objective of understanding all of the major, discrete activities that framed the lives of Tom and Laura documented by this collection. We have now arranged the collection into its fundamental and essential units of meaning. If we, for whatever reason, found ourselves unable to perform any further organizational work on the papers, we would nevertheless have already arranged them sufficiently to facilitate adequate access by researchers. Certainly not ideal, but likely sufficient.

At this stage of arrangement work, we have probably not invested any effort into replacing folders or other containers beyond placing materials in basic archival storage boxes. Nor have we examined any materials within files in enough detail to warrant weeding any out or performing any preservation actions on them. As a result, it is important to note that we have thus far avoided the costliest arrangement work in terms of time, energy, and expense. Avoiding the costly work that characterizes arrangement below the series level may sometimes justify limiting physical arrangement work to the series level and above.

While the physical activity applied in arranging subgroups is largely a matter of shuffling containers about, in processing series we are much more likely to grab handfuls of folders, bound or rolled items, sound and visual media, and to gather them together. It may make sense to start grouping them into archival containers, especially if their file structures are so evident that we can likely avoid repeatedly unboxing and reboxing materials as we perform more granular work later on. Otherwise, we are often better off organizing materials into piles that can be placed in containers later on after their order is further refined. At any rate, this is not the time to have a go at sequencing the files and subfiles within any series. Doing so just distracts us from our immediate objective and can lead us down rabbit holes that slow down the project work overall.

Arrange the files

Here we really roll up our sleeves. The number of record units we are reviewing and manipulating expands at least arithmetically when we move from the series level to the file level. Series, regardless of the form and medium of their contents, generally comprise files and each file typically consists of a sequence of folders or analogous units arrayed in some meaningful sequence. The units comprising a file are closely related to each other in the sense that they are all separate instances of the same sort of record. For example, Tom's Client files probably consist of a number of real or virtual folders, each of them containing the papers documenting his work with a particular client. The types of materials in each client folder(s) are largely the same from client to client.

Arrangement work at the file level typically involves bringing together those folders and sequencing them in a meaningful way, ideally in the original order that Tom established for them and in which he maintained them. File-level work is primarily a matter of sorting the file units until we arrive at an accurate and helpful sequence. In more complex file groups, this often involves multiple sorting actions. For example, the records of a consumer protection agency might contain a large group of files comprising consumer complaints aggregated over a number of years.

Those complaints might end up being arranged first by the issue involved, second by year, and third by name of complainant. So, three sorts would be necessary to finally create the optimal order for the files.

In addition to these sorting actions, several other important processing actions take place as we work through the files:

- *Noting tasks to perform later.*
    - Conservation treatment actions (mending, cleaning, removing rusty fasteners, photocopying bad paper). These tasks might be performed at a later stage in processing, or they might simply be noted as issues to address at some future time.
    - Removing duplicate or unwanted materials, either at this point or as a later project.
    - Reformatting and/or migrating magnetic media to a preservation platform. It is very likely that such technical and time-consuming work will need to be performed apart from processing and perhaps by other staff.
- *Replacing bad folders.* As we arrange files, the majority of our rehousing work takes place. As files are sorted into their final sequences, they will be placed within archival boxes, and the boxes identified with temporary labels. Any replacement of folders and other subcontainers must happen now as well. Whether to replace all existing folders with archival-quality folders or to refolder selectively is a matter of repository policy, but now is the time to implement that policy, as the volume and intended sequence of the files are now apparent and finalized.
- *Initiating the container list.* As we sequence and place the files in their physical or virtual containers, we should be listing them in a structured manner, recording all of the DACS information fields that will form the substance of the detailed finding aid. There is absolutely no point in performing all of this arrangement work and then having to go through the containers a second time to verify and record essential descriptive information.
- *Taking careful notes.* In the majority of processing projects, this is the most opportune time to take more general notes on collection context, functions and activities documented, subject content, collection strengths and gaps, major correspondents, and significant organizations, events, and places. We should also capture information about copyright and other legal, physical, and technical access issues. These notes will eventually populate narrative notes at the collection level and, perhaps, the series and file levels as well.

Arrange the items

Having arranged the materials at the file level, the final step in physical arrangement is to optimize the sequence of the individual items that comprise each file. So, what constitutes an item? An item, like an atomic element, is simply a thing that can't be further divided without destroying a self-contained informational unit. In this sense, an item may be a letter, a 500-page report, a bound volume or a single work in several volumes, a photograph or a photo album, an audio cassette, a document (file) on a digital storage device, a map, a piece of ephemera. All of these things are items, and item-level arrangement simply involves placing them into some sequential order that facilitates research. That sequence may be their original order, or it may involve imposing an order when no useful order is apparent. Either way, at this level of processing, we are examining and manipulating individual items, much like arranging the playing cards in a well-shuffled deck into suits and then into numerical sequences.

In terms of pure physical effort, it is easy to see that this becomes the most labor-intensive level of arrangement work that we can perform. Compared to work at the file level, work at the item level slows processing to a crawl. In a collection of even moderate size, which may contain 10,000 items or more, item arrangement may easily double the amount of arrangement time spent on a processing project. Some units in any archival collection will undoubtedly require item arrangement to make them effectively usable. Without a proper sequencing, the badly disarranged pages in a lengthy loose-leaf diary will frustrate users if we do not invest the time necessary to reconstruct their original order. Item-level arrangement is clearly required at times.

However, many other file units whose contents are also in disarray may not *require* resequencing. A file folder of correspondence may be quite jumbled up but may not depend on a literal sequence of its items to be usable. This may mildly irritate its users but can still accommodate research in a satisfactory way. *This distinction is an important one. Not every series or file requires the same level of arrangement granularity to be usable by researchers.* And, because item-level arrangement is quite costly in both time and dollars, it behooves us to distinguish between those units that really need refined arrangement and those that can get along without it. Bear in mind that, within the same collection, some units may need far less granular treatment than others. It is sometimes easy to get locked into the false logic that the level of work performed on one unit must be performed on all units. Within a single processing project, we can spare ourselves a good deal of unnecessary effort if we consider each material unit as having its own access requirements and therefore its own processing needs. We usually do not have the skill to make this kind of determination at the start of our processing careers, but experience helps us distinguish between the necessary and the unnecessary, between the satisfactory and the perfect.[8]

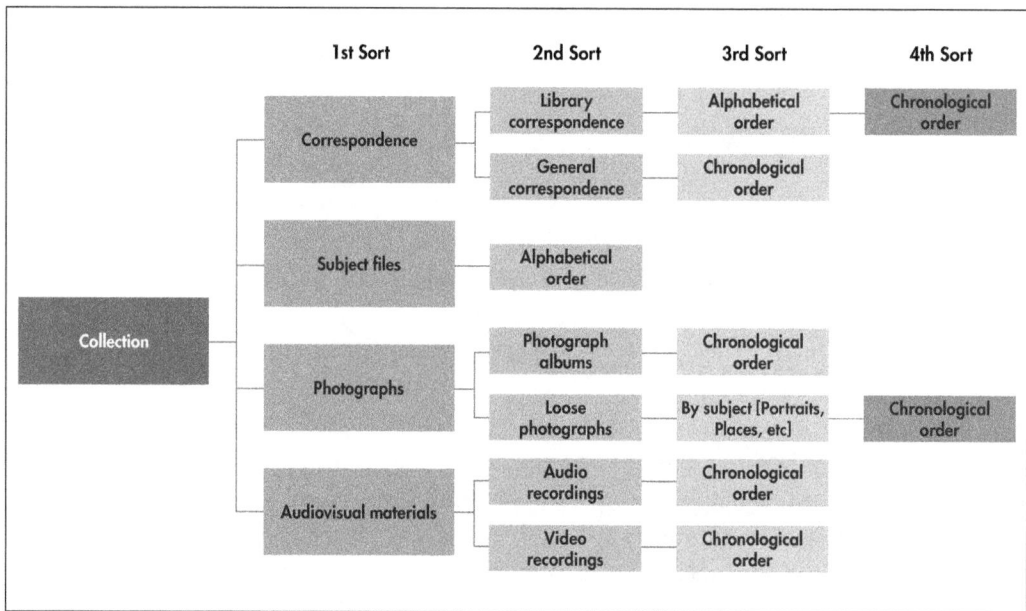

FIGURE 8. An example of the sorting process involved in arranging an archival collection

The work methodology

The last sections should have cemented a few key ideas about how arrangement work should proceed:

1. Any arrangement project ought to proceed in a definite, orderly chain of actions.
2. That chain is generally hierarchical in nature: *subgroup*→*series*→*subseries*→*file*→*item* (as applicable).
3. These actions involve arranging collection materials in any one hierarchical level before doing any arrangement work on materials in the next descending level.

Figure 8 helps explain how this works in practice. The figure depicts the intellectual structure of a modestly complex collection that breaks down into four series, its highest-level components: Correspondence, Subject files, Photographs, and Audiovisual materials. In small collections lacking structural complexity, it is not uncommon for the series to be based on types of records, rather than on major activities of the creator. As emphasized, the physical arrangement of the materials breaks down into a sequence of sorting actions. The initial sort brings the materials constituting the four series together and separates them from the other series. The second sort brings together the main file-level groupings in each series. In the third sort, one of two things happens depending upon the complexity of the files that comprise each series. Either the individual file units (e.g., folders) are arranged into their natural or sensible sequences or, if a given file (like the loose photographs) consists simply of items, then the items themselves are sorted into a natural or useful sequence. Then, in the case of this example, the fourth sort is simply a more refined ordering of the items within each file-level container. Having gone through these iterative sorting actions, the arrangement work is complete.

Why is it so important to arrange materials one level at a time?

- Work on one level, to some extent, informs us about the nature, content, value, and processing needs of the materials at the next level down. This helps us make good decisions about how (and how much) to arrange those materials, as well as how to describe them.
- It is more efficient to work in hierarchical layers. If we drill down to the very items in a series before doing any work on any other series, we are apt to lose our sense of proportion regarding how the nested parts relate to the whole in terms of content and significance. This can cause us to keep going back and forth (and sideways) as we compare materials. We can often end up handling materials multiple times instead of just once. All of this wasted activity bogs us down and slows the project.
- It helps us adhere to our workplan. The workplan we created or finalized following our initial review should have given us some milestones and expectations about how, and how intensively, we process various collection units. Drilling down to the bottom of any one series can make it much harder to stay on the plan simply because we naturally tend to give undue weight and preference to the series we happen to be working on at the moment. Even more critical, proceeding one layer at a time helps us marshal our project resources in the most meaningful and useful way. In discussing arrangement principles in an earlier chapter, I maintained that arrangement and description efforts at higher levels are more impactful and useful to researchers than is work performed at

lower levels. When we perform arrangement one layer at a time, working in a hierarchical way, we can assess our progress and performance after each layer. When we finish work on all of the series, we can easily see how much time we have left to complete the project on spec. Then, we have the ability to decide how much more work we can do, on which particular series, to stay within our projections. Or, we may decide that the original projections were misguided, and we can adjust the plan. Either way, we are in a better position to make an informed decision and to pursue the rest of the project in a controlled and calculated way. Had we processed all the record units in a single series completely before moving along to the next series, we might have already expended 60 percent of our resources on 20 percent of the collection materials. Whenever that happens, we go into scramble mode, and we often end up modifying our workplan in ways that are neither well informed nor calculated to achieve success. When we arrange collections a layer at a time, we are better able to avoid being painted into a corner and to expend our resources in the most effective manner.

Lock in the final arrangement

If we have taken the systematic approach to arrangement that was recommended, little need exists to rethink the collection organization now in place. Nevertheless, now we should review the collection, by way of the container list we have been developing as we arranged the collection units, to ensure that we have not missed anything along the way. As we processed the materials, we should have addressed overstuffed folders or other containers, but this gives us a chance to verify that, as well. We should also verify that the archival containers are packed full enough that the contents do not slump over time and to make sure that none are excessively full. We should resist the temptation to leave space in boxes for potential future additions. Those additions may never materialize, and simply adding new accruals onto the end of the collection is acceptable practice, while ensuring that they are described at the appropriate point in the finding aid in terms of their intellectual arrangement.

At this point, we should review the container list to determine that we have identified all the file units accurately and in consistent phrasing. If changes need to be made to the list in this regard, it is also the opportune time to change the terminology on folder labels and other container units before moving the collection materials out of the processing space and onto storage shelves.

Labeling collection materials

As the physical work on the project winds down, it is important to make certain that all the collection materials are labeled appropriately. Labeling is, of course, essential to ensuring that we can find the materials in our collections. We need to make sure that we can locate containers on our storage shelves or in other locations. We must also ensure that we can correlate the materials inside of each container with the descriptions that appear in the finding aids.

- *Labeling archival containers.* Now that any shifting of materials among containers has taken place, and we have verified the information in the container list, we can replace temporary container labels with permanent labels. Precisely what information goes on a label is largely a matter of repository policy and varies widely among institutions. Here are some of the variations, all of them acceptable:

- Minimal labels contain only the information necessary to retrieve the container and then return it to the proper storage spot. This may include a unique location identifier, name of the collection, container number, or some selection from these. This approach confers a certain security advantage in that no label identifies its particular contents to someone browsing the box labels to find valuable items. Another advantage is that if materials are added to or removed from the box in future, the box labels won't have to be changed or replaced.
- Moderately informational labels might also include names of the series or other significant content units in the container. This might provide some benefit to staff members browsing the collection without a finding aid in hand. It could conceivably benefit reference staff who want to remove and deliver to a patron only some of the materials in a container.
- Verbose labels might include additional pieces of administrative information, including accession number(s), access restrictions, or retrieval and use instructions (e.g., "Gloves required to handle materials in this box"). *Access restrictions* are particularly important to note so that restricted materials are not inadvertently delivered to staff or patrons who have not been granted access permission. It should be considered best practice to indicate the presence of restricted materials in any container. Accomplish this efficiently by using stick-on printed labels that can be easily removed if restrictions lapse.

- *Labeling folders.* The long-standing practice of labeling folders, envelopes, wrappers, phase boxes, and other archival subcontainers using a soft lead pencil remains the most sensible. Pencil can be easily undone if the contents of the container change. Also, it is just plain safer to work around unique collection materials armed with a pencil instead of a pen. More detailed instruction on labeling archival containers can be found in the SAA manual on preservation. The trickier part is deciding which information goes on the folder label. Do we accept the folder title supplied by the creator, or do we supply our own title? I would argue strongly that we serve users better if we take a flexible approach to this question, accepting titles when they accurately and crisply describe the folder content and revising them when they do not. There can be two benefits to modifying received folder (or file) titles:
  - *Accuracy.* A sequence of folders might each be unhelpfully labeled "Financial," when in fact the true contents of the sequence might be "Bank Statements, 2001–2005," "Bank Statements, 2006–2015," and "Brokerage Statements, 2001–2015." Sticking with the folder titles as received would be a real disservice to researchers and searchability.
  - *Discovery.* When we improve file titles to make them more accurate, we also have an opportunity to apply intentional, normalized terminology. Always titling a folder of photo images "photographs," rather than using variants like "pictures" or "photoprints," can improve user discovery by gathering together

closely related materials in a single search. It is an opportunity to use something resembling a controlled vocabulary to more effectively find and identify collection materials.

- *Labeling items.* In times past, some repositories labeled collection items, largely as a security measure. Such "property of" labels, most often associated with manuscript libraries, were usually stamped in ink, often on the *verso* of the item. This practice has become much less common for reasons of practicality (bigger collections) and perhaps because we have become reluctant to permanently alter the appearance of archival materials. An exception that persists is the practice of recording, usually in pencil, the accession number or other identifier on items in extremely small collections. Labeling a dozen or so items poses no great inconvenience, and, arguably, it adds some level of security. Repositories might be especially likely to want to "brand" manuscript items that bear substantial monetary value.

Dealing with Restricted Materials

In the course of arranging materials at the series and file levels, and entering descriptive information into the evolving container list, we should bear in mind those collection units (if any) for which public access will be conditioned in some way. We may need to restrict some access to certain materials for several reasons:

- *Contractual provisions.* The transfer agreement, deed of gift, or other legal instrument will note portions of the records to which access is restricted. The restriction might be absolute, or it might specify a process by which users may request access. Either way, processing archivists have the *undeniable obligation* of being aware of these provisions and identifying affected materials as they are arranged and listed. They need to identify and clearly label the affected unit (series, file, item) itself and to clearly indicate the restriction on the finding aid(s) they are creating. An unhelpful legal document might only characterize the restricted materials, rather than specifying them precisely. No matter how imprecise the injunction, processors must take care not to overlook affected materials. Reference staff, and perhaps legal counsel, will hold them responsible if they fail.
- *Fragile materials.* Sometimes we impose access conditions by our own authority, rather than that of donors. Such is the case with materials recorded on fragile media or carriers, that have already been damaged, or that have other physical problems that make it necessary to restrict access or to control the conditions under which they may be used. For example, if materials must be used under direct supervision of a staff member or only with gloved hands, or they must be copied or reformatted by staff before they can be made available, those constraining conditions need to be indicated clearly. The materials themselves need to be labeled with that warning, and the finding aid(s) needs to contain notes to that effect.
- *Privacy concerns.* This is the most problematic type of restriction, ethically as well as practically, that archivists themselves can impose.[10] We may often find items in collections that we feel could be used to damage someone's reputation or otherwise cause that person, or the collection donor, harm or embarrassment. What to do? Our primary

duty, I think, should be to make collection materials available to users. But sometimes, unfettered access seems risky. We should be loath to impose our own restrictions on sensitive materials, unless we have first discussed them with informed colleagues or our bosses. If we do end up imposing access restrictions for reasons of privacy, we should again take care to label the materials appropriately and make a clear notation on the finding aid(s).

Preservation Actions and Processing

I emphasized in the section on accessioning that a careful assessment of the conservation status and needs of the collection is most appropriately carried out as part of that function. Doing so at that point alerts us to active problems that should not be allowed to persist or worsen while the materials await processing. It also gives us a head start in executing a preservation plan during the hiatus between accessioning and processing, so that all of that important work does not get delayed until after processing occurs. That said, the act of physical arrangement is bound to expose additional specific conditions, some of which will need to be addressed in the course of arranging the records.

When we come across conservation issues during processing, we may either note them for treatment by other staff, perhaps conservators, or we can deal with the issues ourselves at the time. Large problems affecting a number of folders or filing units may need to be left for others, or at least deferred, so that the mitigation efforts don't sidetrack the arrangement work. The units reflecting those larger problems—large amounts of high-lignin paper, a big run of badly curling or cracking photoprints, a large cache of video cassettes in poor condition, a group of slides or transparencies that need use copies printed—if serious enough to prevent use, need to be arranged (to the extent possible), described, and then sequestered until treatment or reformatting efforts can be carried out. But the processing archivist is responsible for most of the smaller and immediate treatment actions necessary.

These sorts of potential treatments fall into a few common types, most of which concern individual items rather than larger groups of materials: damaged, acidic, or fragile paper needing copying or enclosures (polyester or paper); paper items bound together with rubber bands or metal fasteners; dirty materials requiring surface cleaning; photoprints with unstable emulsions in need of interleaving sheets. How much of this work should we routinely perform? How much is truly necessary? Archivists struggle with these questions. In very small collections, such treatments involve a small number of affected items and require very little time. In such cases, we would certainly perform the work as a matter of routine. But, in larger collections, these questions have the potential to significantly affect the timeframe and overall cost of a processing project. In those cases, we need to make workplan-level decisions that will either extend the project timeline or scale back certain treatment actions.

Since the publication of MPLP in 2005, archivists have become somewhat more comfortable airing these questions and treating them as normal business decisions, rather than as unacceptable retreats from best practices.[11] The MPLP research findings suggest that the presence of metal fasteners, high-lignin papers (even news clippings), moderate surface dust and dirt, even rubber bands will not *significantly* reduce the viability of collection materials if the collections are stored in adequate preservation environments. Those storage areas need to be free from continuous UV light exposure (covered windows) and from airborne pollutants (filtered air), and to demonstrate moderate and stable temperature and humidity levels. If those factors can be controlled, then treating the problems noted becomes less necessary and adds less preservation value. As a result, we start to consider them potentially unwarranted costs rather than absolute benefits. As the venerable MIT Processing Manual sensibly advised years ago:

> The sheer bulk of modern records justifies a hard look at the amount of preservation work to be done for each collection. Preservation is very time-consuming. Your preservation recommendations—even the recommendation to refolder papers or remove staples—must be defended on the basis of the collection's research value and the degree of physical deterioration of the records.[12]

It also seems true that being meticulous about item-level treatment actions tends to frustrate our intention to focus our arrangement work at some higher level. Because conservation issues manifest themselves at the item level, seeking them out inexorably draws us back there. This tendency can destroy our project management focus and result in poor processing performance. Another valuable repository processing manual notes that "[t]he level of preservation work you do on any collection is closely linked to the level of arrangement that you complete. For example if you are arranging papers only to the box level, it would make no sense to recommend preservation at the folder or item level."[13]

So, a repository is free to perform conservation treatments at any level it wishes. But, we should bear in mind that many item-specific treatments do not always result in significantly better outcomes and are very likely, in the case of larger collections, to extend the timeframes of processing projects significantly.

Dealing with Accruals

An unremitting problem for archivists is dealing with accruals to existing collections. It often seems that the very fact of publishing a finding aid invites new additions to the collection. Accruals to any given collection may happen once or multiple times. They may be insignificant in size, or they may rival the volume of the original acquisition. Regardless of scale and frequency, each accrual presents the repository with two basic arrangement alternatives: 1) interfile the new materials into the appropriate spots in the existing collection, or 2) simply add the new materials onto the end of the existing collection. Either route is acceptable, and preferability depends largely upon how arduous and expensive interfiling would be. Let's consider the two options:

- *Interfiling*. When an accrual is small, interfiling it into the proper intellectual arrangement of the records is almost always the best alternative. Doing so simplifies access and necessitates the fewest changes to the finding aid, sometimes almost none at all beyond adding a new accession number. However, even if the addition is small, interfiling may become problematic in a couple of cases: 1) the container(s) into which the materials would interfile has no room, or 2) the accrual represents a new format (e.g., motion picture films, audio cassettes, files on a floppy disk) that we do not want to add into the existing container. Either situation discourages interfiling and, instead, encourages us to add new actual or virtual containers onto the collection.

- *Adding onto the collection.* This is often the best solution for larger accruals and for more problematic small accruals, as noted above. A few particular reasons exist for choosing this alternative over interfiling.
    - **Practicality.** Adding a large group of materials, even if only to a single series, usually necessitates a great deal of shifting among the existing containers. This, of course, can take a lot of time and create a substantial processing project in its own right. A better alternative is to "arrange" the new materials *intellectually* without doing any physical rearrangement. Simply insert the descriptions of the new materials into the places in the finding aid where they belong intellectually. Doing this preserves the original order, and the physical materials simply live in a new container(s) at the end of the original collection. This practice has become standard at repositories such as Princeton, Yale, and the Minnesota Historical Society, which have historically managed many large, active, and continually growing collections.
    - **New series.** In some cases, an accrual results in an entirely new subgroup or series, in which case, neither a reason nor a practicable means exists to interfile it. The best alternative is simply to add the materials into new container(s) and place their description into the finding aid where it makes the most sense intellectually.
    - **New format.** The records comprising the accrual may be recorded on media that has no business being interfiled with the materials with which they belong intellectually. In such a case, it makes good sense to store (often after reformatting) the materials in containers or storage locations (e.g., separate cold storage environment) sensible for them and then, again, interfile their descriptions into the proper place in the finding aid.

Some institutions use a somewhat different method, treating the accrual, regardless of the series that comprise it, as a completely new subgroup or series. In such a case, no materials would be descriptively "interfiled" in the finding aid, and users would be advised to search all the separate accrual units for materials that might belong to any given series or other groupings. While this approach may take the least effort, it does place an additional burden on users and may cause some confusion in representing related materials in the finding aid.

This chapter has focused on the mechanics of arranging a collection of archival materials, providing enough information to approach a body of records with confidence in how to proceed. It also sought to communicate a basic understanding of the actions that are necessary to achieve good outcomes for the users of the collection. We have looked at accessioning as the necessary first step in establishing physical, intellectual, and administrative controls over the materials, and we have considered situations in which final processing work might occur during accessioning. We have then broken down the complicated work of arrangement into a sensible sequence of activities: preparing to process the records; reviewing the collection materials *without* performing any arrangement work; developing a realistic workplan that can be adhered to; and finally performing the actual arrangement work. We demonstrated that the most effective approach—in terms of both user outcomes and costs—would be to take a hierarchical approach. Working from the record levels revealed in our review of the collection, we proceed to process the collection, *one level at a time*, beginning with the topmost level present, and working methodically down through series, subseries, files, and items. We also learned that the types and degrees of work performed varies quite a bit from level to level. And this methodical sequencing of actions is germane to both digital and nondigital collection materials.

In the next chapter, we will move from arrangement to description, again focusing on the practical mechanics of describing the records as arranged. Again, we will emphasize approaches that couple good user outcomes with economical tactics.

NOTES

1. F. Gerald Ham, *Selecting and Appraising Archives and Manuscripts* (Chicago: Society of American Archivists, 1993), 81–90; Fredric Miller, *Arranging and Describing Archives and Manuscripts* (Chicago: Society of American Archivists, 1990), 31–44. The SAA *Glossary* has this to say on the matter: "'Accession' should be distinguished from 'acquisition.' As nouns, they are synonymous. However, the verb 'accession' goes far beyond the sense of 'acquire,' connoting the initial steps of processing by establishing rudimentary physical and intellectual control over the materials by entering brief information about those materials in a register, database, or other log of the repository's holdings." Richard Pearce-Moses, s.v. "accession," *A Glossary of Archival and Records Terminology* (Chicago: Society of American Archivists, 2005), 4. For information on the legal and physical transfer of records from the donor to the repository, please see Ham and Miller. This book will treat those considerations as *status quo ante* and will assume that the collection is already in the repository and that legal title has been secured.
2. Miller, *Arranging and Describing Archives and Manuscripts*, 31.
3. Detailed recommendations and advice on performing condition assessments and preparing reports can be found in Mary Lynn Ritzenthaler, *Preserving Archives and Manuscripts* (Chicago: Society of American Archivists, 2010), 26–29 and *passim*.
4. Christine Weideman, "Accessioning as Processing," *American Archivist* 69, no. 2 (2006): 274–83. Weideman coined the catchphrase "accessioning as processing," which has become widely used in repository processing manuals and other writings. Daniel Santamaria, an early adopter of the concept, integrated the approach into processing decision-making and workflows at both Princeton and Tufts Universities. He treats it as an important element of "extensible processing," which he develops at length in his recommended monograph: *Extensible Processing for Archives and Special Collections: Reducing Processing* (Chicago: Neal-Schuman, an imprint of the American Library Association, 2015).
5. Adrien Hilton, *Houghton Library Technical Services Manual*, "Accessioning," https://wiki.harvard.edu/confluence/display/HoughtonTechnicalServices/Accessioning, captured at https://perma.cc/PSJ4-D9WW.
6. T. R. Schellenberg, *The Management of Archives* (New York: Columbia University Press, 1965), 87.
7. A good example of a processing project workplan and directions for completing it can be found in Appendix G of the University of California–Irvine *Archival Processing Manual*, https://staff.lib.uci.edu/departments/sca/docs/Processing_Manual.pdf, captured at https://perma.cc/HDY2-BP26.
8. The concepts and recommendations in this paragraph are developed in much greater detail in Greene and Meissner, "More Product, Less Process," *American Archivist* 68, no. 2 (2005): esp. 236–45. A couple of other works examine and test them further: Weideman, "Accessioning as Processing," 274–83; Donna E. McCrea, "Getting More for Less: Testing a New Processing Model at the University of Montana," *American Archivist* 69, no. 2 (2006): 284–90.
9. The most recent version at the time of this writing is Ritzenthaler, *Preserving Archives and Manuscripts* (2010).
10. Archives professionals truly do need to inform themselves on the issues and vulnerabilities involved with privacy and access. An excellent source of information, and thoughtful reflections on the ethical questions involved, is Elena S. Danielson, *The Ethical Archivist* (Chicago: Society of American Archivists, 2010), especially chapters 3 and 6.
11. Greene and Meissner, "More Product, Less Process," 217–22. This section presents the case for reconsidering extensive conservation treatment actions during the course of processing projects. It also provides a number of citations to literature that both support and challenge this perspective on treatment.
12. Karen T. Lynch and Helen W. Slotkin, *Processing Manual for the Institute Archives and Special Collections M.I.T. Libraries* (Cambridge, MA: Massachusetts Institute of Technology, 1981), 47.
13. Northeastern University Libraries, Archives and Special Collections, *Processing Manual* (Boston, September 2002), 24.

5

Describing the Materials

As the physical or virtual components of the collection are arranged, we begin the process of describing them. I very intentionally begin that sentence with "as" rather than "after." In terms of process, the optimal time to begin recording information into what will evolve into the finished descriptive product is *during* the arrangement of the materials and not after all of that physical or virtual work has been completed. This is more a matter of practicality and economy than of theory; certainly, none of our standards advise us when or how to create the actual descriptive metadata, whether a standalone finding aid document or data values entered into CMS work form fields or data tables. But the economies are very real. If we begin drafting descriptive information as soon as we lock in the arrangement of items, files, series, and so forth, we capture information fresh in our minds that can accurately reflect and, if necessary, explain, the arrangement decisions we have just made. If, instead, we complete all of the arrangement work on the entire collection before drafting any finding aid content, we will need to reexamine many of the materials to identify and explain them. In effect, we would need to reperform a lot of the physical work that we have already carried out. Of course, we would certainly be taking notes throughout the course of our arrangement work, but it can save time-consuming steps if we actually draft the descriptive content in concert with arranging the materials.

And, as stressed in previous sections, the content of archival description is *metadata*—information that identifies and characterizes the content of the collection materials themselves. We should think about our description activities in those data-conscious terms and resist thinking about it as prose. In creating descriptive information about a collection, we don't seek to write an expository narrative, a work of prose that describes the collection. Instead, we create and record data in a structured way so that those data can be manipulated in diverse environments, by humans and machines alike, to create particular and wide-ranging descriptive outputs. The important thing is that we record the various units of descriptive information as structured data, and we utilize the rules and guidelines found in our descriptive standards to form those data so that they can be effectively shared across many systems for many purposes at many different times.

However the descriptive content is discovered and served out, the description *process* is the act of creating metadata so that users can discover an archival collection, or its component parts, and assess its relevance to their research. The whole point of description is to create that collection *surrogate* that will make it as simple and painless as possible for researchers to discover, understand, and locate the particular materials they want to use. As discussed earlier in considering descriptive principles, description *represents* in a visual and textual manner the arrangement of the collection; it is therefore a surrogate for the materials themselves. Our descriptive metadata enables researchers, at some level of remove, to *browse* the collection as though examining the materials themselves. They can visualize the structure of the materials and infer much about their content. The value created by the finding aids saves them the significant labor they would expend by directly browsing the materials themselves to make those same decisions. Researchers can make reasonably informed choices regarding whether they want to use the collection, and which parts they want to examine, without having to visit the repository and sometimes without having to interview an archivist to determine whether the collection is relevant to their purpose.

Our interdependent descriptive standards—structural, content, data interchange, and data value—create a mechanism that lets us identify the information elements crucial to achieving this value for users and conveys how that information should be expressed. And, we must bear in mind that these rules and instructions are appropriate and sufficient at *all* levels of description whenever multilevel description is performed. In discussing the data elements of the description and how we should put them together, I will use DACS as our guide, as it provides the most complete model. The structural standards provide bins to hold information defined in DACS; data interchange standards provide mechanisms to express and share that DACS-defined content.

Constructing Descriptions Using DACS Data Elements

It will be helpful to stress again the fact that the DACS rules are prescriptive only in certain situations. For example, the small set of required elements *must* be included once in every finding aid, generally at the highest level. Beyond that, much is left up to the discretion of the repository. Available resources and local practices will certainly influence the manner in which data elements are used. These considerations are explained in the DACS introduction:

> The rules recognize the necessity for judgment and interpretation on the part of both the person who prepares the description and the institution responsible for it. Such judgment and interpretation may be based on the requirements of a particular description, on the use of the material being described, or on the descriptive system being used. The rules highlight selected, though certainly not all, points where the need for professional judgment is called for, using phrases such as "if appropriate," "if important," and "if necessary." While in no way contradicting the value of standardization, such words and phrases recognize that uniform rules for all types of descriptions are neither possible nor desirable, and they encourage institutions to develop and document a description policy based on specific local knowledge and consistent application of professional judgment. Furthermore, it is recognized that a

particular data element may be formulated differently depending on the intended output system. For example, a scope and content note may be much more extensive in a multilevel finding aid than in a catalog record.[1]

So, a thorough delineation follows of *all* of the information elements necessary to create *any* type of archival description—a catalog record, a detailed multilevel description, units of structured data entered into relational tables, a guide to all or part of a repository's collections, and any other vehicle for sharing descriptive information about collections. Any finding aid that we create is simply a structured presentation of all or part of these information elements defined in DACS. The elements might be used only once in a very short finding aid for a small and uncomplicated collection. Or, they may be used many times over in the multilevel descriptive data documenting a large and complex collection. The point is that, together, they comprise the full suite of data elements, and any archival description is simply a structured repetition of these elements applied to different collection units. Here they are in full.

The identity elements

The identity elements are the core units of information necessary to accurately and unambiguously identify the collection or collection component being described, as well as to characterize its information value in a brief, structured way. That six of the seven are required whenever we are identifying archival information at some level, whatever that level may be, clearly indicates the significance of these information elements. A multilevel description requires these six elements at every level being described. The exception to this occurs when those elements are inherited from their parent in the descriptive hierarchy, or when that element is only applicable at the collection level.

> P7989. J. Harold Kittleson Papers, 1913–1988. 0.9 cubic feet (1 box and 1 oversize folder). *(collection)*
> Accounting Department Files, 1887–1910. 15 linear feet. *(series)*
> Legal Justice Fund correspondence of Anna Quigley, 1976–1986. 2 folders. *(file)*
> Levon Peters scrapbook, 1983–1985. 1 bound volume and 2 folders of loose materials. *(item)*

FIGURE 9. Identity statement examples illustrating usage of identity elements at different hierarchical levels

The seven identity elements follow, the first six of which are required.

Reference code

Required at the collection level, but not relevant at other hierarchical levels, the reference code is simply a character string that uniquely identifies a collection among all the other collections or items in a repository. No requirements exist for forming a code; it simply needs to conform to the repository's own system for administering its collections. It may be a simple serial number, which has the incidental value of providing a running total of the number of processed collections. Or, as in Figure 9, a repository may divide its collections into categories and then number them within each category. Some repositories develop elaborate identifiers that somehow classify the collection within a taxonomy of archival collections to confer a measure of semantic value on the identifier.

A unique identifier not only enables the institution to distinguish any collection from all other collections, it can also be used to create a unique filename for the collection's finding aid(s) within a file directory. It can also be used to distinguish the digital files forming part of one collection from those of another collection. The reference code can be used as the root element for naming digitized collection materials linked to from the finding aid. So, in the Figure 9 example, we might see something like the illustration in Figure 10.

P7989:	Collection reference code.
P7989.inv:	Unique identifier for its EAD finding aid.
P7989-221.pdf:	Unique name of a PDF file made up of a folder of digitized collection items, linked to from the EAD finding aid.

FIGURE 10. Reference code examples

Although they might seem like ideal candidates, using accession numbers as collection reference codes is generally not a good idea. While a one-to-one correlation frequently exists between accessions and collections, there are always exceptions; a single accession may divide into multiple collections, and multiple accessions may combine into a single collection. Needless to say, problems may result.

DACS refers to the reference code applied at the repository level as the *local code*. When an institution's collections are exported into union environments, the local code is combined with a unique repository code, as well as a two-character national code. This identifies the institution that holds the materials and also ensures that all collections in shared environments are uniquely identified.

Name and location of repository

To make it explicit, especially to users at a distance, finding aids should indicate the name and address of the repository. This information is usually generated automatically from reference codes or boilerplate information in EAD and MARC record templates.

Title

Every described unit of materials—collection, subgroup, series, file, and so forth—must bear a meaningful but succinct title to identify and characterize the materials. If the unit has a formal title, that should be used. Otherwise, as is most often the case, the title should be taken or paraphrased from the materials themselves. The title has two parts: the *name* of the creator of the unit and the *nature* of the materials being described. Often, the name part can be inferred from the position of the materials in the arrangement hierarchy. If the collection creator produced all of the collection materials, then the name may not need to be repeated throughout the collection. A file labeled "correspondence" can be inferred to be the collection creator's correspondence. Still, to improve clarity for users, it is advisable to use name elements in all titles in which the creator is not patently obvious.

In the Figure 9 examples, "Accounting Department Files" serves the purpose by identifying the responsible entity and characterizing the content of the materials—"Files"—if only broadly. We can assume that the unit includes *all* the extant files of the accounting department. Similarly, in the

"Legal Justice Fund correspondence of Anna Quigley," the title relates, in the briefest terms possible, the creator, Anna Quigley; the nature of the materials as "correspondence"; and the subject of the correspondence as the "Legal Justice Fund." This level of title information sufficiently explains the contents of these materials to would-be users, which is the real objective of title information. A few other considerations are worth noting:

- Rules for forming the names of individuals, families, and corporate bodies are found in Part II of DACS. These rules are most useful for constructing the name of the creator of the collection as a whole. For names found in collection subcomponents, it is more typical to express them in natural language for purposes of simplicity and brevity (e.g., *U.S. State Department* instead of *United States. Department of State*).
- If more than two entities are responsible for creating the unit, use the name of the one that predominates, or else use a broader characterization (e.g., *Jones Family* instead of *Anne, Bob, and Dave Jones*).
- Always express a name in the same form throughout a finding aid to improve discovery.
- Characterize the content and form of a unit as broadly as necessary to encompass the materials *(accounting records* instead of *journals, ledgers, balance sheets, invoices, and waybills)*.
- Use consistent terminology for collection material forms and media to improve searchability.

Date

The dates of the materials comprising any collection component are an essential part of the title because they give users important information about the scope and boundaries of the content. A researcher interested in the fall of the Berlin Wall is unlikely to be interested in a set of State Department files on East Germany that terminate in 1980. Whenever the title applies to a unit larger than a single item, the date element will be expressed as a range of inclusive dates (e.g., *March 1950–June 1979*). While users are likely to benefit from the most precise dates possible (*March 2, 1950–June 17, 1979*), the economics of processing often dictate that we confine our efforts to supplying less granular information (*1950–1979*, or even *ca. 1950–1979?*). Regardless of the decisions we make in this regard, the date information that we provide must be accurate and helpful (e.g., *[ca. 1920s–1930s?]*, rather than *undated*).

Two distinct types of dates may be communicated in span dates. The most common is *date of creation*, in which the date range reflects the dates on which the materials were themselves produced. The other type is *date of recordkeeping activity*, which reflects the date range during which the creating entity accumulated and managed the materials. In the latter case, most common in organizational records, the management of the information is more important to the informational content of the records than are the literal dates of the materials themselves, which might, in some cases, predate the activity by decades or even centuries.

Extent

Included here are all the informational elements relating the quantity of the materials, as well as their physical nature, form, and medium, all of which can have a significant bearing, not only on their informational content, but also on their accessibility. Common data elements are physical extent (size, volume), physical medium, technical requirements, and physical condition. Analog materials may be described in terms of the linear or cubic footage occupied, the number of containers, the number of items, or some combination of these variables. Electronic records may be described in terms of their disk storage space, number and type of files, volume of storage media, or a combination of these elements.

> 25.5 cubic feet (28 boxes, 1 map folder).
> 15 photographs.
> 27 data processing files (dBase IV) on 3 floppy disks (3.5 in.).
> 3 fragile birchbark letters encapsulated in Mylar.

FIGURE 11. Statement of extent examples

As depicted in Figure 11, for larger collections, indicating the extent of the materials in multiple expressions—the volume in terms of cubic or linear footage, as well as the number and type of containers—can be very helpful. Providing this information helps researchers to understand the magnitude of the collection and the size and complexity of the research project ahead of them. The important thing for us to accomplish is to give potential researchers a reasonably complete sense of the overall scope and scale of the collection in several regards:

- The overall quantity of materials
- The number and types of containers that house them
- The material formats and carrier media that exist, especially when they affect accessibility and suggest content

These considerations can all affect users' interest in some or all of the materials, or their ability to access and use the items. It should go without saying that these considerations are important not just at the collection level, but in title statements at any level throughout a multilevel finding aid.

Name of creator(s)

At the collection level, it is necessary to record the name of the creator or creators in a formal manner. DACS delineates the rules for doing so at great length and accompanies them with a wide variety of examples intended to cover the gamut of situations that archivists normally encounter. It is important to establish locally the authoritative form of any creator name, whether an individual, a corporate body, or a family. That name form should be used in all formal access points in catalog records and detailed finding aids. That way, researchers know how to search for an entity so that all references to the same entity are gathered together in a search. While it is certainly acceptable to record the formal name of the creating entity when identifying collection materials at any level below that of the collection, this ideal level is usually reserved for situations when optimizing search and discovery is desired. To do so in every possible instance would be a poor use of processing resources. Instead, repositories usually embed the creator name into the title of the unit being described only when the responsible entity differs from the collection creator (as in Figure 9).

Administrative history or biography

As was discussed in examining EAC-CPF, it may someday become normal practice to convey this essential contextual information via standalone archival authority records. Until that day arrives, it will remain standard practice to embed narrative historical or biographical sketches (hereinafter referred to as "bioghists" for the sake of brevity) into the identity elements of our finding aids.

As emphasized in discussing the fundamental principles of description, describing content *and* creators are equally important; the latter objective is largely realized through this narrative information. Of the seven identity elements, this is the sole one that DACS does not require. It does, however, consider it an optimal practice and encourages its use at the collection level. So, given the importance of contextual description, why is it optional? Basically, it is a practical compromise acknowledging that such information may be difficult to acquire and therefore too time-consuming to compile. But, this should not prevent us from asserting it to be best practice and striving to include it at the collection level wherever possible. Certainly, bioghists don't need to be lengthy narratives and, for the majority of collections, they can be accommodated in 100 to 500 words. As in content description, users generally appreciate brevity, which results in more approachable and web-friendly finding aids. Although the bioghist may itself be quite brief, we can use it to cite or link out to comprehensive sources of information on the entity being described as a further help to researchers.

While it should be considered best practice to include a bioghist at the collection level, this is not the case at lower levels in a multilevel finding aid. In general, it is a good idea to forego it except in cases where the records are particularly significant and substantial and in which a deeper knowledge of the circumstances of their creation is crucial to understanding them. This may occur most typically at the subgroup level in large and complex collections and sometimes at the series level.

Information for biographical and historical sketches can be found in published materials and in the collection materials themselves. Biographical dictionaries, encyclopedias, academic articles and monographs, corporate and government reports, websites, and genealogies are typical sources, but the collection itself often provides sufficient reliable information about the creator. In cases where two or more creators are responsible for the collection, multiple bioghists are advisable. What information elements are pertinent in constructing good bioghists? These vary somewhat between corporate bodies and persons, so I will consider them separately.

Corporate bodies

- Functions, activities, mandates, and name changes
- Dates of formations and dissolutions (whole and parts)
- Geographic locations
- Key events and individuals (especially if relevant to collection content)
- Administrative structure
- Predecessors and successors

Individuals and families

- Important activities, roles, and occupations
- Names, name changes, and genealogical information
- Key relationships with persons and organizations

- Life dates
- Places of residence
- Education

Content and structure elements

This group of elements includes those informational pieces that explicate the content of the materials being described and the manner in which they are organized, rather than information about the entities responsible for the materials. At certain hierarchical levels, there may be extensive textual notes about the informational content of the unit being described. Common data elements include scope and content notes (narratives), notes about the arrangement of the materials, and controlled vocabulary access points.

Scope and content notes

These notes are the most important elements in content analysis. They also tend to be the fullest and the most frequently found notes throughout the finding aid. DACS requires them in every finding aid, but only at the highest level present. In multilevel description, they are optional at all descending levels of arrangement. But, as was the case with bioghists, the fact that they are not required does not diminish their value in explaining and characterizing the informational content

---

HISTORY OF THE CAMDEN AREA COMMUNITY CONCERNS COUNCIL

Inspired by other attempts at neighborhood activism and frustrated with a perceived lack of social services in the community, the Camden Area Community Concerns Council (CACCC) was formed in 1975 to work with citizens as well as city, school, and library officials to assess community needs and recommend plans and projects for community improvement. The goals of the organization were to further community development, educate residents on civic matters, engage in job development for underemployed and unemployed youths, improve the economic condition of senior citizens, and to generally improve the welfare of the Camden Community. The group sponsored and supported such projects as the establishment of a community center, neighborhood beautification efforts, creating a volunteer network to provide support services to senior citizens, and the reform of harmful real estate sales practices.
—Finding aid for the Camden Area Community Concerns Council Records, Minnesota Historical Society

BIOGRAPHY OF NIKKI DARLING

Nikki Darling is a third generation Angelino on her father's side and Neomexicano on her mother's. From South Pasadena, she was born June 6, 1980 and attended various schools in the area including Holy Family School, Ramona Convent, and the Los Angeles County High School for the Arts. Darling graduated high school in 1999.
  Darling attended Eugene Lang College, the New School for Liberal Arts in New York, majoring in writing and earning her Bachelor of Arts in 2006. She earned a Masters of Fine Art in Critical Studies from the California Institute of the Arts in 2010. She is a candidate in the Creative Writing/Literature PHD program at USC.
  Nikki Darling's music criticism and essays appear regularly or have appeared in the Los Angeles Times, LA Weekly, Art Book Review, Tomorrow Magazine and Public Books. As well, she is a columnist at KCET, Artbound. Her essay "Appropriate For Destruction" was included in Best Music Writing 2010. She is finishing her first novel, Fade Into You, a memoir of mixed race identity in the San Gabriel Valley during the 90's.
—Finding aid for the Nikki Darling Papers, UCLA, Chicano Studies Research Center

---

FIGURE 12. Examples of bioghist notes

of the materials found in any archival unit. Therefore, we should consider it best practice to include a scope and content note for every notable unit of materials in a collection for which the identity elements themselves do not adequately characterize the materials. Of course, we should expect that these notes will generally grow briefer and briefer as we move down the records hierarchy. The main scope and content note at the collection level will usually be much more extensive than one at the series level and so forth down the chain. Because we can expect the information found in materials at the lower levels to be more focused in topic and format, these notes rarely need to exceed a sentence or two. As in all narrative description, our goal should be to provide the leanest wording possible to accomplish our objective.

And what should that objective be? Obviously, it is not possible to describe the myriad people, organizations, places, events, and topics that will be encountered, and evidenced, in all the documents that comprise any archival unit. The information in any collection or component is simply too diverse and wide-ranging to contemplate doing so. How then to say just enough? Schellenberg, the Dutch writers, and other theorists come to our rescue by emphasizing that the archivist's responsibility is simply to *characterize* the collection materials, rather than to enumerate them, to analyze them, to promote them, or to debate them. Archivists should leave that work to the users of archives and should never take on that role themselves. This is good advice for several reasons:

- As already noted, we lack the capacity to engage with the documents in a collection at such a granular level. Our productivity will plummet if we attempt to do so.
- Verbose content notes can yield bulky finding aids that become impenetrable and confusing to the researchers using them and that are difficult to manage online.
- The *evenhandedness* of our descriptions becomes compromised. Experience tells me that when we immerse ourselves in evaluating and explaining the collection materials, we run a great risk of suggesting that our own perspective is the only lens that matters in summing up the content and research value of the collection. When this happens, we are just as likely to mislead users about the content of the collection as we are to enlighten them.

But, if we restrict our notes to *characterizing* the overall content of the unit we are describing, as accurately and succinctly as possible, we will go a long way to preventing the problems just noted.

What types of information, then, should we include in our scope and content notes to achieve that characterization of the materials? DACS suggests the following guidelines for information in scope and content notes (my comments appear in italics):

- The function(s), activity(ies), transaction(s), and process(es) that generated the materials being described. *(This applies mostly to notes at lower levels in multilevel description. At the collection level, this information will usually be found in a bioghist, which would probably not appear at a subgroup, series, or file level.)*
- The documentary form(s) or intellectual characteristics of the records being described (e.g., minutes, diaries, reports, watercolors, documentaries).
- The content dates, that is, the time period(s) covered by the intellectual content or subject of the unit being described.
- Geographic area(s) and places to which the records pertain.
- Subject matter to which the records pertain, such as topics, events, people, and organizations. *(In the interest of accuracy and conciseness, the subject matter mentioned or discussed should be limited to things that are essential or central to the collection materials being*

described. It is unhelpful to suggest to users that the records include information on topics too scanty to support research.)
- Any other information that assists the user in evaluating the relevance of the materials, such as completeness, changes in location, ownership, and custody while still in the possession of the creator, and so on.[2]

The key in creating a useful and sufficient scope and content note is to record the relevant types of information from the list above in the form of a brief narrative that encapsulates that information to suggest content and significance.

System of arrangement notes

While it is essential to explain and characterize the topical content of the materials, it is no less important to help users understand how the materials are arranged. I emphasized earlier that description *represents* arrangement. Arrangement notes help users to visualize in a brief and basic way how that arrangement plays out. While the finding aid as a whole provides a single exhaustive view of the collection's arrangement, and of all its component parts, an arrangement note summarizes this information at a glance via a brief narrative statement or, perhaps, a structured outline.

DACS does not require an arrangement note, but instead considers it added value. Why not require it? Some collections, because of their size or organizational simplicity, may not benefit from a note. This would be most typical in a small collection consisting of a couple of folders; in that case, awareness of an arrangement scheme offers no research advantage. Some collections may simply have no arrangement, perhaps existing in a received state that exhibits no structure. In others, for example a collection consisting entirely of correspondence in a single chronological

---

Records of an organization founded in 1975 to promote positive activities in Camden Community (located in north Minneapolis) and to address community concerns. *(MARC record: collection-level note)*

Papers of Macfarlane, Northern Pacific Railway Company president (1951–1966) and chairman (1966–1969), who began service with the company as its western counsel in 1934. The papers concentrate on his personal and family life (1920s–1970s), documenting the management of their household, family interrelationships, trips, the education and marriages of his four children, and family finances. Business correspondence documents the organizations and events in which Macfarlane participated as a Seattle lawyer (1922–1930) and King County Superior court judge (1930–1934), as well as a railroad executive. *(Full finding aid: collection-level note)*

Materials from Mondale's US Senate career include schedules and appointments, meeting files, bill and committee files, outgoing correspondence, sampled constituent correspondence and constituent service records, press releases, speeches, radio broadcasts, and news clippings. A large set of wide-ranging issue files kept for each year by Mondale's Senate office concern federal departments, international affairs, domestic matters, and state issues. *(Full finding aid: subgroup-level note)*

Includes minutes, financial statements, memoranda, correspondence, reports, and other materials. Minutes document the theater's study and analysis of its audience, funding efforts, and marketing strategies. They also include information on the theater's expansion and reorganization in 1990. *(Full finding aid: series-level note)*

Packets organized by monthly board meeting include director's reports, board and committee meeting minutes and reports, project and financial reports, financial statements, surveys, and related administrative materials. *(Full finding aid: file-level note)*

FIGURE 13. Scope and content note examples

sequence, a simple reference to that fact might be made in a scope and content note, eliminating any need for a separate note. However, I would argue that it is almost always useful to some degree to include a structured note in a predictable place simply to make the arrangement status clear to the user. I would maintain that something as simple as "Arrangement: unarranged" is better than nothing. It also lends predictability to a repository's finding aid system if each and every finding aid can be counted on to contain an arrangement note in a predictable place. While not required, I believe it is useful and should be considered a best practice for finding aids.

As is true with nearly all DACS elements, an arrangement note can exist at any level in a multilevel description. While most common and necessary at the collection level, it can be helpful at any other level, especially when the materials in a subgroup, series, or file are organized in an unexpected way ("Letters in this correspondence file are arranged by the sender's location"), or have a complicated arrangement ("Organized in annual groups, thereunder by local chapter, and thereunder by name of writer"). In either case, users might benefit from foreknowledge.

> The collection materials are organized into the following sections:
>   Administrative Records.
>   Project/Issue Files.
>
> **Arrangement:** chronological
>
> Arranged chronologically by file number.
>
> General Correspondence Files are organized by year, thereunder by name of correspondent.

FIGURE 14. Arrangement note examples

Controlled access points

Another useful way to provide content information is through embedding controlled access points in our finding aids. Traditionally, we use these as the added entries encoded in MARC catalog records. However, EAD also provides fields for including search terms derived from controlled vocabularies, as do collection management systems. It can be a boon to discovery and collocation, especially, to include a judicious number of these terms in any finding aid. Embedding terms derived from authoritative vocabularies helps researchers pull together related collections in a single search without having to dream up every way in which a particular topic might be expressed. Terms employed should be limited to collection topics that are particularly significant to the collection and may include names of persons and corporate bodies, geographic locations, and topical subject headings. Rules and guidelines for applying controlled search terms are available in bibliographic name and subject cataloging resources.

Because archives, unlike books and other published materials, are not generally about particular subjects, it can be less helpful to researchers to focus topical analysis on the sort of subject headings used in bibliographic cataloging. Archives are not so much about *things*, but they are most definitely about *activities*. Emphasizing subject terms that denote particular activities—whether

> **Topics:**
> Booksellers and bookselling—Minnesota—Twin Cities Metropolitan Area.
> Bookstores—Minnesota—Twin Cities Metropolitan Area.
>
> **Places:**
> Minnesota—Duluth—Authors.
>
> **Persons:**
> Banning, Margaret Culkin, 1891–.

FIGURE 15. Examples of access points

business, political, scientific, educational, social, or the like—or functions, such as legislating, merchandising, publishing, cooking, and so forth, therefore greatly benefits users.[3]

Conditions of access and use elements

This group of elements conveys what is often very important information to help users understand the terms and conditions that affect their ability to 1) gain access to collection materials and, then, 2) to make further use of the materials beyond the mere act of reading them. These elements are also important for public service archivists in determining whether and how they may facilitate access to collection materials.

Conditions governing access

This is one of two access and use elements required by DACS, and it is only required at the collection level in multilevel description. The purpose of the element is to clearly state the conditions under which users may gain access to materials in the collection and, specifically, whether any or all of the materials are restricted. Access restrictions are delineated in a deed of gift or other legal documents governing the repository's acquisition and administration of the collection. The language in those documents should be accurately conveyed in the access note. If access restrictions are in force, it is important that the note communicate 1) which portions are restricted, 2) the duration of the restrictions, 3) to whom they apply (if they are not universal), 4) special conditions constraining how and where the materials may be viewed, and 5) how the researcher may request access to them.

Although the access note is crucial in cases where materials are restricted, it is also useful for unrestricted collections simply to make explicit to potential users that no obstacles exist to gaining access. This is why the element is required and not optional.

Physical access

In some cases, access is not constrained by legal requirements, but by the physical nature of the materials themselves. Such conditions might include their location, which could delay access to the materials because of retrieval issues. Some materials (e.g., photographs, sound and visual recordings) may suffer from such poor image or sound quality as to badly compromise researchers' ability to use them. Fragility and similar preservation conditions might limit or control where and under what conditions researchers could handle certain items. The physical condition of the materials could also indicate that, as in the previous case, users should only access copies, rather than the

> **Access Restrictions:**
>
> Restricted, in part. With the exception of the publications series (see Box 2), access to materials less than 25 years old requires written permission.
>
> Records in unprocessed sections are closed to the public.
>
> Access to records less than 25 years old requires written permission. News releases, clippings, photographs and commonly available publications are excluded from this restriction.
>
> **Use Restrictions:**
>
> For records less than 25 years old quotation or publication beyond the fair use provision of the copyright law requires written permission. News releases, clippings, photographs and commonly available publications are excluded from this restriction.
>
> Documents in this collection may not be reproduced.

FIGURE 16. Examples of conditions of access and use notes

originals themselves. In all such conditions, it is helpful to alert users in advance that their access may be conditioned by particular physical exigencies. Because these factors are not commonplace, and because they are rarely deal breakers in and of themselves, DACS does not require the element. But it should be considered best practice to include a note when physical access conditions exist.

Technical access

Some materials are problematic to access, not because of their physicality, *per se*, but because they require some special equipment, software, or other technologies to view and make sense of them. These technical resources might not be available within the repository. Even if they are present, they may require special access spaces or that particular staff members assist users. All of these things can understandably place severe obstacles in the path of would-be users. Therefore, a technical access note is quite important to include whenever conditions suggest that gaining effective access is likely to frustrate users. In some cases—consider the presence of many 35mm slides, but no projector—access is limited, but not severely hampered, and the inclusion of a note is much less important. Perhaps for that reason, DACS does not require the note. Consult DACS for specific guidance on how to express the access requirements of digital files.

Conditions governing reproduction and use

Although not a required element, it is nevertheless extremely important to refer to the copyright status of collection materials, as well as to any particular conditions governing their publication, reproduction, display, or other use researchers might make after viewing them in the repository. These notes must express concisely and accurately the legal rights and obligations of users with regard to the materials in the collection. Clearly expressing all of these considerations in a single note is the best alternative. In many cases, different use considerations will apply to different groups of materials in the collection, requiring multiple separate notes for clarity and comprehensiveness. The source of information is generally the gift or transfer agreement, or else related legal documents signed by the transferring entity. Essential information breaks down as follows:

Copyright status. It is important to indicate the legal status of the collection materials or particular parts of them. It is good practice to include a statement even when all of the materials are in the public domain to save users the trouble of having to make that determination themselves. In this instance, quoting the concise DACS commentary on this note, which states the important considerations succinctly, is useful:

> The statement of copyright status of a work indicates whether or not it is protected by copyright and, if it is protected, the duration and owner of the copyright. The copyright status is determined by the copyright legislation of the country in which the archives preserving the work is located. Where the term of copyright protection has expired, it is useful to indicate that the work may be used freely for any purpose without the permission of the copyright owner or the payment of royalties. Where the work is still subject to copyright protection, it is useful to indicate the duration of copyright protection and the copyright owner, should the user require permission to use the work for purposes other than private study, scholarship, or research. Copyright laws provide the copyright owner with other rights in addition to copying, including the right to control publication, distribution, broadcast, public performance, and so on. Copyright laws may also permit archives and libraries to copy items in their holdings for limited purposes, such as research or preservation, without the permission of the copyright owner, provided that certain conditions are met.

Conditions governing reproduction. Reproduction refers to copying collection materials by any mechanical or digital means. It does not refer to any later *use* that is made of the copies. Like access restrictions, the donor usually imposes reproduction restrictions, but they may also be imposed by the repository either because the materials are under copyright or because materials are too fragile to permit copying. The reproduction note should state which materials may not be reproduced, which entity imposed the restriction, the reasons for the restriction, the date when the restrictions cease, if ever, and instructions for petitioning to make copies in the meantime. DACS does not require a note about reproduction and, indeed, most repositories would assume that any and all materials may be copied for patrons if no note to the contrary exists.

Conditions governing publication and other uses. While the reproduction note covers the making of copies, this note specifies the uses that may be made of those copies, including display, public viewing, broadcast, presentation on the Web, and so forth. The note should specify the nature of the restriction (some uses may be allowed, while others not), the period in which it is in force, the authorizing agency, and procedures for gaining permission to publish. DACS does not require a publication and use note, but it is certainly good practice to include one whenever restrictive conditions are in force.

Languages and scripts of the materials

As is true with the various constraints on access and use, the language of collection materials, as well as the alphabet or script in which their information is recorded, can have a profound effect on researchers' ability to make effective use of the collection. For this important reason, DACS requires a language note. Any such note should indicate which materials are in a language, script, or character set different from the language of the rest of the collection; the language of those materials; and the script or character set in which they are recorded. This is a case in which multiple notes may appear throughout the finding aid, as different units of the collection may well be in different languages. In a multilevel finding aid, a general language note should appear at the collection level (e.g., *Most of the collection is in English, with some materials in Portuguese*). Then, additional notes will be placed within the descriptions of subunits that are in another language. Because the note is required, a note should at least exist at the collection level (e.g., *In English*).

Finding aids

This optional note is used to record the existence of additional "finding aids" to the collection apart from the finding aid in which the note appears. It is common for donors, repository staff members, or users to create other descriptive tools such as lists of letters or correspondents, calendars, indexes or databases to particular series or files, or essays about the collection or creator. It is also common enough for the collection materials themselves to include useful tools like correspondence registers or indexes, box lists, and so forth. Sometimes, a parallel finding aid may exist online, the creation of some entity with a strong interest in the collection. The finding aid note calls attention to any such tools that may be helpful to users.

Acquisition and appraisal elements

This set of optional elements provides a place to record information that does not describe the collection materials themselves, but instead documents important administrative actions performed by the repository in the course of acquiring, preserving, and managing the collection. While this information has obvious value for repository staff, it can also be very helpful to users in explaining the history of the collection during its custodial phase of existence and how it may have changed from its original state as archivists and other professionals repeatedly shaped and acted upon it.

Custodial history

This note records custodial changes that occurred to the records subsequent to leaving the custody of their creators. Such a note rarely has value in the most typical situation in which records are transferred from creator to archives and subsequently stored. However, in cases in which records may have passed through multiple hands, or multiple archival institutions, on their way to their current location, the note can be useful. This is especially true if it helps to explain anomalies in the completeness or condition of the materials.

Immediate source of acquisition

This note provides a place to record the person or agency from which the collection materials were received by the repository. This note should generally include the name of the transferring entity, the entity's relationship to the materials (e.g., creator, inheritor, purchaser), the date of acquisition, the method of acquisition (e.g., gift, transfer, purchase), accession or collection identifying numbers, and any other information the repository finds to be relevant and useful. Not all repositories wish to publicly share information about donors, purchase details, and other things they may consider sensitive in nature. Therefore, the information included in these notes should reflect policy decisions by the repository.

Appraisal, destruction, and scheduling information

This note (or notes) provides a place to document those of its decisions and actions that have affected the extent and content of the collection as it currently exists. It is, of course, routine for repositories to appraise potential collections prior to donation or transfer, thereby taking possession of only some portion of the original body of materials. Over the course of its custody, the collection may be reappraised (especially at the point of processing); it may be deaccessioned in part or in whole; it may be reduced or augmented through scheduled records management actions; it may be destroyed following its reformatting (e.g., digitization or microfilming); some records may be redacted. At any rate, these notes (usually a separate note for each transaction or event) comprise a record of all actions taken by the repository that have shaped and determined the materials available to researchers. These notes should contain all data points relevant to questions that users might reasonably ask: which materials were removed or added; on what date; by which means; for what reason; by whom; by whose authority. The chronology of notes thereby provides a complete record of all changes to the collection over the course of its archival custody.

Accruals

Many collections, especially those acquired from living donors and agencies with active mandates, are subject to recurring accruals of additional records from time to time. This note provides a place to advise that additions to the existing collection are expected and, if they occur regularly, the frequency with which they are expected. This simply arms the user with awareness that more relevant materials may become available in future.

Related materials elements

This set of optional notes exists to call users' attention to other archival resources that may be related by content or provenance to this collection. Those resources may exist in the same repository, in an external institution, or in private hands.

Existence and location of originals

In some situations, the materials being described in the finding aid are not original records, but are copies of originals located elsewhere, not in the same repository. The note should indicate the extent of the originals (whether they comprise the whole or a portion of the materials being described), the holder of the originals, contact information, and any identifying numbers for the originals.

Existence and location of copies

In other cases, copies of the original materials being described in the finding aid, in whole or in part, may exist in some other public repository and are available there for research access. Because the copies may be more convenient for some researchers to use, it is helpful to include a note about them. This is especially true when the copies may be available for sale or interlibrary loan. The note should indicate the extent of the copies (whether they comprise the whole or a portion of the materials being described), the holder of the copies, contact information, and any identifying numbers for the copies. This note is *not* intended to indicate copies that may exist in private hands. If a copy of all or part of the materials being described is also available in the repository holding the originals, it is useful to include a note providing information about the medium and location of the copy, any identifying numbers, and any conditions on the use or availability of the copy.

Related archival materials

Notes on locations of originals and copies concern materials that are intellectually part of the same collection. Related materials notes concern materials that comprise collections that are separately cataloged, but nonetheless closely related by virtue of 1) sharing the same creator(s) or provenance, 2) documenting the same or related topics, or 3) documenting the same or related activities. A single creator might be responsible for multiple separate collections in the same or different repositories. A close relative or the same corporate body may have created another collection. A variety of known collections may contain closely related information on topics or activities documented in the collection being described. A note for any of these reasons may help a researcher locate other useful archival resources. As the number of these notes could quickly get out of hand, we should take care to restrict them to referencing collections that are very closely, not tangentially, related.

Publication note

Collections that have been around for some time often become fundamental sources for scholarly and other publications. This note provides a place to record citations to publications based significantly on the collection being described. Especially pertinent are sources that analyze the collection materials or that constitute annotated versions of them.

Notes element

While DACS provides structured notes for the most common and necessary elements of description, occasions often arise when we need to include helpful information that does not appear to fit in any of these places. That is the reason for this element—just a place to include any sort of textual note that might benefit users of the materials. The most common uses for a general note might be:

- *Conservation notes.* These notes explain conservation actions that affect the appearance, formatting, or accessibility of materials (e.g., *Materials in this folder were removed from a scrapbook that was disbound in 2007.*).
- *Processing notes.* It is sometimes useful to explain changes made to the received arrangement of collection materials or other notable processing actions. These actions by processing staff are frequently more significant than they may at first appear. They

---

Conservation Information:
Newsprint materials in *Correspondence* series were deacidified in 1987.

Preferred Citation:
[Indicate the cited item and/or series here]. St. Philips Episcopal Church. Minnesota Historical Society. See the Chicago Manual of Style for additional examples.

Accession Information:
Accession numbers: 11,709; 11,924; 15,251; 15,418.

Processing Information:
Processed by: Lara D. Friedman~Shedlov.
Catalog ID number: 09-00320301.

FIGURE 17. Examples of general notes

are often neither trivial nor neutral. They may introduce bias and may preference a certain perspective on the records and on the agents and activities that produced them that, in turn, influence the understanding and use of the records by researchers. So it is important to note decisions and actions taken by archivists, including significant arrangement and description choices, that have profoundly shaped the collection as it currently exists.
- *Citation notes.* Many repositories use notes here to indicate their preferred format for citing materials from the collection.

Descriptive control element

This note is used to record information about the creation of the finding aid itself. Most commonly, one would record important conventions or rules used (e.g., *Description based on DACS*), the name of the person who created the finding aid, the date of its creation, and the dates of significant revisions to the finding aid.

A core set of elements for multilevel description

I emphasized earlier that, with few exceptions, the DACS elements are available at every level of archival description. As I defined and explained them in the preceding section, it can easily seem as if I was describing a catalog record or some other generalized description of the entire collection. And that certainly could be the case; the DACS elements are all useful and necessary in describing the overall collection at that highest level. But, at every other level in a multilevel description—subgroup, series, subseries, file, item—we draw from the very same set of elements in creating the description. And the same DACS rules, element definitions, and practical recommendations apply.

So, that being the case, how do we prevent some sort of massive overkill or description bloat from taking over our finding aid, which we would also like to keep as lean and compact as possible to protect readers from confusion and fatigue? It becomes apparent quickly that if we employ these many elements in describing each unit of information—each series, each file, each whatever—our finding aid will be alarmingly huge. And then consider the effort needed by the archivist to compile and record all of those information elements for what may well turn out to be hundreds of subunits in even a moderately sized collection! It fails any sort of practicality test. When we get down to the file level and below, how useful are information elements like language, or custodial history, or arrangement system, or related materials? The answer, I think, is *not that useful*. Most DACS elements are meaningful, often necessary, at the collection level, but, as we descend the hierarchical chain, fewer and fewer remain useful or advisable.

However, *a small set of DACS elements is useful at all levels and in most situations*. This "core" set of DACS elements communicates necessary information to users at any archival level; it lets us focus on recording the key descriptive information; and it helps our descriptive labor become efficient because we are not continually asking ourselves what information we should be entering and how we should be expressing it at every link in the hierarchical chain. As a result, we quickly learn to assess any given archival unit for a few key pieces of information to enter into our finding aid. We soon develop expertise and confidence.

What are these elements? Kathleen Roe, in the previous version of this manual, identifies them as follows:[4]

- **Name:** Which entity created this unit of materials, <u>if different</u> from the creator of its parent unit?
- **Title:** What is the nature or topic of the materials in this unit?
- **Dates:** What are the inclusive, or meaningful, dates of the materials in this unit?
- **Extent:** What are the quantity, volume, and type of materials in this unit?

This small set of elements almost always answers researchers' main questions once they get below the collection level: *What is this stuff and how much of it is there?* By recording this modest amount of structured information for every unit of materials being described, the archivist conveys an essential and meaningful information package that is seldom more than a line or two in length.

So, this information is always necessary, but is it always adequate? Of course not. Even well below the collection, or even the series level, it will be necessary for some units to include other DACS elements to communicate important information to users. The additional DACS elements that most frequently have utility below the series level tend to be

- Access or use restrictions
- Physical or technical access requirements
- Language or script
- Arrangement
- Scope and content

These elements might have some direct bearing on users' ability to make effective use of the materials. Scope and content notes are probably the most likely to be used, but for many files, for example, the title of the materials might be insufficient to characterize their contents. Generally speaking, these additional descriptive elements become more necessary and commonplace as we move up the descriptive hierarchy in a multilevel description. At the *subgroup* and *series* levels, most of the additional DACS elements will be relevant and valuable.

Creating Descriptive Metadata

DACS provides a means for organizing archival description—information created by archivists about archival records, the events and people they provide evidence of, and interventions that change the nature of records by creators, archival repositories, and other parties during the records' life cycle. As a content standard, DACS includes a set of elements that will populate our descriptive tools (based on the ISAD(G) structure), as well as a set of rules we can use to form and express these elements.

DACS, of course, does not tell us (outside of a few examples) how the finding aids we create will be displayed (in print or on the Web) nor what sort of data entry tools we might use to capture archival description. We should see this as a feature, rather than as a shortcoming. DACS, like all our descriptive standards, aims toward *output neutrality*. We can use the rules to create a standalone EAD or HTML document, to define the fields in a flat Access database, or to define and connect the tables in a more powerful relational database. By understanding DACS as a structure and a set of rules for recording descriptive metadata, we can prevent painting ourselves into a corner by creating finding aids that cannot be easily shared or repurposed.

For as long as archives have kept holdings, archivists have found ways to make their contents known to a wider public through inventories, registers, catalog entries on cards, and printed catalogs. Printed union catalog projects (efforts to describe holdings across repositories for a general audience of researchers) in the later twentieth century helped create an administrative and political structure for computerized union catalogs like the RLIN project. While libraries were quick to realize that to share information about their holdings in a consistent manner (and to capitalize on the reuse of records for books held by more than one library), they needed to create encoding, transmission, and content standards, archives were slower to grapple with the question of standardization.[5]

The advent of standardization and networked technologies means that we now live in a golden age of archival access. Most reference archivists have encountered patrons who had previously never set foot in an archives but came to do research because they found the archives' holdings about a particular hobby or interest as part of a web search. At institutions that hold materials in the public trust, we are now abler than ever before to share them with a wider public.

In his very helpful SAA description module, Daniel Santamaria points out that despite the emergence of powerful encoding and communication tools (MARC21, EAD, XML databases), despite the wide uptake of descriptive standards, and despite the availability of software helper tools and web services, "many archival repositories struggle to provide access to their holdings."[6] For reasons already stated, it behooves all repositories to begin putting their finding aids online within some system that enables user discovery. A continuum of approaches exists to make this happen, ranging from least costly (time, effort, money) to very costly. Santamaria describes these approaches, and you should turn to his module for thorough and specific advice. What follows here is largely a distillation of his guidance.

At the very heart of his advice is the clear directive to start thinking about the information captured in our finding aids as *data*, rather than as text, and to think of the finding aids themselves as data repositories or packages, rather than as documents. Why data? The simple answer is that when we enter and manage descriptive information as data—that is, in a structured way—we create information that can later be exported to other structured data stores or tools, such as EAD, databases, spreadsheets, institutional repositories, and so forth. Information parsed and organized as data is flexible and can be reused many times to different ends. It should not be necessary to re-enter this same information manually at any future date. Create one time, use many. If we draft finding aids using the methods suggested in the preceding section, organizing them carefully as prescribed in DACS and the structural standards that support it, then we will have created structured data.

The suite of tools at our disposal in performing the totality of our descriptive work breaks down into two basic types: *input solutions* that we use to enter data into our finding aids or other structures and *output solutions* that we can use to publish and share the metadata. We will look at these tools as they occupy that continuum of approaches.

Input Solutions: Creating and Managing Descriptive Metadata

Our input tools may build a finding aid directly (an EAD-encoded text file, for instance)[7] or may simply capture and organize the metadata to use it to produce a formal finding aid at a later time (for example, a spreadsheet organized by DACS elements). With either approach, we should be entering information into some sort of template or framework that *maps* the discrete pieces of information that we enter into specific DACS fields and that uses DACS rules and formatting guidelines to constrain the information that we enter. Some alternative approaches for capturing and managing all of the descriptive information necessary to create a detailed finding aid as an output follow.[8] The necessary levels of expertise and the costs vary among them, but they certainly include options for nearly every technical proficiency and budget. One helpful report published by OCLC Research provides some crisp advice that can help adopters of descriptive technologies ease the learning and encoding curve.[9]

The traditional finding aid document

For the past twenty years, archivists have been moving away from description based on static, disconnected, sometimes monograph-length documents—we might call them traditional finding aids—and toward description based on structured data that is flexible, interconnected, and easily sharable. Despite that paradigmatic sea-change, it is safe to say that, as of the date of this writing, the great preponderance of descriptive metadata in American archives is expressed via traditional finding aids wherein the entirety of a collection is described in a single hierarchical structure purpose-built as a textual document. Because of its ubiquity, long history, and track record as a suitable tool for researchers, I will examine it first as a device for capturing and managing archival description.

Before starting in, let me re-emphasize that the best way to produce an EAD finding aid is not to hand build it, as such, but to produce it instead as an output product using the metadata captured in some more data-friendly structure like a CMS or other database or a spreadsheet. It is a more difficult process to transform a native EAD document back into pure structured data—disassembling it back into the data tables of a CMS system, for example—than it is to reverse the process by capturing it at the outset in some tabular structure. So, the section that follows, in which we sequentially capture DACS-defined metadata into an EAD structure, should be viewed as pertaining equally well to the process we would go through to capture the same data in, let's say, a set of CMS work forms. I will be considering the same hierarchical levels of metadata and the same sequence for capturing the pertinent data.

In the text that follows, then, I will be working under the assumption that we are creating an EAD finding aid, as this is the preeminent platform for building and expressing the full content of a detailed finding aid at the time of this writing. Even if a repository does not choose to use the EAD format, the standard nevertheless provides a sound model for structuring all of the descriptive content in any detailed finding aid. It is also important to keep in mind that we should think of all the information we record in our finding aids as *structured data*.[10] We are not creating a free-text document, regardless of the software we may be using to draft the finding aid. Instead, we are entering data in a carefully structured manner. DACS gives us rules that, if followed, ensure that the data we enter into any description are consistently parsed, identified, and formed. Therefore, even if we don't encode our finding aids in EAD, by structuring our data carefully, we will at any time be able to export that data into some structured system. It might be a database, it might be an EAD-encoded file, or it might be a simple spreadsheet. By following DACS rules and recommendations, we are at least not foreclosing the opportunity to migrate our finding aid information into more sophisticated systems at some future date as resources permit.

What input software will we use to create an EAD document *directly*? We could, of course, use the thing most familiar to us: a word processor. But doing that would, at the end of the road, leave us with a document almost impossible to transform into structured data that could be repurposed or machine-processed. Much better to use XML editing software that can encode the information we enter as truly structured data that retain their semantic value. These text editors have improved greatly over the years and thus remain the finding aid authoring choice of many repositories. Increased functionality in software packages like *oXygen* and *Notetab Pro* accommodate tools like templates that can supply much of the boilerplate information found in a typical EAD instance (greatly reducing data entry), validate text as it is entered, and highlight the particular tags (data fields) that the archivist needs to complete for each subcomponent. They can also be used to constrain the DACS elements used by processors to control the granularity of description. This greatly speeds up data entry and helps ensure a well-formed (valid) output. These software packages remain very affordable, and numerous community-developed tools are available to bring data entry and finding aid transformation within the reach of repositories with modest budgets and limited technical resources.

In a certain sense, we construct the detailed archival finding aid in the same way we arrange the collection materials: we proceed from the general to the specific, describing first the collection as a whole, then describing its major subdivisions (whether subgroups or series or files), and finally describing the subcomponents of those sections. Of course, when the collection is small and structurally flat (lacking hierarchical levels), we describe it only at the collection level. The successive steps after that pertain only to multilevel description. Again, Kathleen Roe sums it up well in her manual:

> Archival description should proceed from the general to the specific. That is, descriptive information should be provided for the broadest aggregation of records (at the group/collection or fonds level when appropriate), and when useful, for additional levels (series, sub-series, sub-sub-series, item). At each level, the core elements of description . . . should be provided. The descriptive levels should be consistent with the levels of arrangement existing within the records. However, even if records are physically arranged at a more detailed level, it may not always be necessary to provide separate descriptive elements for each level. Based on the potential use and users of a group of records, the archivist needs to determine when it will be useful and productive for access to describe records at each succeeding level. There is no hard and fast rule that can effectively be applied regarding what level of description to apply beyond the imperative to describe records first at the most general level of aggregation.[11]

Describing the collection

We begin by recording the information required for the DACS *identity elements*, which include our four core elements. We need to enter an identifier for the collection, which is determined by the repository's collection naming system. We also record the name of the collection, which is generally the person, corporate body, or other entity responsible for creating it. Then, collapsing all of the information from the container list that evolved during our arrangement work, we provide a title for the collection and record its dates and extent. The *title* should be broad enough to cover the whole of the collection materials, but also as specific as practicable. So, while it is typical to title something as broadly as "records" or "papers," if an organization's records pertain only to its legal department, then the title should indicate that (Acme Company. Legal Department Records). Collection *dates* should express in the most accurate way possible the true date range of the collection materials. This is usually managed with a single range of dates (1829–1914), but it may also be constructed to indicate substantive gaps (1950–1965, 1980–2010) or the dates that predominate in the materials (1893–2015, bulk: 1909–1976). Precision is good, but there should be a point to it. The *extent* of the materials can incorporate a number of helpful measurements: overall volume (20 linear feet), number of containers or items (4 boxes, 3 map folders, 5 phonodiscs), and physical and technical characteristics (27 audio files on 1 CD-ROM disc; 14 bound ledgers in oversize box). The important thing is to characterize the overall extent of the collection in a way that helps the user understand the nature and volume of the materials, as well any information about its physicality that could affect access and use.

Contextual information, generally biographical narratives or administrative histories, usually follows these fairly spare identifiers. At the collection level, where context description is most likely to occur, this should be sufficient to characterize the nature, experiences, and activities of the creator(s) while remaining brief and crisp. As emphasized earlier, few users really want to read long-winded narratives, especially online. Stick to the information that helps to explain the things documented in the collection. Notes made during arrangement, augmented judiciously with published information, should supply all the information necessary. Even for a substantial collection, a contextual narrative can usually be kept to a few paragraphs. In a more complex collection where several different entities share responsibility for its creation, we might create separate sketches for each entity. This is more common in family collections where we may want separate biographical sketches for multiple family members. It is also good practice to augment the narrative with a timeline of events when doing so helps to explain the context more clearly than could be done with narrative text.

The informational content of the collection can then be expressed in a *scope and content note*. Here again, at the collection level, our objective is to characterize the content of the collection as a whole, without digging deeply into the series and other components that make it up. We are very briefly noting names, places, events, activities—topics that play overarching roles in shaping the informational content of the collection. And, as with contextual description, our scope and content note ought to be kept to a few paragraphs.

If we can briefly say something useful about the overall organization of the collection materials, we should include an *arrangement note*. This note may simply identify the major groups into which the collection divides (*arranged into 5 series: . . . .*) or indicate the overall arrangement in a flat collection (*arranged chronologically*). Anything more complex is best left to the hierarchical container list to explain.

We also need to include notes explaining the *conditions governing access and use*. As I discussed in the DACS elements section, we may need to include notes explaining ways in which access to some or all materials may be limited or conditioned due to contractual provisions (access or use restrictions), physical condition, technical requirements, or language. A separate note should be made for each condition that applies, and DACS should be consulted for appropriate language. If none of these conditions apply, it may still be a service to researchers to include a note affirming that no restrictions exist on access or use of the collection.

A *related materials* note is used to indicate the existence of archival materials in another repository that are related to the collection by virtue of shared provenance. This is not a place to indicate materials related only by shared subject matter. Similarly, a *location of originals* note may be used to specify the location of the original records in those cases when all or part of the materials described in the finding aid are actually copies of originals located in another repository. Both of these notes can be a great help to researchers who may want to access closely related materials.

To improve discovery of the collection in online search environments, it is also useful to include *name, subject, geographical, form, and genre terms* taken from controlled vocabularies. For reasons of both economy and accuracy, these should be limited to a small set that truly characterizes the topical content of the materials. It can be very frustrating for users to be led to a collection by way of an index term only to discover that the documentation of that subject is negligible.

Finally, a number of elements comprising *administrative information* about the collection are relevant at the collection level:

- **Source of acquisition** identifies the donor or transferring entity, as well as the date(s) of acquisition and, perhaps, the accession number(s) comprising the acquisition. Each acquisition that fed into the collection might have a separate note. Institutional policy will determine whether donor information is shared publicly.
- **Custodial actions** notes alert users of actions taken by the repository that have altered the collection from its received state. They might include notes on appraisal and weeding actions taken, preservation treatments performed, reformatting of materials, or subsequent returns of materials to the donor.
- **Preferred citation** provides a place for the repository to indicate model language for citing materials from the collection.
- **Processing information** notes can communicate when the collection was processed and by whom—again, a matter of institutional policy.

With this information recorded, our finding aid successfully describes the collection as a whole. In a single-level finding aid, this constitutes the entire description. In a multilevel finding aid, this information typically displays at the top section. A container list, sometimes called a "detailed description" or "description of component parts," follows and goes on to describe in a similar—but less verbose!—fashion the full hierarchy of collection units.

Producing a catalog record

The preceding section presented the collection-level portion of a detailed finding aid. However, this same process and content describe equally well the preparation of a catalog record for repositories that produce and share such things. The only substantive difference is one of encoding. This level of description in a detailed finding aid is likely to be encoded as an EAD file (or some other structured data file); in a catalog record it will be encoded in the MARC21 format. See Appendix E for an example of the content and encoding syntax for a MARC21 catalog record.

Describing the collection components

In the simplest terms, describing the collection components is a matter of 1) fleshing out our existing container list into its full and final form and, then, 2) adding it onto the end of the collection-level description. Of course, the actual mechanics of this and the form it takes in the end depend upon the finding aid system employed by the repository. The objective in describing the component parts is to describe, to the extent necessary, each collection unit using the same set of DACS elements that we used in the collection-level description. We will use far fewer of them in describing any collection component and fewer and fewer still as we work our way down the arrangement hierarchy.

We start by describing the first (as sequenced in the arrangement) of the highest-level components, whether they happen to be subgroups or series. And then we keep drilling down through its nested, descending units until we reach the lowest level that we choose to describe, usually the file level. We follow the same process through the components of each of the other top-level arrangement units. We want to keep in mind, as we describe the descending units, that the most important and the most frequently used DACS elements will be the *core set* explained earlier: *name, title, dates, and extent.* These four building blocks will always be present in the description of every single component of the collection. Additional DACS elements may augment them, but they will not be replaced. Let's look at the requirements for effective (and efficient) component description at the generally recurring arrangement levels.

Subgroups and series. In any multilevel arrangement scheme, the highest level will be a subgroup or a series, dependent only upon the complexity of the relationships among the records themselves. In most cases, when we describe these units, the finding aid sections will include more than the core DACS elements. Subgroups and series will represent major discrete functions or activities of the creating entity—different divisions or business lines in an organization, different departments or mandates in a government, different individuals or pursuits in a family or personal collection. Because of the significance of these components, we may need to expand their description with some combination of the following:

- **Reference code.** This might be a number (*Series 2*) or a location (*Stack range 3.B*) that distinguishes this large component from other large components.
- **Bioghist note.** The creator and the context of creation and use for this component might be rather different from that which characterizes the collection as a whole. If so, it might warrant a brief bioghist note of its own.
- **Scope and content note.** As it probably relates to a discrete function, activity, or mandate of the collection creator that the other collection components do not share, this subgroup or series probably merits a note describing the record types and content of the materials it comprises. The rules and expectations here are the same as those for notes at the collection level, except that they need to focus specifically on the component being described and nothing beyond that.
- **Conditions of access and use.** High-level components are much more likely to have access and use conditions aimed at them specifically, so such notes may be necessary. Make as many separate notes as apply. However, if such restrictions or conditions pertain *only* to a subcomponent of these materials, then make the note only at that level.

- **Arrangement.** It is certainly likely that the materials constituting one subgroup or series have an internal structure or arrangement that differs from the rest of the collection. If so, a note describing that structure may be helpful to users.
- **Processing actions.** As is true at the collection level, it may sometimes be important to note decisions and actions taken by archivists, including significant arrangement and description choices, that have profoundly shaped the collection as it currently exists.

The structuring of this information in the finding aid is similar to that used in describing the collection as a whole. Exact sequencing and appearance will be a matter for local repository guidelines.

Subseries and files. The basic set of core elements is much more likely to satisfy the descriptive needs of these lower-level components. In cases where these components are large or complex, it may be necessary to include one or more of the notes already discussed, but, as always, they should be resorted to only when they are likely to substantively improve user success. At this level, the most commonly occurring note might be one on access and use conditions.

Items. When it becomes necessary to describe individual collection items, the four core elements are almost always sufficient. Again, a note on access and use conditions (especially technical or physical requirements for access) may be the most common, but a scope and content note might be necessary on rarer occasions.

We follow this hierarchical process for each subgroup or series in the collection to complete the finding aid data capture. The next stage in our work is publishing it in our finding aid system.

The downside is that the metadata captured within an overtly EAD structure is somewhat more cumbersome to transform into some other data structure. It is considerably less flexible when stored as an EAD instance than when encoded into a collection management system or even a spreadsheet. Nevertheless, it can be done using stylesheets written in XSLT, JavaScript, or some other language capable of transforming the native EAD instance into some other structure, like a web page.

Spreadsheets

Santamaria makes the important point that, in the current century, simply no good reason exists to persist in the practice of authoring finding aids in "docucentric" software like Microsoft Word. Word processors are likely to yield attractively formatted descriptive text that resists subsequent efforts to parse it into meaningful data like DACS elements, no matter how carefully we have followed DACS rules in entering the information. In the end, we are left with a finding aid that will never be more than static text and that cannot be easily repurposed into any more flexible form (e.g., fields in a database). If we ever desire to manipulate that descriptive information in more powerful ways, we will probably need to re-enter it. This makes no sense. The least expensive alternative, requiring the lowest amount of technical expertise, is to use a simple, "datacentric" option like a spreadsheet.

Spreadsheets are very effective tools for creating component-level descriptions in multi-level finding aids. Visualize a simple spreadsheet in which the rows contain descriptions for each hierarchical level in the collection, and the columns contain each of the DACS data elements. The first column could be used to indicate the hierarchical level (<c01>, <c02>, <c03>. . . , in EAD usage) of the description on that line. While not an elegant or a very user-friendly presentation of the information, it is nevertheless a brilliant input and storage mechanism. All the information required for *component description* is compactly recorded in a form that can be, with some tinkering, migrated successfully into another format for expressing structured data, including a Word or HTML document for public use. Collection-level information, especially substantial narrative information, might alternatively be recorded in another platform and then cobbled onto the component-level description derived from the spreadsheet. That collection-level information is most easily, and typically, imported from the MARC21 record for the collection, if one exists. Software tools are available that can, in successive stages, readily transform the raw spreadsheet data into an EAD-encoded text file or into other outputs.

Figure 18 depicts such a spreadsheet. This small collection—records of the Burlington Northern Clown Club and Band—are enumerated with considerable granularity. The collection consists of ten files (too hierarchically flat to comprehend series), the latter of which—*audiovisual materials*—includes item descriptions. The columns of the spreadsheet accommodate all the necessary DACS elements: container, title, dates, extent, and scope and content notes. Because this is an example of multilevel description—it delineates two hierarchical levels—additional columns (level 1 title, level 2 title) accommodate that complexity. More columns would be added, as necessary, to express a more complex arrangement hierarchy.

Because these data are well structured, the spreadsheet columns can be mapped to DACS elements or to EAD, METS, MARC, or any other ontology. This makes the spreadsheet a serviceable and economical way to capture and store archival descriptive data.

Local databases

Affordable database applications like Microsoft Access or FileMaker Pro provide a slightly more sophisticated alternative to spreadsheets. As is true with spreadsheets, the structured information stored in the database file can be output, using some macros or transforming tools, as an EAD, PDF, or HTML finding aid. The database structure (especially in relational databases) also affords the advantage of being able to constrain data values to enforce DACS rules, or to map to DACS elements in a more nuanced way. Also, it is relatively easy to set up data input forms to speed up and simplify data entry for each descriptive subcomponent in the finding aid. One final advantage of databases is that, even if a repository lacks the resources to output the data as, say, EAD finding aids, the database itself provides an electronic discovery and access tool that staff members and researchers can use directly.

Archival collection management systems

For repositories willing to devote resources toward a local collection management system, options exist that not only facilitate the management of their archival collections, but also expedite greatly the data entry, transformation, and web publication of archival finding aids. At this time, the preeminent system purpose-built for archives is ArchivesSpace, a Lyrasis product.[12] As

Box #	Level 1 Title	Level 2 Title	Date	Quantity	Scope Note
					The Burlington Northern Clown Club and Band began as a community service under the former Great Northern Railway Company, probably as early as the 1950s. The band performed along the rail line at community festivals, charity events, and at children's hospitals, senior citizen residences, and schools for the underprivileged. It was especially active during the St. Paul Winter Carnival. George Donnay and Robert W. Achterling coordinated the activities of the band.
1	Correspondence and miscellany [Great Northern file]		1958–1970	1 folder	
	Correspondence and miscellany [Great Northern file]		1970–1985	5 folders	
	Directory of members		1979, 1981, 1983	1 folder	
	Member notices		1966–1979	1 folder	
	Procedures		1970s	1 folder	
	Publicity		1970s	1 folder	
	Skit material		undated	1 folder	
	Thank you letters		1959–1980	3 folders	
	Winter Carnival Committee		1964–1973	1 folder	
	Audio-visual materials:				
		Clown films	1971–1977	1 videocassette	Master tape
		Band music, calliope music	1973, 1977, 1979	1 stereo cassette	
		Clown show (aquatennial)	1977	1 stereo cassette	
		Clown show	1979	1 stereo cassette	
		Clown show/spike tones/3 Stooges/Christmas	undated	1 stereo cassette	
		Clown show	undated	1 stereo cassette	
		Ding-a-long song	undated	1 stereo cassette	

FIGURE 18. Burlington Northern Clown Club and Band records. Minnesota Historical Society.

a comprehensive, integrated collection management system, ArchivesSpace supports the archival functions of acquisition, accessioning, and arrangement and description of all digital and non-digital materials; authority and rights management; preservation management; and reference. It enables the creation of separate authority records, which can then be linked to multiple resource records. It can also manage collections by tracking custodial events of all sorts and producing a variety of administrative reports. It incorporates a DACS-compliant metadata authoring tool supporting multilevel description and is capable of generating a variety of outputs, including EAD, MARCXML, MODS, Dublin Core, and METS formatted data.

Most important, ArchivesSpace is an *API-first application*. In this context, the ArchivesSpace API is a set of protocols and tools that make it possible to safely and powerfully import, export, and change the data stored in ArchivesSpace. Archivists can now, much more easily, change their data in bulk. For instance, it was standard and correct in the days of APPM to provide the name of the creator "Martha Washington" in the creator element and to then give the name of the collection as simply "papers." It would be laborious for an archivist to rename each collection that follows this pattern, but the ArchivesSpace API makes it easy to identify collections that follow this pattern and update them with DACS-compliant titles, in this case, "Martha Washington papers."

As an input tool for structured metadata, ArchivesSpace utilizes a data-entry template that allows the archivist to enter the appropriate DACS-specified data for any collection unit in a single-level or multilevel description. In fact, when ArchivesSpace was being built, system architects looked to DACS as the data model to determine which fields should be present and how they should work.

Figure 19 shows an input screen on which an archivist is describing an archival series. The top portion of the screen is a navigational device that shows the developing hierarchical structure of the collection description and the position of the current unit within it. The left-hand bar enables linking from the unit being described to various external resources: agents, rights information, preservation assessments, and so forth. The central portion of the screen is the worksheet in which the desired content information for the unit being described—Native American Community Board—is entered, field by field. Apropos of DACS, the same worksheet appears for any collection unit at any level, as the same DACS elements would be available for each of them.

Another archival collection management system, AtoM,[13] is supported by the International Council on Archives and used by many repositories outside of the United States. It manages standards-based archival descriptive information in a database that users can search directly from the Web, allowing for very sophisticated searching of structured archival data. Currently, AtoM supports the following import/export formats: EAD, EAC-CPF, CSV, and SKOS.

The main advantage of acquiring any integrated collections management system is the fairly seamless support the system provides for the phases of archives management: acquisition, accessioning, description, and public access. Information captured during acquisition and accessioning, for example, may be utilized during description, eliminating a lot of redundant data entry and helping to ensure that each part of our practice is integrated. And the incorporation of customizable data-entry forms, and back-end conversion tools, can greatly simplify finding aid production and repurposing over time.

Integrated systems give our practices the opportunity to be more integrated. A field archivist can start an accession record (or update the historical note for the organization whose records

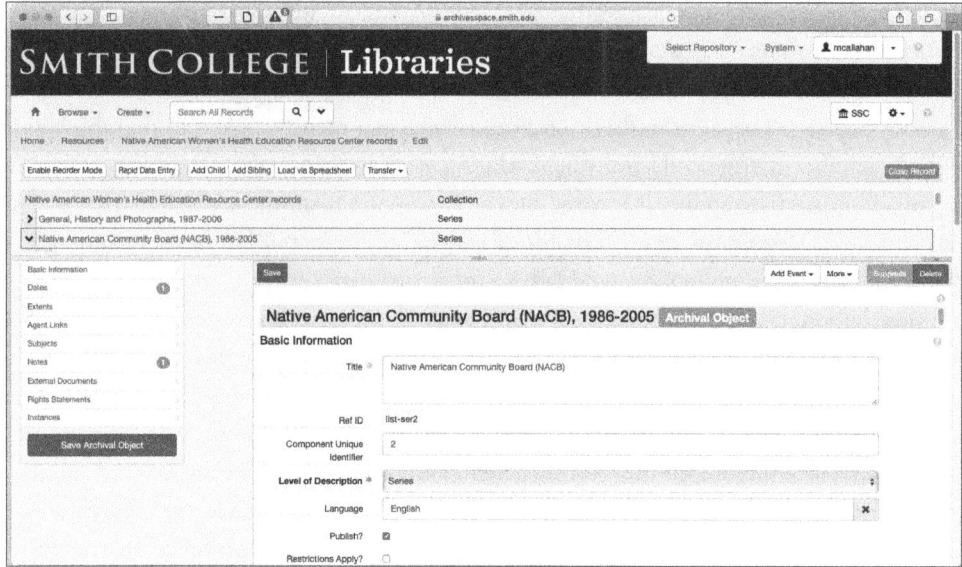

FIGURE 19. Input screen with series description in process. Image courtesy of Special Collections, Smith College Library.

she's collecting); the accessioning archivist can then add information about the materials as they were received, including the containers' sizes, conditions, and locations in the repository; a description archivist can update the finding aid to include this new accrual; and, finally, a public services archivist will immediately know where the new acquisition is shelved and can retrieve it for a patron.

A repository may bear the cost of annual licensing fees and support for such integrated systems, though both ArchivesSpace and AtoM are open source software and can be downloaded at no cost. And a certain level of technical expertise, as well as some basic institutional technical infrastructure, is necessary. However, when all costs involved in supporting any description and access enterprise are considered, a collection management system could be a cost-effective solution. It certainly simplifies archival work by bundling many input, management, and output activities into a single system, and it rolls many disparate description and access costs into a single cost center. A CMS may prove the most workable alternative for many repositories.

Output Solutions: Publishing and Sharing Descriptive Metadata

Having descriptive metadata stored and managed in a flexible form, mapped to standards, and capable of being exported and repurposed in multiple ways are important first steps for a repository. The next step, equally challenging, is to output that information into a *publishing system* able to deliver effectively searchable finding aids to users. The issues regarding institutional resources—technical expertise, digital infrastructure, and dollars—that influence our choice of input tools also affect our choice of output tools. As was the case in discussing input tools, this manual will provide the broadest of overviews. More detailed and technical guidance will be found in the Santamaria module and in the resources categorized on the SAA Standards Portal.

The finding aid that we have constructed serves no purpose, beyond providing a rather grandiose internal inventory of the collection, until we find a way to share it with the repository's users. The easiest and least costly way to do this is to simply print the finding aid and to make it available in our public service area, along with the finding aids for all of our other collections. All well and good, but unless our finding aids are few in number, we need to create some sort of index to go along with them so that researchers don't need to paw through binders full of collection descriptions to find the one they are looking for. The index would presumably point to a collection's reference number, that identifier providing the simplest organizing scheme for the finding aids. Still, an index only gives users one search parameter to go on, presumably the DACS name element. So, unless researchers already know the collection they want to see, and would not be interested in any related collections, name access won't be adequate on its own.

To promote really robust discovery, our simple index is going to have to expand almost geometrically into a *catalog*. The catalog will afford collection discovery by creator name (provenance), as well as by the names of other persons and corporate bodies (agents) responsible for substantial collection materials, subjects (topics, themes, and events) documented in the collection, major functions or activities evidenced in the materials, occupations of creators, geographical locations important to the records, and perhaps also the forms and genres of documents when they have a notable bearing on research. Traditionally, archivists have done all of this in labor-intensive and inflexible forms like card catalogs. Clearly nothing is to be gained in repeating these approaches.

Let's look at common approaches to publishing our descriptive metadata online in an arc running from simplest and least costly to complex and most costly. The simplest of all is to capture our data in an electronic form and then save it as a PDF or HTML document. These output documents can then simply be added to a web directory located on the public side of the repository's domain, and then users can be directed to that page from appropriate locations on the website. Easy peasy. The downside, as noted, is that by capturing the finding aid as a weakly structured, word-processed document type, we may never be able to repurpose its information in a more structured way to support future technical opportunities, at least without some restructuring and rekeying. A somewhat more robust alternative might be to use the spreadsheet or database input method already described, and then produce, say, a Word document from either of them as an intermediate step. We still get the PDF or HTML output, but the descriptive information is preserved as structured data rather than as text. And the output documents are amenable to text searches by users.[14]

A more sophisticated and powerful publishing scenario takes advantage of the input tools considered in the previous section that result in data that are either already EAD-encoded or that can be turned into an EAD file by using internal or external transformation tools. Having our finding aid encoded in EAD provides us with a fairly powerful data structure from which to produce a variety of published finding aids. That EAD instance is a great package for organizing and storing descriptive data, but it is a lousy access tool, as the EAD markup in Appendix D attests. The simplest way to publish a user-friendly version of that mess is to *transform* the raw EAD file into a nicely formatted and searchable document encoded in either PDF or HTML. Either of those document types, as they are created, can simply be added to a web directory located on the public side of the repository's domain and linked to some sort of user search box. Such a web directory comprises a browsable list of hyperlinks to the individual finding aids. The PDF- or HTML-published outputs can be rendered from the EAD file using XSLT stylesheets, CSS stylesheets, or other web programming tools, many of them freely available on SAA's EAD Related Resources pages.

Employed in its most basic form, this solution requires users to seek out the repository's website on their own before they can discover the directory of finding aids. A more robust enhancement is to embed indexing terms into the search-engine-friendly headers of the finding aids (using, for example, Dublin Core discovery elements) and then to expose the finding aid directly to web search engines. Users can then discover finding aids using a simple Google search without first locating the repository (or even understanding what a repository is). Embedding this additional discovery layer certainly adds steps to the finding aid creation process, but much of it can be programmed once, fully or partly, via a transformation stylesheet that automates the process for all future finding aids.

Finding aid aggregators

A more powerful solution for publishing EAD finding aids, and perhaps finding aids in other encoding schemes, is to contribute them to an aggregator that allows users to search across finding aids contributed by many repositories. Such aggregators free a repository from having to develop its own discovery and access platform. They also might offer more powerful indexing and display features than are available to a repository on its own website.

One such aggregator used by many archival institutions is ArchiveGrid, an OCLC service free to participating repositories that are willing to have the corpus of their finding aids harvested and freely shared. As described on its website:

> ArchiveGrid includes over 5 million records describing archival materials, bringing together information about historical documents, personal papers, family histories, and more. With over 1,000 different archival institutions represented, ArchiveGrid helps researchers looking for primary source materials held in archives, libraries, museums and historical societies.[15]

Such a service allows a repository to expose its finding aids to a much wider audience and also provides a richer discovery layer, as its indexing tools are designed in part to exploit the semantic complexity of EAD. ArchiveGrid also routinely studies the system's usage and user behaviors, using that data to improve its indexing and display functions. Other aggregators, including the Northwest Digital Archives and the Online Archive of California, have been developed to serve members of particular consortia of libraries, archives, and other cultural institutions.

The two-stage approach

The system of finding aids that has become the current model for many archives, especially those operating within academic and research libraries, is a two-stage system of consciously linked finding aids. The first stage is the catalog record already discussed in some detail. The catalog record may be thought of as a very high-level finding aid, whose first purpose is resource discovery. Within a catalog of resources—it might be an institution's local catalog or a union catalog for a large consortium—the catalog record (expressed in the MARC21 format) permits researchers to identify and distinguish a particular collection from among all the other resources (books, periodicals, audiotapes, artifacts, other archival collections) comprising the library's holdings. Following discovery of the collection, the catalog record's next purpose is to describe, in very general terms, the collection as a whole. The objective is to characterize the collection well enough to allow the researcher to decide whether to investigate it further.

The second stage in the system of archival description is the detailed finding aid, which is usually linked directly to the catalog record. Archival repositories variously call this finding aid an inventory, a register, a collection guide, or other names, and though its appearance differs somewhat from institution to institution, it always serves a definite set of roles, which both follow from and contrast with those played by the catalog record. First of all, whereas the first objective of the catalog record is to permit researchers to find the collection as a whole, the initial purpose of the detailed finding aid is to help them find the individual components (series, files, folders, items) that comprise the collection. So, while the catalog record demonstrates low granularity (describing the collection as a whole in quite general terms), the detailed finding aid shows high granularity, focusing as it does on all the structural and informational pieces that make up the collection. And, whereas the catalog record is a bridge from resource discovery to collection-level description, the detailed finding aid acts as a bridge from that collection-level description to component-level description.

From this, we start to get a picture of how this two-stage finding aid system works in practice. Researchers initially discover the collection in an online catalog via access points (controlled vocabulary terms) embedded in the catalog record, the text of which provides an encapsulated narrative summary of the entire collection. The catalog record then refers researchers to (or directly links to) the detailed finding aid, which begins with a greatly amplified description of the collection as a whole, but then enumerates and describes the informational components that comprise the collection, so that researchers can decide which specific pieces to study.

The majority of archival repositories have adopted this general mode, and it is used in local catalogs, as well as in union catalogs mounted by various consortia and large bibliographic utilities like OCLC WorldCat and ArchiveGrid. But the ability of finding aids to intermix successfully and intelligently in these catalogs, and to share a helpful presentational uniformity, requires a huge amount of standardization on the back end. As described at length earlier, archivists have been actively developing and building a head-spinning array of conceptual and technical standards over the past twenty years. And they have been doing so for the primary goal of maximizing researcher access to archival collections.

Acceptance of these key points and the standards that underlie them have led to the model for archival finding aids—both catalog records and detailed finding aids—currently in use. The model identifies several basic parts, each of which has applicability at every hierarchical level in the description.

Collection management systems

The archival collection management systems I have described provide a publishing alternative more sophisticated, but perhaps less daunting in terms of necessary expertise. Typically, descriptive metadata stored within the database structure of a CMS can be served out to users as web pages, perhaps as fully formed EAD finding aids or else as separate component-level descriptions.

ArchivesSpace, for example, has a Public User Interface module that permits archivists to convert the data stored in their tabular structures into fully formed finding aids displayed as

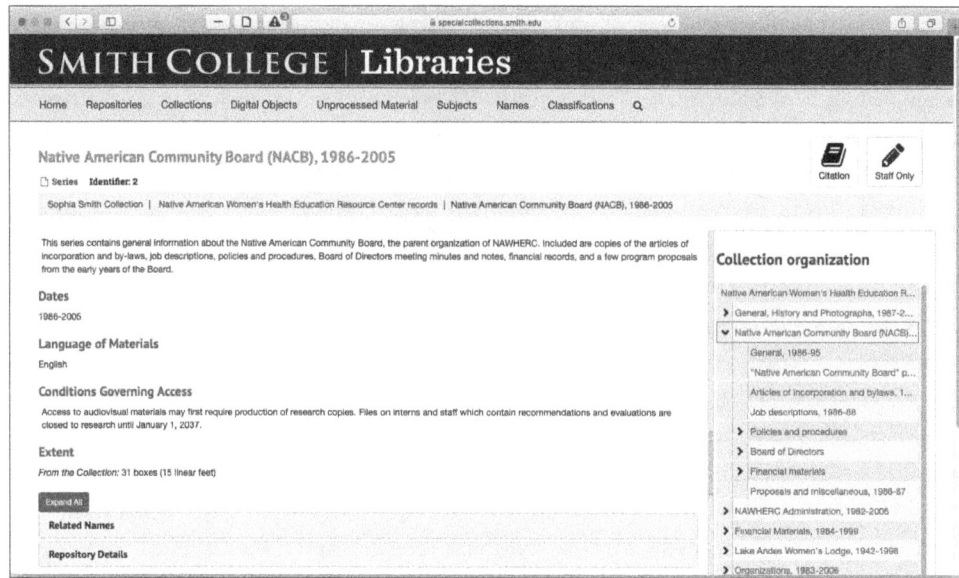

FIGURE 20. View of finding aid metadata from ArchivesSpace Public User Interface. Image courtesy of Special Collections, Smith College Library.

interactive web pages in response to user queries. Let's use ArchivesSpace as an example of how such a CMS-based system can work. The software indexes all of the descriptive metadata entered into the staff interface during collection description. The index creates a web page for the collection, as well as landing pages for each of the component descriptions that comprise the collection. In response to a user query, the EAD instances that satisfy the request are returned to the user as web pages that present the collection description as an EAD document, the components of which may be browsed or further searched. Figure 20 shows one of several views of the metadata. The full component descriptions appear in the scrolling primary window, while the tree structure of the EAD instance is displayed in the right-hand window to preserve the hierarchical context.

CMS-based systems relieve us from the significant work of creating our finding aids directly, because the system produces descriptive outputs as a largely automated function, as well as from the labor of providing a discrete public discovery and access platform.

A more complex alternative is to serve out EAD finding aids through an *XML publishing platform*. This type of publishing system uses an XML database structure to manage EAD-encoded information in a relational database that actually stores the data in an XML format. Because EAD is an XML language, a database such as this parses out the EAD elements in a finding aid into data tables based on EAD tags (data elements). Users can then search the database through a query layer that understands the semantic meaning of the EAD elements. The great advantage of such a platform is its ability to search on the basis of discrete and meaningful data elements (name, title, bioghist), rather than simply searching for character strings within, say, an HTML or PDF document. This functionality is also present in the AtoM system, which stores descriptive metadata in an XML database. But, such an XML-based platform makes huge demands on a repository in terms of the technical proficiency and staffing and infrastructure needed to manage such a system. It is almost certainly beyond the capabilities of most small and medium-sized repositories. However, it may be within reach of repositories banding together in consortia to support public access systems. The Online Archive of California uses such a system to power its archives description management and access system for the University of California Libraries.

This chapter has provided a thorough overview of the practical mechanics of archival description. We have studied each of the many DACS data elements with an eye toward understanding how to form the informational content that is recorded in each of them, as well as how to determine how much content is needed in each of them in the course of preparing single-level and multilevel archival description. In doing this, we have re-emphasized the important consideration that effective description is based upon structured data—carefully formed and appropriately applied.

We also looked carefully at the mechanics and alternatives for both capturing and sharing descriptive metadata. We considered a variety of approaches and software tools for both purposes, and we learned that input solutions and output solutions are best treated as separate categories that may require very different software tools. I hope we also appreciate that these tools and approaches comprise some of the more rapidly changing components of archival description, with new techniques and systems emerging all the time.

In this chapter, as in the chapters that preceded it, we have considered concepts, approaches, and practices that are largely applicable to *all* archival holdings, regardless of form or medium. But in the following chapter we will look briefly at a variety of nontextual record types and consider how they may at times call out for more distinctive or special approaches to their arrangement and description.

NOTES

[1] *Describing Archives: A Content Standard*, 2nd ed. (Chicago: Society of American Archivists, 2013), 4, https://www2.archivists.org/standards/DACS.

[2] *Describing Archives: A Content Standard*.

[3] T. R. Schellenberg, *The Management of Archives* (New York: Columbia University Press, 1965), 138–42.

[4] Adapted from Kathleen D. Roe, *Arranging and Describing Archives and Manuscripts* (Chicago: Society of American Archivists, 2005), 73–74. In these pages, Roe does a thorough job explaining the role and importance of these four key data elements.

[5] In the library world, Anglo-American Catalog Rules and the Machine-Readable Cataloging Standards (MARC) have co-evolved since the 1960s, although theories of how to classify and describe books have existed for much longer. The following sources may be useful for information about the history of standards adoption in archives. Society of American Archivists, *Inventories and Registers: A Handbook of Techniques and Examples: A Report of the Committee on Finding Aids* (Chicago: Society of American Archivists, 1976), https://catalog.hathitrust.org/Record/000719473, captured at https://perma.cc/LC9L-G6ND. Steven Hensen et al., "Thirty Years On: SAA and Descriptive Standards (Session 706)," *American Archivist* 74, no. Supplement 1 (2011): 1–36, https://doi.org/10.17723/aarc.74.suppl-1.15011hj3lg56t0t3; Jean Dryden, "Developing International Standards: Lessons from the CUSTARD Project," *Comma* 2005, no. 2 (2005): 1–6, https://doi.org/10.3828/coma.2005.2.14.

[6] Daniel Santamaria, "Designing Descriptive and Access Systems," in *Trends in Archival Practice: Archival Arrangement and Description*, ed. and with an introduction by Christopher J. Prom and Thomas J. Frusciano (Chicago: Society of American Archivists, 2013), 148. He remarks that as late as 2010, only 44 percent of archival collections in the United States were described in online finding aids. So, repositories that have yet to get their descriptions online need not feel they are alone or outliers. These repositories have an opportunity to work together to meet our users' expectations for easily accessible information about archival holdings.

[7] Michael Rush et al., "Applying DACS to Finding Aids: Case Studies from Three Diverse Repositories," *American Archivist* 71, no. 1 (2008): 210–27.

8. This basic manual lacks both the space and the technical expertise necessary to explain these input and output alternatives sufficiently. It is in no sense an operating manual for implementing any of the described solutions. Guidance at that level is readily available from better sources. One is certainly the SAA descriptive module authored by Santamaria, "Designing Descriptive and Access Systems." His work provides an excellent jumping off point, and it directs the reader to external sources of a more technical nature, specifically community-based help pages, discussion forums, and a variety of technical helper tools, most of them freely available. To dig deeper, the SAA Standards Portal contains a wide variety of information resources and helper tools to guide archival description practitioners. The largest section is devoted to preparing, manipulating, and transforming EAD finding aids. Among the most helpful resources are the community-supported information resources, including rich examples, maintained by SAA's Encoded Archival Standards Section, https://www2.archivists.org/groups/encoded-archival-standards-section/resources-maintained-by-the-eas-section, captured at https://perma.cc/WL3A-6NE9; and dozens of technical helper tools available at https://www2.archivists.org/groups/technical-subcommittee-on-encoded-archival-description-ead-disbanded/encoded-archival-description-ead, captured at https://perma.cc/6ECZ-VKZA. These tools automate many tasks, large and small, that both assist in creating EAD finding aids and then transform them into a variety of user-friendly, sharable finding aid outputs. In addition, continuing education workshops are available from SAA and other organizations that can train us to perform the most common of these technical tasks.

9. Michele Combs, Mark A. Matienzo, Merrilee Proffitt, and Lisa Spiro, *Over, Under, Around, and Through: Getting around Barriers to EAD Implementation* (Dublin, OH: OCLC Research, 2010), http://www.oclc.org/content/dam/research/publications/library/2010/2010-04.pdf, captured at https://perma.cc/NAH7-Z936.

10. Santamaria, "Designing Descriptive and Access Systems," 145–215. The author, throughout this work, does an admirable job of explaining and reinforcing the importance of treating finding aids as structures for recording and manipulating descriptive data.

11. Roe, *Arranging and Describing Archives and Manuscripts*, 71–72.

12. ArchivesSpace is the active, community-supported platform for previous users of Archon and Archivists' Toolkit, as well as for new users. ArchivesSpace is free and open source software. This means that any archives can download, install, and use ArchivesSpace for no charge whatsoever. However, many archival repositories may wish to participate in the governance and future directions of the ArchivesSpace software and can do so by becoming paid ArchivesSpace members. Additionally, archival repositories with no technical support staff to maintain the software and server environment may wish to contract with a vendor to provide ArchivesSpace web hosting. ArchivesSpace boasts an active user-support community—more than 350 repositories are currently members—and a variety of fee-based service providers on top of the technical support provided by Lyrasis as basic member support. More information about the technology behind the project, the governance model, and possible implementation solutions are available on the system website, http://archivesspace.org.

13. AtoM is an open source system aimed at direct public use. It manages a database of Archival Descriptive information that users can interrogate directly through a web-based query layer. More information is available at https://www.accesstomemory.org/en.

14. This manual does not venture into a repository's management of its existing hoard of legacy finding aids, many of which are probably in the form of typescript paper documents. Instead, this manual looks at policy and practice moving forward. So, how to deal with that dark archive of finding aids that are not discoverable or available online? Perhaps the most practical—certainly the most economical—solution is to simply scan the finding aids, OCR the scans, and then save them as PDF documents. Although the PDFs cannot expose any of the semantic value locked up within the finding aids, at least the text can be crawled by search engines. The PDF documents can be served out directly from a "Finding Aids" landing page, or they can be linked to from MARC records in an OPAC. At any rate, it gives the repository a workable means to bring its legacy descriptions online as it moves ahead with a superior regimen for its day-forward descriptions.

15. This description is found on the landing page of ArchiveGrid, https://beta.worldcat.org/archivegrid, captured at https://perma.cc/2ZZS-MNPS.

6

Arranging and Describing Nontextual Formats

Arranging and Describing Sound and Visual Materials

To treat this broad class of nontextual records, I will divide them into two classes: photographs, and sound and moving image materials. With regard to either class, I will summarize important points, but will refer you to substantive, specialized titles that treat these complicated and idiosyncratic formats with the detail and nuance necessary to fully understand and work with them in processing projects.

Photographs

In general, we should accept the reality that photographic images,[1] while unique in format, content, and documentary utility, are still archives whenever they form part of an archival collection. They are neither strange nor "other" and should not be treated differently from other collection materials, apart from the fact that their physical characteristics may require particular sorts of housing and storage. Processing photographs in archival contexts does not require format "experts" and does not compel us to segregate the photo images into their own subgroup or series, separated from the rest of the records, simply because of their nature as photographic materials. In times past, it was common practice for some institutions to remove photographs from their contexts, transferring them to a separate audiovisual library or else banishing them to completely artificial series within the collection. We should consider this bad practice and refrain from perpetuating it. Photographs should, in most circumstances, be retained in and described as part of the series or file in which they are situated. If they must be gathered together as a separate physical unit for storage purposes, they should nevertheless be described as part of the unit into whose original order they fall. Photographs should certainly comprise a separate intellectual unit when they were created as part of a discrete activity apart from the activities that produced the other records. But this situation is entirely different.

Processing photographs involves a few particular activities not often necessary with textual materials:

- *Identifying the chemical process that produced them.* Are they direct prints or were they produced from a negative? What does their coloration or mounting say about how they were produced? Do these conditions affect their treatment, storage, or commercial value? These questions become less important when we are dealing with modern-day commercial prints or snapshots but can affect how we deal with earlier photographic products.
- *Identifying their media and formats.* These considerations can affect the stability (acetate base) of the materials, safety issues (nitrate base), or the ability of researchers to access and use the materials effectively (slides, negatives) without special equipment or reformatting.
- *Identifying their context and content.* Textual materials usually contain enough identifying information to help us understand who created them, for what purpose, and how they came to reside where we found them. This is often not the case with photographs. Unless they are meticulously labeled—and they rarely are—we are left with incomplete or nonexistent information about them. This affects our ability to arrange and describe them, to assess their research value, and to determine whether they should be retained.
- *Identifying treatment and storage needs.* Photographs may be curling or cracking and may require some stabilization efforts and some special housing to halt or slow down the degradation. Nitrate- and acetate-based items may need to be removed and reformatted. Some images may require interleaving sheets to keep them separated. Different formats and media may have particular requirements in terms of folders and boxes to store them.
- *Identifying redundancy.* Photographs derived from negatives may result in many redundant images throughout a collection. An identical image (in terms of content and composition) may appear as a film negative, a 35mm slide, and multiple prints of various sizes. Which one(s) to keep depends upon your documentary goals for the collection, the time you have available to compare and evaluate the images, and perhaps other considerations.
- *Identifying user access needs.* Any photographic materials may require users to wear gloves to touch them. Beyond that, some formats (e.g., slides) may require special equipment like a light box or a projector. We need to specify these conditions in our descriptions so that reference staff and researchers are aware of them in advance of requesting materials.

So, while the principles of arrangement and description advise us to treat photographs as normal archival holdings and give us basic procedures for doing so, photographs nevertheless present us with a number of challenges we must address. We may address them in part through processing policies or through decisions about processing granularity objectives spelled out in our workplan, or we may need to deal with situations case by case as we proceed through our arrangement work. The important thing is to be aware of these considerations and to have a plan for addressing them in our work. I strongly advise studying the SAA manual on photographs[2] and the SAA preservation manual for more detailed and authoritative advice.

Sound and moving image materials

These audiovisual materials are challenging in many of the same ways that photographs are challenging. They require us to understand very different formats and media, housing and storage requirements, and user access needs. In addition, they impose the more significant hurdle of requiring special equipment simply to access them. For the most part, we can view photographs directly in the same way that we do textual materials. Most audiovisual materials are unknowable at first glance, apart from whatever labels they came to us with. To know anything more, we need to interrogate them in a complicated process. That interrogation must often happen in real time; skimming for content is more difficult than with written materials or photographs. This affects how we arrange and describe the materials, and it certainly affects their accessibility to users.

Megan McShea, in her very helpful *Guidelines for Processing Collections with Audiovisual Material*,[3] identifies three general areas that determine processing decisions, actions, and productivity when dealing with these records:

- *The quality of existing housing.* Are existing containers adequate, or will some or all need to be replaced with specialized containers suited to the records' format?
    - **Magnetic media.** Audio reels and cassettes, and video cassettes, should be placed in new plastic containers if their containers are missing or broken. Store cassettes on edge, rather than on sides. Tape down the exposed ends of open reel tapes to prevent unwinding. Retain label information.
    - **Motion picture film.** Airtight, rusted, or cardboard cans should be replaced with plastic, vented cans. Retain label information, and tape down loose ends. If vinegar syndrome is present, wrap in tissue paper to contain odors. Small reels can be stored vertically in folders, while larger ones will need to be stored flat. Any film mounted on cores will need to be stored flat as well.
    - **Grooved discs.** Older, glass-core discs are fragile and need to be tissue wrapped and sandwiched between cardboard. Vinyl discs are sturdier and need no wrappings. Those smaller than twelve inches can be stored on edge, while larger ones should be stored flat.
    - **CDs and DVDs.** Tyvek or polyester sleeves are good protection, but if they are already in jewel boxes, those can be retained instead. Small numbers may be stored vertically; larger numbers should be stored in archival shoe boxes of the correct size.
- *The quality of media labels and documentation.* The media units may carry labels of any quality: some descriptive and easy to interpret, others bearing cryptic notations understandable only by their creators. Some may lack label information entirely. Related documentation like transcripts or production notes may exist, especially when

the materials were part of an audiovisual production project. Missing or unhelpful labeling forces us into a decision about the granularity and intensity of processing. As in all processing workplans, it is legitimate to choose a particular level of processing work to apply to the audiovisual materials:

- ***Minimal processing.*** Record the label information as it exists, and describe those lacking information as "unidentified." Don't spend time playing the media.
- ***Intermediate processing.*** Accept label information as is, but make the effort to play unlabeled media, perhaps sampling content at various points along the playback. That way, some level of useful description is available for all media.
- ***Full processing.*** Play all media with ambiguous or no label information so that accurate descriptions can be prepared for everything.

- *The complexity of the AV material and the quality of the existing arrangement.* As with photographs, sound and moving image materials should be arranged (at least intellectually) and described in their appropriate series and file units throughout the collection. They are almost always less valuable as a category based on format than they are as part of the documentation of the overall activity or function (series) for which they were created. The only caveat to this recommendation concerns groups of audiovisual materials created as part of a *production project*. Those media projects often result in their own series (or files), as they represent a discrete activity. Other considerations also apply to production projects. Weeding out redundant copies, or variant versions, of a particular title will require more thought. Some or all of those variations may be key to documenting the project as a work in its own right. Ideally, the processor faced with such a situation would consult staff members involved with acquiring the collection.

One final consideration applies to audiovisual materials on analog magnetic media. When we accession and process those materials, leaving them in their existing formats, we introduce ticking time bombs into our collections. A bit like plutonium, they are degrading every day. And, unlike digital files on a preservation server, they are not being inspected, evaluated, refreshed, and updated. They are simply aging and dying. The best possible practice is to digitize these materials either during accessioning or processing. Understandably, we usually lack the time, staff, or technical resources to do this work at the time we should. As a result, most of such materials enter the stacks in their received state. Whenever that is the case, we should prepare a form or memo for our administrative files to remind us later that we need to address the problem as soon as we have the means to do so. Otherwise, we simply incarcerate the materials on our own death row.

Arrangement and Description in a Digital World

So, does the emerging world of digital archives foreshadow the end of the approaches and methodologies I have explained and recommended in the rest of this manual? Not as much as we might fear. In the end, I would argue strongly that the principles of arrangement and description remain intact and that they persist as important guides to influence our practice. The methodological stages and steps involved in arranging and describing our collections continue to be relevant as well, although they certainly need to be adjusted in a number of ways to satisfy some unique requirements of digital archives. The influential report produced by the AIMS (An Inter-Institutional Model for Stewardship) working group emphasizes that success in arranging and describing natively digital records depends on the same things that we require in working with traditional materials:[4]

- Preserving the context in which the records were created, managed, assembled, or accumulated irrespective of their format;
- Establishing intellectual control over the materials;
- Providing a finding aid or other means of discovery.

The current generation of archival educators and digital curation theorists has been wrestling with the continuing relevance of archival approaches and principles for twenty years. They end up, with some important cautions, affirming the power and utility of core precepts of arrangement and description. Anne Gilliland, for one, asserts that "[a]pplying these concepts makes it possible to unite related digital, nondigital, and predigital according to their intellectual rather than their physical characteristics. These concepts build context, which is a powerful and underused tool for facilitating understanding and ultimately creating knowledge."[5]

Provenance, original order, collective arrangement and description, and natural whole-to-part relationships are all concepts that help us to explain and manifest intellectual structure within materials that may seem to lack such a framework as they array themselves in the storage devices in which they come to us. Arguments have been made that, in the world of digital records, arrangement is a pointless activity. Better to simply search text across a storage device and skip the frustrating work of arranging an opaque profusion of electronic files. This, I think, is misguided, although undoubtedly at times we must settle for that. It is incumbent on us as archivists to ascertain and express the intellectual structure that surely exists within a collection of digital records in the same way that it exists in nondigital collections.

This may not be as daunting as it seems. In the first place, individuals and organizations will tend to maintain their digital files in some degree of order in the same way that they keep nondigital records ordered. It may be crude and inexact, it may be jumbled, but some intellectual structure exists—some breakdown into basic activities or functions that gives us a place to start. I think about my own digital documents. In my work life, I create a directory folder for every key activity. As files accumulate in that folder, I eventually subdivide it into subfolders to make it easier for me to find things. An intellectual structure emerges. I find that I do pretty much the same things with documentation of my personal life. Perhaps a looser structure, but I still need to be able to find things, so I maintain a structure that helps me do so. Naturally, a few junk drawers hold the files and objects that don't go anywhere else, but we're used to that in the nondigital world as well.

Even if we can go no farther than to separate digital files into key groupings, we have at least taken the requisite step of identifying and establishing major series of records. A digital collection probably comes to us from a lot of directions too: an internal computer drive, external drives of all sorts and sizes, optical and floppy disks, and cloud storage. A lot to pull together into an intellectual structure, but the analytical work is not essentially different from what we routinely face when we bring together a nondigital collection previously stored in a motley host of liquor boxes, office file drawers, storage lockers, and what have you. The work is the same in principle, though different in the technical mechanics, as we cannot skim most of the contents with our eyes. Fortunately, a wide variety of software tools exists that can help us skim, and thus identify, digital materials.

The fact that most of the collections we will be receiving into the foreseeable future will be *hybrid collections* comprising both digital and nondigital materials in varying proportions also helps our arrangement work. Hybrid collections confront us with a number of arrangement questions and possibilities, as the digital and nondigital materials will always be stored and accessed in radically different ways. Notwithstanding that, having a body of nondigital materials at hand may help to provide a basic intellectual structure for the collection as a whole. The digital materials may very well interfile with (or at least augment) the rest of the collection. This gives us a leg up in arranging the digital portion. Or, the digital records may prove to stem from activities, entities, and functions unrelated to the nondigital materials. Still, what we know about the creator and the context of creation from the nondigital materials will provide some guidance in determining the nature and purpose of the digital files.

So, as different as digital files may be from the materials we have traditionally dealt with, they nonetheless comply with our core arrangement principles and methodologies. We can use this similarity to arrange digital archives effectively. This is a good time to hark back to another core principle of arrangement: that the rules governing the treatment of archives are the same regardless of their form or medium. Throughout this volume, in treating different aspects of arrangement and description, I have tried to make the point that our intellectual approaches and our descriptive practices apply to digital materials in the same way they apply to any other archival holdings. This is certainly true in the main. Some caveats exist, however, as noted at the beginning of this chapter. The remainder of the chapter outlines the steps involved in arrangement and description as presented in the previous two chapters, applying them to digital materials. However, it only focuses on those situations for which the treatment of digital materials varies in practice from the treatment of the nondigital. Otherwise, it can be assumed that the approach does not differ significantly.

In presenting this information, I am indebted to the extensive research and clear expression found in Gordon Daines's SAA module, *Processing Digital Records and Manuscripts*.[6] What follows is summarized to a great extent from that work. I strongly encourage you to consult that work for fuller and more authoritative explanations, as well as for its references to many other relevant and more detailed publications.

If you seek a more comprehensive framework, and granular recommendations, for arranging and describing digital collections, you may want to consult the *Digital Processing Framework*,[7] published by ten archivists on Cornell University's eCommons digital repository, which proposes a minimum processing standard for digital archival content. The framework is intended to bring archival processing practice together with digital preservation activities. The authors recommend it for experienced digital archivists looking for a decision-making framework to guide the arrangement and description of any body of digital materials, and who are familiar with the OAIS Reference Model[8] for digital preservation. The framework breaks digital archives processing projects into twenty-three separate, nonsequential activities:[9]

- *Survey the collection.* As with analog collections, this activity establishes the overall information about the records, including extent, scope and content, copyright and access issues, date ranges, provenance and accessioning notes, physical media, preservation concerns, creator context, and notes on any original order.

- *Create processing plan.* Draft a plan that considers how you will deal with access requirements, levels at which arrangement and description will occur, necessary resources (including time, equipment, and expertise), and relationships between analog and digital components (if a hybrid collection).
- *Establish physical control over removable media.* Carefully identify and inventory the existing media, focusing on identifiers, type, capacity, file formats, stack locations, and existing labeling. Stabilize media and transfer files from unsafe carriers. Photograph existing media to document received state and to simplify further work with them.
- *Capture digital content off physical media.* Determine satisfactory capture method and implement it using standard operating system tools, specialized file copy tools, or (for wholesale content capture) by creating disk images.
- *Create checksums for transfer, preservation, and access copies.* Determine preferred algorithm (e.g., MD5) and create checksums before transfer to archives, after transfer, and at the time that the normalized version of the file is created. Record checksums in collection documentation, CMS, or another stable repository.
- *Determine level of description.* How will researchers most likely use the materials, and what level of description is needed to accommodate that—collection vs. series vs. file? If part of a hybrid collection, how does description of the digital component need to interplay with that of the nondigital? How does description level affect choice of access mechanisms—finding aid, catalog, institutional repository, and so on?
- *Identify restricted material based on copyright/donor agreement.* Determine necessary actions to take with materials that must be restricted in some fashion, and flag those materials for appropriate action during the processing workflow.
- *Gather metadata for description.* Compile information on access status for collection components; standardize language to be used in descriptive metadata (titles, dates, digital extent, and so forth); determine whether existing technical and descriptive metadata can be reused; review existing file directory structure to assess its potential as an arrangement structure; record information on file system properties.
- *Add description about electronic material to finding aid.* Determine the component levels in the finding aid to which information will be added about the digital records in particular. These might include statements on access, dates, extent, processing actions, scope and content, use conditions, arrangement, and formats. Insert that metadata into the input mechanism.
- *Record technical metadata.* Document software and tools required to use the materials, date and method of file acquisition, as well as file-specific data such as filenames, size, path, checksums, originating software, format, file systems, and so forth.
- *Create SIP (Submission Information Package, per OAIS Model).* The SIP comprises the full package of digital resources and metadata as received into the archives. At this time, document the technical metadata, the content checksums, the full package content, and basic administrative metadata like rights and access information.
- *Run virus scan.* With the SIP complete and intact, this is the appropriate point at which to run the repository's antivirus software against the digital files. Results should be documented in the administrative system.

- *Organize electronic files according to intellectual arrangement.* First, determine whether the existing arrangement suffices or if digital files must be restructured. Then, organize and describe the files at the previously determined level of arrangement. This may involve creating a new file directory list and new folders or hierarchies to reflect the intellectual arrangement (especially in hybrid collections).
- *Address presence of duplicate content.* If it is simple and straightforward to identify and delete duplicates, this can be done during the course of arranging the digital files. Decisions and actions should be documented in the collection management system and/or the finding aid.
- *Perform file format analysis.* It is necessary to run a software tool (like JHOVE or the NARA File Analyzer) against the files to verify their format and readability, and then take preservation actions if problems exist.
- *Identify deleted/temporary/system files.* A more intensive step not mandated at baseline processing levels is to run those analytical tools to discover deleted, duplicate, temporary, and hidden files. Such files can then be appraised for possible deletion.
- *Manage personally identifiable information (PII) risk.* Based on donor and accessioning information, files can be selectively opened for risk assessment. Files with problematic personal information can then be flagged for restriction, redaction, or deletion as necessary for legal or ethical compliance.
- *Normalize files.* Source files, sometimes proprietary in nature, will often need to be converted to formats that are more accessible and stable, and that can be easily shared on the Web. Determine the software needed to perform file normalizations, and then migrate the converted files onto new storage media. Source files, of course, may need to be preserved in the form they were received, as dictated by the repository's preservation policies.
- *Create AIP (Archival Information Package, per OAIS Model).* The AIP constitutes the exhaustive compendium of information aggregated to this point and becomes the essential and inviolable package to be maintained for preservation purposes. It may include the original transferred files, disk images, files normalized for preservation, files normalized for access, redacted files, metadata (technical, administrative, descriptive) about the digital content files, and documentation created throughout the process (checksums, logs, reports, and notes). This ragtag compilation can be bundled using specialized software such as Bag-it, or via something as pedestrian as a .zip or .tar file.
- *Create DIP (Descriptive Information Package, per OAIS Model) for access.* The DIP comprises another aggregation of files, all of which are aimed at users of the digital records. Pull together relevant access and use information, capture file system metadata, and create a file directory list and a list of access files. The conceptual package includes all the user access files, which are then transferred into the public service delivery mechanism.
- *Publish finding aid.* Following transmittal of the DIP, create or edit an output finding aid (probably an EAD instance). Alternately, the DIP content files and metadata may simply persist within a CMS or digital repository until served out to a user in response to a query.

- *Publish catalog record.* If the repository exposes its metadata through an OPAC of some sort, it also needs to create or edit a MARC record.
- *Delete work copies of files.* Finally, confirm that preservation and access copies exist and are stored in the appropriate locations, and then delete all working copies that may have accumulated throughout the process.

This framework articulates three possible levels—baseline, moderate, intensive—at which to approach each activity, depending upon the resources that the repository is willing and able to devote to processing the digital collection.

Accessioning

In terms of the required workflow outlined here, it is in the accessioning phase, in which we take formal possession and establish the first physical and intellectual controls over collections, that our practices for digital materials veer most markedly away from our procedures for nondigital records. As Daines points out, "[t]he key lies in taking [physical] custody in a way that preserves the authenticity of the digital records and manuscripts."[10]

Ingestion

As noted before, we are likely to receive digital files from numerous locations via various platforms and media—floppy disks, hard drives, FTP transfers, and Dropbox locations. Unlike receiving most nondigital materials, digital materials are almost always received in a vulnerable state, and we need to address and mitigate that vulnerability as the first link in the chain of custodial actions by the repository. The records' vulnerability has several aspects requiring varied responses.

Files must be moved from unstable or inaccessible media. Collection materials will need to be migrated onto a repository server before any further work is done. This server should quarantine the new accession from other collections or internal administrative files until the received files are determined to be stable and secure. Staff cannot work on the materials while on their received media or locations, nor can effective and sustainable access be provided while they remain in that state.

File content must not change during migration. The acts of migrating and viewing digital materials have the potential to change their data in minor or significant ways. Because an important ethic of archivists is to preserve records unchanged and unharmed, it is incumbent upon us to prevent any errors from occurring during the process of migrating the files. Forensic software tools are readily available to migrate an uncorrupted image of the files on the received media and allow them to be viewed and moved without introducing errors. Daines explains them in detail.[11]

Files may already be corrupted or infected. The repository needs to assure itself that the files can be accessed and that they are free of virus infections. Mounting checksum and antivirus software on the accessioning server, along with the other forensic tools, can automate and validate the security, safety, and functionality of the records.

The "archival" records cannot be manipulated during processing. Because viewing, evaluating, moving, and otherwise manipulating files has the potential for damaging them, work from a copy of the file of record. Again, software tools are available that allow us to preview and inspect digital materials.

Preservation assessment

A crucial accessioning task is to assess the preservation status and conservation needs of the collection and, if necessary, create a mitigation plan for the accessioned materials. As I emphasized in discussing accessioning in a previous section, this assessment is more appropriately performed as part of accessioning, rather than later as part of the physical arrangement of the records. This is even more important in the case of digital materials, which cannot afford to sit around for any length of time absent a complete understanding of their preservation status and an immediate plan to mitigate problems. As is also true with nondigital materials, the process is threefold:

1. **Identify problems.** Obviously, digital materials diverge sharply from analog in that problems are rarely apparent to the senses. Determining their existence requires analytical tools like antivirus software. Repositories must also validate the integrity of the files to determine whether they have suffered from bit rot or other damage resulting in loss or corruption of information. Daines discusses useful analytical tools in some detail. I should perhaps emphasize here that, to a degree almost unknown with nondigital materials, conservation assessment is a continual, regular, and frequent preservation activity throughout the custody of the materials. Providing this postaccessioning assurance and mitigation is, of course, a responsibility that passes on to the repository's digital preservation program.

2. **Segregate problematic items.** In the same sense that serious problems like mold and pests require removal of materials to a safe, separate environment, infected and corrupt digital items need to migrate to a server environment that both quarantines them from the rest of the materials and contains forensic and treatment tools that can repair the items.

3. **Plan for mitigation.** If we're lucky, treatments may be accomplished simply and immediately. But, in some cases, a substantial quantity of affected items or deeper problems may exist. In those circumstances, we need to utilize the available forensic tools to develop a treatment or mitigation plan for the materials. As with nondigital materials, this plan should identify a critical path of actions that might stretch some time into the future. As Daines emphasizes, a robust action plan for digital materials should be in place *before* problematic materials are encountered and, as part of that advance planning, the repository will have "the resources necessary to implement that plan as part of the subsequent processing steps."[12]

Rights assessment

Because digital records will be served out to users directly, it is imperative that we understand the rights and permissions for access and use for all digital files. As is true with analog archives, some files will have been restricted by their donors or transferring agencies, and some will be judged by the archivists to contain sensitive materials that cannot be legally or ethically shared. A novel wrinkle affecting digital records is whether some private entity holds copyright in the materials. In nondigital records, researchers have always borne the burden—with some education and coaching from archivists—of understanding and respecting copyright in the collections they are using. In the case of digital records, however, archivists bear more of that burden and may be prevented from displaying some copyrighted materials online, as doing so is tantamount to publication and reuse.

Fortunately, Peter Hirtle, an archivist who has specialized in copyright laws respecting archives and unpublished cultural materials, has created a chart and supporting resources in Cornell University's Copyright Information Center that provides immeasurable help in deciding how to proceed in determining which materials may be shared and to what extent.[13]

Nevertheless, all digital objects will need to be flagged (encoded) during some phase of processing to either allow or disallow their publication. This is an essential task during digital arrangement and, as is true with nondigital materials, it can be applied with a broad brush (entire files or even series) or with precise granularity: digital file by digital file. Staff at OCLC Research have invested considerable effort in pursuing cost-effective solutions to managing access to digital materials whose rights status may be unclear.[14]

Arranging the records

Daines notes several tasks associated with arranging collection materials that need some rethinking when processing digital records.

Rehousing

This pivotal function in digital preservation will often occur as part of accessioning or as an immediate follow-on. Digital materials intended for public access *must* be migrated to servers that are routinely backed up and managed as part of the institution's preservation environment. Ideally, continuing management of the server spaces will include the full suite of recommended digital preservation actions, but at the least they should include two things: regularly scheduled and automated backups, and multiple copies of all collection items. At the least, the latter would consist of a master copy on an internal server and an access copy on a public web server.

Intellectual arrangement

In the case of a collection composed entirely of digital materials, we should make the greatest *reasonable* effort possible to identify all of the electronic files sufficient to organizing them into an intellectual hierarchy (subgroup, series, files, etc.), as one would with any new collection. And, if no original order can be deduced from the existing contextual information or from the materials themselves, then a new order that facilitates research must be established by the processor. It will be left up to our descriptive tools not only to express the intellectual structure that we end up with, but also to provide a direct access mechanism for the user. User access to the records themselves will almost always occur directly from the descriptive metadata, most likely in the form of hyperlinks to digital objects. In the case of a *hybrid collection*, however, a basic decision must be made that gives the processor essentially two choices:

1. **Integrate the digital files, as much as possible, into the intellectual structure that already exists for the nondigital materials.** In many ways, this results in a superior outcome for researchers as it yields one intellectual structure to present and to explain. It also reinforces the principle that records are records and that digital materials, while different in their physicality and manipulability, are not intellectually distinct from nondigital materials.

2. ***Create a new subgroup or series for the digital records.*** Past common practice has been for archives to accord a separate "series" status to groups of materials (e.g., maps, artifacts, photographs, video recordings) that are both physically different and semantically distinct from other collection materials. This has been done for reasons both good and bad. In its best light, it has allowed archivists to describe these materials in terms of their unique characteristics better than would be possible if they were atomized throughout the other intellectual groupings within the collection. This can certainly be true with digital records. They are accessed directly from the finding aid, which creates an entirely different storage and retrieval mechanism that may require explanatory notes that are easiest to present within a series that consists entirely of digital materials. Significant content and functional differences important to the digital records (patrons' ability to sort or further query the use copies served out to them) make it sensible to separate them into their own intellectual structure.

Whichever way we decide to handle intellectual arrangement, important distinctions arise in arranging digital materials. The first is that arrangement is a *purely intellectual* endeavor. All of our processing work will be performed at computer workstations, which really changes the space and equipment requirements for processing, not to mention how much exercise we get during our workdays. And, because the arrangement is intellectual rather than physical, records can be arranged in multiple ways and any file or directory folder can be represented in multiple series. This arrangement and rearrangement can be performed by the user as well as by the archivist. The AIMS Report summarizes this important consideration quite well:

> At its most fundamental, arrangement in the digital world is the representation of relationships between items. The organization of material into a "folder" and "file" is representational only—the data of the digital items themselves are not organized this way on the physical hard disk or other storage medium. Metadata captured at the point of accessioning can be reused during processing to represent this organization. Born-digital material can have multiple arrangements (or rather, multiple arrangements can be represented), such as the original order of the files as they were received or a different order applied by the archivist. Files could even be re-organized (or differently represented) by the user through manipulation of the metadata and data online—for example by sorting a collection into date order, by title or by file format, etc.[15]

The second distinction concerns how we *view* and *rename* collection materials. In nondigital collections, we continually "open up" and view materials, and we routinely assign different names to the files that comprise series to more accurately represent their content to users. In digital collections, both of these activities are fraught with danger, as either of these actions can end up changing the digital records in unintended, and perhaps archivally destructive, ways. Again, technical tools at our disposal allow us to perform these routine activities in ways that don't produce harmful consequences.

A final item of great importance for our users is to ensure that the digital records in our user-pointed web server are all in web-friendly formats supported by browsers (PDF, JPEG, MP3, MP4, etc.). When transformations are necessary, it is important to retain the original version of the converted file on the internal server.

Describing the records

Description is a function that does not change significantly in working with digital records. The one distinction worth emphasizing is that, when we describe digital materials, we are not only creating descriptions of the context and content of the materials, we are also facilitating access to those materials *directly* from the finding aid itself. We therefore need a metadata technical platform in place that can encode hyperlinks to various digital objects. Certainly, PDF and HTML files satisfy that requirement, as do databases with robust discovery layers that can return digital objects as query results. Beyond that consideration, description occurs simultaneously with arrangement in processing digital materials.

The objective of description in managing digital records is really a matter of adding value to the acquired or created digital records. This is accomplished through the addition of descriptive metadata to the technical metadata that already exists in the digital objects. A few important decisions must be made concerning the description of digital records, whether they are natively digital or the result of digitization projects:

- *Determine a level at which to present and describe the materials.* Digital records, like nondigital materials, can be described at a variety of levels. It has typically been assumed that digital materials ought to be described at the item or object level, so that a search can retrieve individual electronic files. However, more recent efforts at mass digitization challenge that assumption in some circumstances, arguing that scarce resources, combined with the growing demands for digital access to archives, call for a less granular and resource-hungry approach. In such a regimen, all of the items in a physical file folder may, for example, be concatenated within a single PDF file and simply linked to the finding aid description for that folder. Users cannot search for a document but must instead browse for it. Search precision has been lost, but access to much more digital material gained. The access goals of the repository will suggest the level at which description should occur.
- *Determine a metadata schema for the digital objects.* A digital object will consist of the content file itself joined to a metadata record by way of a digital wrapper that binds them together. Especially if descriptive metadata is being captured at the item level, it will need to be expressed in an encoding schema—EAD, MODS, Dublin Core—that is understandable to, and actionable by, web search engines and other appliances. As an illustration of this, the Minnesota Historical Society, when it digitizes collection records at the folder level, concatenates the individual scans in a PDF/A file to hold and display them. The XMP schema is used to record a few DACS-compliant elements of descriptive metadata into the header of the file.[16]
- *Determine an input software solution.* CMS software can simplify the creation of metadata for digital files by providing input work forms that capture the content file and the metadata elements, while establishing and preserving the contextual linking of the digital objects back to the metadata record for the archival unit that they either comprise or form a part of. The system can use internal scripting tools to wrap the digital objects appropriately within a variety of output formats, such as EAD, that may be served out on request. Digital repositories and other institutional information systems will possess

some or all of that functionality as well. In hand-coding an EAD finding aid, by contrast, the links to the digital objects will need to be intentionally encoded into the EAD instance.

Either in their native state, or as the result of ingestion processes, the digital objects comprising a unit of digital records may already each contain some level of descriptive metadata in their headers, perhaps encoded as Dublin Core elements. Digital objects may also, in the course of ingest and arrangement, be individually wrapped within a METS file, which can further preserve important contextual information. Despite that, there is value in contextualizing the objects within the structure of an archival finding aid, which can express the relationships among the parts of the collection and among the responsible entities.

A useful set of best-practice guidelines for arranging and describing digital and hybrid collections is found in the United Kingdom's Paradigm Project, a research partnership between the University of Oxford and the University of Manchester. The project's products include a *Workbook on Digital Private Papers*,[17] which recommends arrangement and descriptive practice for various sorts of digital files (emails, websites, and so forth), as well as EAD templates and advice on applying descriptive standards.

This chapter has examined some common nontextual record types—photo images, sound recordings, moving image records, and digital records—to identify processing requirements that are specific to those formats. Photographic, sound, and visual materials often require special handling due to their physical formats and media, due to their chemistry, and due to technologies affecting their access and use. More problematic still are digital archives, which typically require extraordinary tools and protocols for their ingestion, preservation, arrangement, description, and public access. Nevertheless, we can rely on our core principles and processes to guide our work in the main, and the new tools and protocols that may be required are certainly within the reach of most archivists.

This chapter also concludes the content of this work as a practical manual for arranging and describing archival collections. Over the arc of these six chapters we have studied the nature and purpose of arrangement and description as an essential function of archival work. We have examined the long-standing principles upon which that function is based. And we have walked through the practical activities and mechanics involved in the everyday work of arranging and describing an archival collection. The content of these six chapters is also supported and enhanced by the appendixes that are found in the final portion of this work.

However, the following chapter—"Emerging Trends and Theoretical Shifts"—takes a sharp turn away from utilitarian processing advice. In that chapter, we will look at some aspects of our thinking and practice that exist on the boundary between established and emerging practice. Some of this represents a natural evolution in our thinking; some represents new abilities afforded by changing technologies; and some represents emerging challenges to long-standing assumptions. The directions and outcomes of these conversations and opportunities will surely affect the future of our work in arranging and describing archives and manuscripts.

NOTES

1. For ease of expression, I will refer to all varieties of photographic images simply as "photographs" when speaking of them as a broad class. So, when I use the term "photograph," I am not referring to any particular type of image.

2. Mary Lynn Ritzenthaler and Diane L. Vogt-O'Connor, with Helena Zinkham, Brett Carnell, and Kit A. Peterson, *Photographs: Archival Care and Management* (Chicago: Society of American Archivists, 2006).

3. Megan McShea, *Guidelines for Processing Collections with Audiovisual Material* (Washington, DC: Smithsonian Institution, Archives of American Art, 2015), https://www.aaa.si.edu/documentation/guidelines-for-processing-collections-with-audiovisual-material, captured at https://perma.cc/5JBZ-GD8L. Much of the content in this section is based on her guidelines, and I strongly recommend her work for quick, practical processing advice. Deeper discussion of all phases of managing audiovisual materials is found in Anthony Cocciolo, *Moving Image and Sound Collections for Archivists* (Chicago: Society of American Archivists, 2017), especially "Chapter 2. Accessioning, Arrangement, and Description," 24–40.

4. Adapted from AIMS Work Group, *AIMS Born-Digital Collections: An Inter-Institutional Model for Stewardship* (2012), 32, https://dcs.library.virginia.edu/files/2013/02/AIMS_final_text.pdf, captured at https://perma.cc/P7QK-98AV. Chapter 3—"Arrangement and Description"—of the report is a very helpful guide for planning a processing project for digital records, as well as for understanding the policy and technical considerations that are key in achieving a successful outcome.

5. Anne J. Gilliland-Swetland, *Enduring Paradigm, New Opportunities: The Value of the Archival Perspective in the Digital Environment* (Washington, DC: Council on Library and Information Resources, February 2000), https://clir.wordpress.clir.org/wp-content/uploads/sites/6/pub89.pdf, captured at https://perma.cc/XH4N-QTLV. See also Christopher A. Lee and Helen Tibbo, "Where's the Archivist in Digital Curation? Exploring the Possibilities through a Matrix of Possibilities and Skills," *Archivaria* 72 (Fall 2011): 123–68.

6. J. Gordon Daines III, "Processing Digital Records and Manuscripts," in *Trends in Archival Practice: Archival Arrangement and Description*, ed. and with an introduction by Christopher J. Prom and Thomas J. Frusciano (Chicago: Society of American Archivists, 2013), 87–143.

7. Susanne Annand et al., *Digital Processing Framework* (August 2018), https://hdl.handle.net/1813/57659.

8. The *Reference Model for an Open Archival Information System* (OAIS) is maintained by the Consultative Committee for Space Data Systems and is a technical specification for use in developing a broader consensus on what is required for an archives to provide permanent, or indefinite long-term, preservation of digital information. The high-level conceptual model describes an information system divided into several phases—ingestion, storage, management, description, and access—specifying for each certain required information packages to gather the digital information being managed and transmitted. Three packages—SIP, AIP, and DIP—are referenced in this framework for arranging and describing digital collections. The full OAIS Reference Model documentation is available at https://public.ccsds.org/Pubs/650x0m2.pdf, captured at https://perma.cc/TKD2-US6E.

9. Adapted from Annand et al., *Digital Processing Framework*.

10. Daines, "Processing Digital Records and Manuscripts," 101.

11. An exhaustive list of digital forensics tools, with links to their product websites, is maintained at https://forensicswiki.org/wiki/Tools, captured at https://perma.cc/44KA-GWXT.

12. Daines, "Processing Digital Records and Manuscripts," 104.

13. The Copyright Information Center resources are available at https://copyright.cornell.edu/publicdomain, captured at https://perma.cc/RE29-T6ZX.

14. Much of their work is distilled into the small document, "Well-intentioned Practice for Putting Digitized Collections of Unpublished Materials Online," https://www.oclc.org/content/dam/research/activities/rights/practice.pdf, captured at https://perma.cc/RUC9-ZD6S.

15. AIMS Work Group, *AIMS Born-Digital Collections*, 31.

16. This practice is defined and enforced in a local processing manual chapter: *Finding Aids: PDF/A Standards for Digital Reproductions*. In its overview it states that: "Added metadata should identify the original characteristics of a reproduction, provide a citation to its parent collection and repository, and provide generic information indicating that the material may be protected by copyright. Document properties that describe the creator, title, and source of an archival component are always to be added to the Extensible Metadata Platform (XMP) header of any PDF/A file. XMP is a labeling technology that allows us to embed data about a file into the file itself. Data that we typically record includes descriptive metadata naming the creator and title of the original collection component, the title of the collection and Minnesota Historical Society as the holding repository. As well as providing descriptive information about the file, these properties are essential to web indexing performed by search engine crawlers," http://www2.mnhs.org/library/findaids/CMToolkit/BestPractices/FindingAids_PDFA-Standards.pdf, captured at https://perma.cc/3SLQ-MPHC.

17. Paradigm, *Workbook on Digital Private Papers*, http://www.paradigm.ac.uk/workbook/index.html, captured at https://perma.cc/4NGD-EAL4.

7

Emerging Trends and Theoretical Shifts

As if you didn't have enough to worry about—absorbing the history, principles, standards, rules, and practices surrounding archival arrangement and description—it is now necessary to mention that the ground you are standing on is shifting in a seismic way that, in time, may well call some long-standing assumptions and approaches into question.

Challenges to the Concept of Original Order

Despite its prominence as a core principle of archives, original order has always elicited skepticism from various quarters.[1] For example, what does original order mean when multiple transfers of records over the years have changed (perhaps several times over) their created order? How do we deal with filing systems of dubious or unknown legitimacy? What happens when original order frustrates usability by prioritizing the system of arrangement of record creators over an arrangement that best suits future users and researchers?[2] What is so "original" about original order, and how do we know it to be so? Even if we accept that a single ideal ordering scheme exists, which one is it: The one at the end of the records' life cycle, just before transfer to the archives, or the way records were kept and used at the beginning of a project? Or when the project was in full swing? Or toward the end, when competing priorities meant that members of an organization weren't as attentive to recordkeeping as they might have liked? Or at the beginning of the tenure of a new project manager, when the entire project was reconceptualized?

And how can we assert a *single* original order in situations wherein a series or file has, at various different times, comprised part of multiple *fonds*, record groups, or collections? In government records, especially, it is not uncommon that responsibility for a subgroup or series will have shifted from one department to another, perhaps many times, over the course of its active existence. How can we represent its "original order" when it has lived within diverse hierarchies? A single original order that we might impose is often neither unique nor inevitable. Different, equally reasonable arrangement decisions might have been made. Several archivists have puzzled over this problem, eventually arguing that archival units may have *relationships* with multiple creating entities over time and cannot be fixed in a single relationship with one creator. Although they may be physically filed within a single records hierarchy, they may have equally strong intellectual positions within other records hierarchies. Out of this quandary arose what has come to be known as the Australian Series System, in which records of government are controlled at the series level, rather than at any higher level, and are related to one or many *fonds*, sub-*fonds*, and so forth.³ In this system, the *relationships* among groupings of records are emphasized, rather than a static original order.

As emphasized in chapter 2, the value of original order has always resided in the utility it creates in terms of simplifying arrangement and description, and thereby helping researchers use archival collections effectively. As one archival educator put it:

> From a practical viewpoint, the principle of original order obviated the need for resource-intensive and contentious rearrangement according to subject. From an intellectual viewpoint, it preserved the objectivity of the records and provided insight into the functions, processes, and personal relationships of the records creator as reflected in the arrangement of the records.⁴

But what happens to the expectation for a meaningful (and necessary) original order in a world of digital archives, a world apparently lacking an inherent order? If the reason for adhering to original order is one of utility and practicality, rather than some higher philosophical principle, then the importance of identifying a fixed original order diminishes.

First, if we are not bound by something being located or described in one place and one place only, then why not take advantage of that freedom? It has been pointed out that tools like the *Forensic Toolkit* can help us get digital archives to describe themselves.⁵ Such appliances could lessen or obviate the need to articulate a single hierarchy of the records in a collection, instead allowing a search to serve up a set of record units that satisfies the search parameters and that contextualizes the records in the way that purpose-built finding aids have traditionally done. It is easily conceivable that documents in a collection are only "arranged" at the point of being requested by a user. In effect, a web service may organize the presentation of the materials in real time and the arrangement may well change with each query. In such a scenario, a collection may be "arranged" in many different sequences, presenting itself in multiple different hierarchies. Each of these hierarchies represents a different relationship among the components comprising the collection. No single original order predominates or needs to.

Second, if the purpose of description really is to serve and empower users, why not move in directions that amplify that service and power? It has been persuasively argued that diverse users "have diverse needs and may not always want, or may not obtain maximum benefit from, groupings of records based on provenance.... In digital realms, there is no restriction to a single mode of grouping.... If fixed groupings do not accommodate the needs of all users of archives, might we not apply technological approaches to allow—or even encourage—users to combine items differently?"⁶

Given the technological means to do so, users will inevitably form their own "collections" of digital records. These user-created collections may consist of a subset culled from a single archival collection, or they may encompass related objects pulled from multiple collections. This scenario is far from imaginative and represents the emerging reality of scholarship in digital archives. The key to user success (from an archival point of view) in these endeavors is the ability to adequately contextualize the compiled digital objects so that users understand the source of each, as well as its historical relationships to creators, to activities and functions of creators, and to other records. If those contextual semantics can be preserved, then the archival integrity of the materials is ensured.

Accomplishing this difficult objective to a great extent depends upon the capture of item-level metadata by archivists. As a noted thinker on this topic has characterized it, the researcher does not want to drag along all the informational baggage of a finding aid to preserve the important information about the creation, maintenance, and relationships surrounding the digital objects she is gathering. "[I]nstead, she wants the information about the context of each item to travel with the item when it moves into her collection and to remain with it when she subsequently manipulates it within the collection and beyond."[7] Being able to pull together diverse but related items, along with simple contextual metadata, into a sort of metacollection permits archivists and users alike to explore and represent a much richer web of relationships existing among records. This is truly more powerful than the single predefined grouping of objects found in traditional finding aids.

Of course, the devil in all of this lies in our ability to automate the creation of item-level metadata so that it becomes a practical and affordable processing activity. Tools to enable this are certainly under development. When encouraging pilot projects mature into practical tools, we might enter a future in which the potential for exploiting the rich relationships among digital objects moves us to abandon the notion of original order.[8]

Revolutionizing Our Models of Description

Records in Contexts (RiC)

As mentioned in chapter 1, an ICA Expert Group in Archival Description (EGAD) has been working since 2012 to develop a new standard for archival description that marries several existing standards, resulting in a new conceptual model (2016) and an ontology—a machine-readable version of the model—developed in Web Ontology Language (OWL) to express it, aimed at achieving a more multidimensional approach to describing archival resources. Rather than viewing description as an essentially top-down, isolated account of a single collection, Records in Contexts (RiC) aims at comprehending archival description as a more complete expression of the multidimensional web of relationships that exist among diverse records, collections, people, and functions. This web of relationships is nonhierarchical and dynamic rather than hierarchical and static. This introduces a previously unimaginable flexibility into describing archival resources, and it places more of the descriptive burden on computers, which are able to infer semantic relationships and deliver results accordingly.

RiC divides the category of archival records into three levels: the *record*, or item, itself; the *record set*, which comprises multiple records within a collection or across collections; and the *record component*, which accommodates component parts of a complex record (thus accommodating all possible granularity). These three levels form three separate entities. Those record-based entities may in turn be related to each other; to all possible agents (persons and groups who are creators, subjects, and so forth); to mandates, functions, and activities of business entities; as well as to such entities as dates, places, and concepts.

Having defined the disparate entities that may be in some way related to one another, the model then enumerates forty suggested *types* of relationships that may exist between any two entities (e.g., record→was authored by→agent). That way, all the potential relationships relevant to an archival description can be expressed as RDF (Resource Description Framework) triples,[9] thus allowing the descriptive metadata to be shared over networks in ways that preserve the semantic value, and contextual relationships, of records no matter which collection units (series, file, item) are being delivered to users.[10]

While still a long way from practical implementation, RiC offers us a real opportunity to move from the multilevel description of a standalone records hierarchy into *multidimensional* description in which, for example, a person entity may be related to many different records and collections. Similarly, a records series may be related to multiple creating entities, which helps solve the problem in organizational archives wherein ownership of a persistent series of records gets shuffled over time among multiple business units within the organization, or even across organizations.[11]

Linked open data

Part of the revolutionary appeal of RiC is that it eschews apprehending a body of archival resources as a single, fixed hierarchy in favor of a fluid perception of them as a nonhierarchical web of relationships that change in response to different user requests. Users' queries for information deliver not a static, unchanging finding aid but, instead, a targeted set of records that are grounded by pieces of contextual information that explain their relationships to creating entities, to the activities that generated them, and to other resources (archival and nonarchival). It also utilizes the power of the semantic web, employing RDF expressions to encode specific relationships among various entities and resources.

That crucial contextualization of the search results depends upon *linked open data* as a technology that actualizes the connections between an archival unit and related entities and resources. Descriptive metadata based on the emerging RiC model would incorporate RDF triples to indicate relationships in the structured data. Those triples can then be actuated as hyperlinks among objects located within data structures exposed to web search engines. As one archivist puts it: "Using the semantics encoded in the RDF vocabularies, it is possible for a computer to surf those links just like we surf links on the human-readable web."[12]

To visualize some of the power of linked data, we can turn to our hypothetical collection of Jane Doe Papers introduced early on in Figure 1. One of the series in that small collection was

Environmental Issues
- Sierra Club membership files
- Orange County Clean Water Initiative fund-raising files

If our descriptive metadata employed RDF triples to identify relationships among the entities in the collection, a search that returned the file-level unit "Orange County Clean Water Initiative fund-raising files" might also be able to contextualize that piece of information through returned hyperlinks so that users would also see that 1) Jane Doe was the creator of the file, 2) that the file formed part of her activities relating to environmental issues, and 3) that her environmental activities occurred in a particular place and time. They might also include links to a full authority record for Ms. Doe (formed according to the EAC-CPF standard), to other works she had authored (in external archival or nonarchival resources), to external works relating to the Clean Water Initiative, and so forth. Linked open data functionality in archival description gives archivists the potential to enrich and enlarge their metadata without having to manually encode the necessary links or even to imagine them in advance. By adhering to linked data practices, they enable computing resources across the Web to establish those links automatically.

To facilitate the power of linked open data in the future, we need to be creating descriptive metadata *today* that meets some basic thresholds of supportive practice:[13]

- That it is available on the Web with an open license;
- That it exists as machine-readable structured data;
- That it is in a nonproprietary format.

MPLP and Its Aftermath

In 2005, Mark Greene and I published findings and recommendations from a research project that interrogated long-standing arrangement and description practices and suggested changes that we felt would achieve better processing performance and user outcomes. The More Product, Less Process project, or MPLP as it came to be commonly abbreviated, argues in favor of a more economical, less resource-intensive approach to arranging and describing *most* archival collections.[14] It contends that many of the more item-focused actions performed in the course of processing do not add value to the collections in terms of improving user outcomes or in preserving the materials themselves. Those item-focused actions include (among other things) cleaning and mending documents, carefully sequencing documents within files and subfiles, and inventorying individual documents in finding aids.

Regrettably, many practitioners focused almost exclusively on methods, provided in the article by way of example, for increasing efficiency and, as a result, missed our larger and more important conclusions. Many archivists still see MPLP as a set of minute prescriptions for processing the records in any collection. In fact, we hoped that the real value of MPLP would be a theory of resource allocation—an approach that gives archivists tools to address any processing project in a way that preserves the collection and makes it usable in the most economical way possible. Most important, it encourages archivists to make small decisions in the context of the larger needs of the repository. In this way, any processing approach is relative rather than absolute. It is sensitive to the larger body of work not yet done and the larger context of user needs. Leaving behind any absolute advice about removing staples and other trivialities, here are some of the essential arguments of MPLP.

- *User access is paramount.* Processing archivists truly add value to a collection when they open it up to research, and our efforts are only helpful and necessary when they enable that result. Any actions that do not produce a demonstrable benefit for users should be questioned. Item-level sequencing of documents, minute conservation treatment actions, and excessive description may not, in many situations, make it easier to use collections. In such cases, we waste our very limited resources performing unnecessary work and—worse yet—we forego the opportunity to process some other collection. Backlogs grow, and research resources languish while we perform unnecessary labor. So, a crucial question that we must bear in mind as we approach each and any processing project is: *which arrangement and description actions, at which archival levels, will create value for users—and which will simply add unnecessary costs to the project?*

- *Think like a manager.* MPLP is not really about doing, or not doing, specific things in every processing project. Instead, it is about viewing every processing project as a new opportunity to manage a repository's resources—time, money, people—carefully and, therefore, to achieve the greatest impact from our resource investment. Resources saved in one project can be applied to some other needful project. When we operate by rote, performing the same actions at the same levels in every collection, we are not behaving creatively, nor as managers. As professionals, we should apply managerial thinking to every project, creatively making decisions about what approaches to take and which actions to perform. When we develop an annual workplan for our repositories, we consider available resources and how to deploy them in some optimal way among all the projects in front of us. We should really do no less in developing a plan for each individual processing project.

- *Embrace flexibility.* In making processing decisions, we should *expend the greatest effort on the most deserving or needful materials*. We waste resources and show little sensitivity for user needs when we assume that all collections must be processed with the same intensity or to the same level. Many collections call for a light touch, while others demand very intensive work, sometimes at a very granular level. We need to adjust our approach in each case to achieve a similar outcome in terms of usability. The resources we save in the former case will be available to us in the latter case when we really do need them. Similarly, we should not assume that every series (or file, or whatever) in a single collection must be processed with the same intensity. Typically, some units will require little or no attention, while others must be dealt with at some more granular level. Again, we save resources in one portion so that we can apply them in another. The result is that all collection units support researcher access in a fairly equal way.

Because MPLP is managerial, resource sensitive, and user focused, it has proved itself adaptable to domains other than archives, including electronic records, library special collections, and museums.[15] As Greene and I declare in a follow-on article clarifying its objectives and assessing its impact:

> It offers a broad approach to leveraging our collective ability to provide access to research collections: a general mindset, rather than a constraining manual of practice; a determined prioritization of access and user needs; ROI-based strategies and tactics; an approach in which perfectionist dreams don't impede progress toward the possible; and an agnostic approach vis-à-vis techniques, formats, and institutions. All these extensible features have encouraged a variety of cultural institutions to take a serious look at it as a generalizable tool to help shape practice.[16]

We continuously remind archivists that MPLP is one tool among many and that, while applicable in many situations, its more specific recommendations are not relevant or appropriate in all situations and institutional contexts. It is certainly not a processing manual; rather, it is better thought of as a decision-making framework that archivists can use in approaching processing projects and in creating broad institutional approaches to arrangement and description.

Influences from Critical Theory

Starting in the 1990s, archivists began reacting to various tenets of postmodernism—especially those emanating from *critical theory*—and making use of them as a framework from which to reexamine and challenge some long-standing assumptions about archives. Among the convictions questioned were that archival documents possess some objective meaning that can be agreed upon, that archives can be described in a neutral fashion that would present that meaning, and that archivists are passive administrators of the records and perform no role in shaping them. Many archivists came to disparage, or at least deprecate, those traditional assumptions and argued that we needed to make significant changes to our practice in light of the problems critical theory had exposed. Dominique Daniel captures the movement in a nutshell:

> Speaking from a wide range of perspectives and expressing varied views postmodernists explored at least two aspects that bear on archival theory: an assault on objectivity and impartiality, and a call to dismantle the dominant discourse and recover the voices of marginalized and oppressed groups.[17]

Many of those recommended changes have been aimed at our arrangement and description convictions and practices. As one archivist has written, postmodernism "reconsiders the archivist's role in arrangement and description. No longer neutral or objective, it instead recasts archivists as the mediators of archival records. . . . In short, as mediators, we mold archival collections through our arrangement and description."[18]

Debunking the myth of neutrality, exposing the archivist

Archivists have for generations been cautioned, in describing the materials in their care, to be as neutral as possible in representing them. Postmodernist views of communication suggest that this is a fantasy; there is no such thing as a neutral voice, free of cultural or personal bias and capable of expressing an objective perception. As archival theorist Tom Nesmith puts it: "A hallmark of the postmodern view of communication is that there is no way to avoid or neutralize entirely the limits of the mediating influences which, thus, inevitably shape our understanding. Our understanding, then, is not simply affected by such mediations, but is a product of them."[19] In the same way that our own cultural frameworks shape our descriptions of archives, the archives we describe are themselves cultural constructs lacking objective meaning. They are shaped not only by their creators, but also by archivists who have in turn influenced their meaning by *selecting* them from among other documentation and then *arranging* them into some sort of meaningful construct. Through these actions, we make ourselves cocreators of the documentation we seek to preserve. But our conventional approach—to withdraw ourselves and our actions from the users' view—has served to hide our own influences on the meaning conveyed by the preserved materials. It is therefore incumbent upon us to not mask these mediating constructs and actions but, instead, to expose them as completely as we can. As Heather MacNeil succinctly puts it, "archival description involves conscious and deliberate decisions about the representation of archival documents. And because description constitutes the frame of reference that shapes the meaning and significance of those documents, archivists are obliged to render an account of our role and responsibility in the process of our representation."[20]

Those mediating actions undertaken by archivists in arranging and describing materials may include adding more recently acquired records into existing collections and series; rearranging collection materials; and changing the descriptive metadata. All of these events can occur multiple times over the course of a collection's archival custody, and all of them can change the contextualization and, therefore, the meaning of the records. DACS certainly provides metadata elements (e.g., custodial history, appraisal, and description control elements) that can help us be more transparent about how we have shaped and reshaped a collection over the course of our stewardship. Periodic notes about arrangement and description actions, as well as user actions, can help to expose custodial influences on the materials and to lessen the unintended inference of neutrality by communicating changing views of users and archivists regarding the nature, purpose, and value of the collection materials. One early suggestion was to increase transparency through the use of colophons in finding aids:

> . . . the colophon for a finding aid, like its pre-modern antecedents, represents a certain self-conscious perspective that acknowledges the processor's role in shaping a collection and presenting a specific view of it to patrons. It signifies an approach that may call a researcher's attention to the mediating "I" present in both the finding aid and the materials it describes.[21]

CMS systems certainly have the ability to capture data, within an integrated system, about the decisions that we make in terms of what we preserve, how we happened to organize it the way we did, and why we described it as we did. Such actions can help mitigate the misperception that the arranged and described collection is an unambiguous reality rather than a constructed cultural resource.

Culturally competent description

It has been frequently noted that history is written by the victors, resulting in a one-sided viewpoint that may be prejudicial and is almost certainly insensitive to the vanquished. A similar problem can be said to be ubiquitous in archives, which often comprise records composed and passed down by powerful elites and which may misrepresent the experiences of groups lacking power. We archivists contribute to the problem when we simply erase the less powerful actors from the archival record by failing to call attention to their presence in the records when we create our descriptions.

This failure to note the presence of marginalized voices is a perennial problem and can perhaps be addressed most successfully by training ourselves in the tools of cultural competence, which, among other things, helps us wake up to the commonplace biases that always exist in our perceptions of the world around us. Improving our competence as observers and interpreters can help us be more aware of and sensitive to the voices of records agents (creators and subjects) who may be very present within archival documentation, but nevertheless lost to the dominant voice of the agent that produced the records and caused them to be preserved in the archives. As one archivist summarizes the problem:

> It could . . . be argued that this view of the former failures of finding aids is not so much about silence, but about bias. Clearly the two are connected: if bias leads to the judgement that some archival content or actors are not worth mentioning in a description, then silence results. If material is represented in hierarchies of power, then the voices at the top of the hierarchy are more likely to be heard. Some voices will not make it even to the bottom rungs of the ladder, and the resulting silences can be profound.[22]

Descriptive standards and technologies cannot ameliorate the problem; it is up to us to be alert and sensitive to all of the voices that ought to be surfaced in our descriptions of collections.

Inviting multiple voices into description

MacNeil argues that web-based descriptive metadata, through its ability to link multiple, diverse descriptive pathways into a given collection, has the ability to dislodge the traditional authoritatively voiced finding aid by giving users multiple descriptive viewpoints to explore or ignore as they see fit. "It could provide users with the opportunity to create new pathways by incorporating spaces in which users are free to contribute additional perspectives and alternate readings on the records and their representation."[23]

An insight from the Revisiting Collections program of the United Kingdom's Collections Trust is that

> . . . in certain situations contributions made by users about records can offer information or interpretation that has a significant value and that ways need to be found to incorporate them within archive catalogues. The sea-change here is the notion that the single, neutral, authoritative voice of the archive catalogue might be expanded, amplified, and interpenetrated with a range of other, attributed voices.[24]

User annotations to archival metadata can be an effective (as well as cost-effective) way to bring users of records, the subjects of records, and other previously unheard voices into archival descriptions. Valerie Johnson relates a local project in which the Koorie people of Victoria, Australia, were invited to "add their own stories and versions of other stories to records held in public archives." The project, which has come to be known as the Koorie Annotation System, has afforded the opportunity for indigenous people to comment on the accuracy of information about them found in archival collections.[25]

Social tagging provides archivists another opportunity to invite other, nonarchival voices into their standards-based description to provide an added layer of description that offers different perspectives that can augment and perhaps challenge the perspective of the archivist. Anne Gilliland suggests its power and potential:

> Social tagging . . . is a process whereby users of the Web can annotate resources they encounter, add descriptors, or, taking the use of social media one step further, contribute their own content. . . . By so doing, anyone using the Web can contribute expertise different from that of professional describers or catalogers, fill in gaps in missing knowledge about a resource, and contribute alternate perspectives and additional tagged content. If a sufficient amount of social tagging occurs, it may be possible to discern emergent community vocabularies or

ontologies, often different from those applied by the archivist or librarian, and even generational shifts in vocabulary and language conventions.[26]

Taggers from diverse social, political, religious, and cultural communities can possibly help users to see the records through different lenses, perhaps contributing to a fuller understanding of the materials being thus described. This can be a relatively low-cost, high-impact way to enlarge archival description. And, it can be accomplished without losing the voice of the archival professionals amid the voices of nonprofessional communities, as the social tagging represents a separate layer (or layers) of description linked technically to the standards-based archival description.

Who controls identity?

Postmodernist thought has certainly exposed weaknesses in our reasoning about identity as it relates to the actors and subjects in archival collections. Identity is a fraught concept in that a person's identity may be a very complex construct, involving many variables and facets. Archivists have many times collapsed a rich and complicated identity into a one-dimensional characterization. A person, over a lifetime, may claim multiple identifications with different persons, groups, events, and experiences. Allegiances and involvements change. We may tersely identify an agent in a collection as a Native American activist. That person may see himself, perhaps more importantly, as a former soldier and a Vietnam veteran. A collection user may see his vocation as a spiritual leader eclipsing the other roles.

Elisabeth Kaplan summarizes the situation quite well:

> [M]ultiple, intersecting circles of belonging and difference are not usual. . . . [T]hinkers in the area of identity politics have theorized that identification with one group does not preclude another, that individual identity does not preclude multiple group identities, that people inhabit multiple "worlds" at once. Shifting, evolving, continually negotiated and renegotiated, individual and group identities co-exist, although their characteristics may not always be consistent. Identities themselves are socially constructed in response to external conditions and needs.[27]

It is important that we not allow our descriptions to bury the complexity of identity. Although archivists cannot abdicate their role to characterize a person's identity in creating descriptions, it is also important to consider that person's right to define his or her own identity, as well as to take account of the perspectives of other actors.

How do we effectuate this when we describe records? As was true in dealing with silent and marginalized voices, it really comes down to thoughtfulness and sensitivity in identifying persons, communities, and other agents. Have we characterized them thoroughly and fairly? Have we considered how they would characterize themselves? Description in this regard can really depend upon our own astuteness and sensitivity as observers of what we see in the records themselves and our knowledge of the actors represented in those materials.

Looking at critical theory's influences overall, how ought we apply the thinking to description? The relevant archival literature is often long on rhetoric, but short on practical advice. Our ability to use it successfully may come down to a few things that we need to do better:

- Increase our own cultural awareness and sensitivity to make ourselves better observers and interpreters of the information content and the agents interacting in our collections.

- Accept the reality that our descriptive metadata can never be objective, and the language we use can never achieve neutrality. A definite perspective will always be present in what we choose to call out in our descriptions and how we choose to communicate it. We must simply be aware of this and keep a critical eye on our choices and expressions.
- Employ real care and sensitivity in evaluating the relationships, interactions, and information in records. Whose voices are we representing and whose are being ignored, deprecated, or judged?
- Invite other voices into archival description through the use of user annotation, social tagging and, perhaps, more formal contributions.

This chapter has taken a sharp turn from the confident advice contained in the rest of the manual and has examined some areas of practice that only are beginning to emerge into the mainstream of arrangement and description. We have seen strong challenges to such long-standing assumptions as original order and to prevailing models for description. We have looked at the impact of MPLP thinking and to increasing postmodernist influences from areas like critical theory. Professional assumptions and the technologies that both shape and facilitate our work are clearly in flux. The directions and extent of that instability is unknown, but we can count on the fact that arrangement and description will remain in the crosshairs of that change.

NOTES

[1] Jefferson Bailey, "Disrespect des Fonds: Rethinking Arrangement and Description in Born-Digital Archives," *Archives Journal* (June 2013), http://www.archivejournal.net/essays/disrespect-des-fonds-rethinking-arrangement-and-description-in-born-digital-archives, captured at https://perma.cc/JT86-ZDPB. Bailey summarizes the critique against original order, essentially contending that it was a creature of its times and that its value ought to be reassessed in a world increasingly defined by digital archives. He makes the interesting point that, at the bit level in which digital records are created and inscribed, meaningful original order does not exist. Therefore, all arrangement is an act of subjective rearrangement.

[2] Frank Boles, "Disrespecting Original Order," *American Archivist* 45, no. 1 (1982): 31.

[3] This problem and solution were originally described in Peter Scott, "The Record Group Concept: A Case for Abandonment," *American Archivist* 29, no. 4 (1966): 493–504. The practical approach to this was more fully developed in C. Hurley, "The Australian ('Series') System: An Exposition," in *The Records Continuum: Ian MacLean and Australian Archives First Fifty Years*, ed. Sue McKemmish and Michael Piggott (Clayton, Vic.: Ancora in association with Australian Archives, 1994). It was more recently argued in Terry Eastwood, "Putting the Parts of the Whole Together: Systematic Arrangement of Archives," *Archivaria* (January 2000), http://archivaria.ca/index.php/archivaria/article/view/12767/13959, captured at https://perma.cc/J23R-B6G4.

[4] Anne J. Gilliland-Swetland, *Enduring Paradigm, New Opportunities: The Value of the Archival Perspective in the Digital Environment* (Washington, DC: Council on Library and Information Resources, February 2000), https://clir.wordpress.clir.org/wp-content/uploads/sites/6/pub89.pdf, captured at https://perma.cc/XH4N-QTLV, 12–13.

[5] Maureen Callahan, "The Value of Archival Description, Considered," *Chaos—>Order* (blog), April 14, 2014, https://icantiemyownshoes.wordpress.com/2014/04/04/the-value-of-archival-description-considered, captured at https://perma.cc/96AC-P5P4.

[6] Geoffrey Yeo, "Contexts, Original Orders, and Item-Level Orientation: Responding Creatively to Users' Needs and Technological Change," *Journal of Archival Organization* 12, nos. 3–4 (2015): 171.

[7] Yeo, "Contexts, Original Orders, and Item-Level Orientation," 175.

[8] Jinfang Niu, "Archival Intellectual Control in the Digital Age," *Journal of Archival Organization* 12, nos. 3–4 (2015): 190–92. Niu points to a number of initiatives, especially in government archives, that have potential to automate affordable metadata at fine granularity, while also acknowledging that the necessary technological tools are currently beyond the reach of most repositories.

9. RDF is explained fully on the World Wide Web Consortium website, https://www.w3.org/2001/sw/wiki/RDF, captured at https://perma.cc/2FLN-795Q.
10. A thorough and authoritative explanation of EGAD's work and the RiC project is available in Gretchen Gueguen, Manoel Vitor Marques da Fonseca, Daniel V. Pitti, and Claire Sibille-de-Grimouard, "Toward an International Conceptual Model for Archival Description: A Preliminary Report from the International Council on Archives' Experts Group on Archival Description," *American Archivist* 76, no. 2 (2013): 566–83; and International Council on Archives' Experts Group on Archival Description, *Records in Contexts (RiC) An Archival Description Draft Standard* (paper presentation, ICA Congress, Seoul, 2016), https://www.ica.org/sites/default/files/session-7.8-ica-egad-ric-congress2016.pdf, captured at https://perma.cc/3C29-72UL.
11. See, especially, Scott, "The Record Group Concept: A Case for Abandonment," 493–504. The conundrum led to the development of the "series concept" of arrangement within Australian government archives, in which the record series predominates as the key level in description, allowing a given series to be the child of multiple business unit parents, whose responsibility for the series is temporal rather than absolute.
12. Rubenstein, "Sharing Archival Metadata," in *Trends in Archival Practice: Putting Descriptive Standards to Work*, ed. Kris Kiesling and Christopher J. Prom (Chicago: Society of American Archivists, 2017), 25. Rubenstein's module provides a useful overview of the mechanics of linked open data as they would play out in practice.
13. Rubenstein, "Sharing Archival Metadata," 30–31. These practices are taken from Tim Berners-Lee's "5 Stars of Open Linked Data," https://5stardata.info/en, captured at https://perma.cc/6WT4-FQVL.
14. Mark Greene and Dennis Meissner, "More Product, Less Process: Revamping Traditional Archival Processing," *American Archivist* 68, no. 2 (2005): 236–54.
15. Early case studies in applying MPLP in particular repositories are examined in Matt Gorzalski, "Minimal Processing: Its Context and Influence in the Archival Community," *Journal of Archival Organization* 6, no. 3 (2008): 186–200.
16. Dennis Meissner and Mark A. Greene, "More Application while Less Appreciation: The Adopters and Antagonists of MPLP," *Journal of Archival Organization* 8, no. 3 (2010): 177.
17. Dominique Daniel, "Documenting the Immigrant and Ethnic Experience in American Archives," *American Archivist* 73, no. 1 (2010): 90.
18. Sara White, "Crippling the Archives: Negotiating Notions of Disability in Appraisal and Arrangement and Description," *American Archivist* 75, no. 1 (2012): 122.
19. Tom Nesmith, "Seeing Archives: Postmodernism and the Changing Intellectual Place of Archives," *American Archivist* 65, no. 1 (2002): 26.
20. Heather MacNeil, "Picking Our Text: Archival Description, Authenticity, and the Archivist as Editor," *American Archivist* 68, no. 2 (2005): 272.
21. Michelle Light and Tom Hyry, "Colophons and Annotations: New Directions for the Finding Aid," *American Archivist* 65, no. 2 (2002): 225–26.
22. Valerie Johnson, "Chapter 6: Solutions to the Silence," in *The Silence of the Archive*, ed. David Thomas, Simon Fowler, and Valerie Johnson (Chicago: ALA Neal-Schuman, 2017), 149.
23. MacNeil, "Picking Our Text, 276.
24. J. Newman, "Revisiting Archive Collections: Developing Models for Participatory Cataloguing," *Journal of the Society of Archivists* 33, no. 1 (2012): 58.
25. Johnson, "Chapter 6: Solutions to the Silence," 147–48.
26. Anne J. Gilliland, *Conceptualizing 21st-Century Archives* (Chicago: Society of American Archivists, 2014), 120.
27. Elisabeth Kaplan, "We Are What We Collect, We Collect What We Are: Archives and the Construction of Identity," *American Archivist* 63, no. 1 (2000): 129.

Conclusion

This book has provided a pretty exhaustive introduction to archival arrangement and description. I hope it has not been exhausting, as well! I have tried to impress upon the reader that the prosaic work that encompasses processing occupies a crucial nexus in the continuum of archival work. These activities unlock the potential value in our received collections and enable us to deliver their full value to all of our users.

By way of summary, I want to re-emphasize a few important considerations that I highlighted along the way.

- Arrangement and description are time-consuming and expensive activities. The preeminent reason for expending that great effort is to serve the eventual users of the records by providing effective access. User access should drive the processing decisions that we make and the work that we perform. Because that work is expensive, we should perform it as economically as we can, letting user outcomes serve as our most important metric.
- Despite all the physical work involved, arrangement and description are essentially intellectual activities. The most important work we do in processing archival records is to determine the natural, or at least useful, structure into which the materials fall and to express that arrangement in the descriptive metadata.
- That intellectual work is grounded in long-standing theoretical concepts and principles, the most fundamental of which are *respect des fonds*, provenance, original order, and the hierarchical levels of arrangement. But, as important as these principles are, they are still just tools that we use to guide our work. They can and should be reinterpreted and adjusted in the face of evolving knowledge, user needs, and technologies.

- The general principles, rules, and procedures that we follow apply to all of the materials found in archival collections, regardless of their form or medium. We should resist the urge to deviate from them except in truly special circumstances. And these archival approaches apply to manuscript collections just as much as to archival records.
- There is a generally optimal structure and sequence to processing work that should be rigorously followed to achieve the best results. Crucial to that sequence is first understanding a collection's composition before attempting any arrangement work and then performing that arrangement in a top-down manner, one level at a time.
- Description represents arrangement and serves as an explanatory map to the arranged materials; it should be as spare as possible to efficiently guide and inform the user. We should treat that description as structured data, parsed according to DACS data elements, to maximize its potential for manipulation and understanding by humans and machines alike.
- Finding aids can take many forms; there is no single format that defines a finding aid. Their content is captured with data input tools and is then serialized as outputs. Those outputs may be text documents, tabular data, or something else that satisfies a user's request for information. Finding aids may be constructed intentionally or may be assembled on the fly in response to a query.
- To achieve these ends, description must be grounded in standards. There are important interdependent data structure, content, interchange, and value standards that archivists must comprehend and apply to produce descriptive metadata that is understandable, predictable, and sharable across institutions and networks.
- The finding aids that we produce must describe the creators, agents, and contexts of the records just as deliberately and thoroughly as they describe the informational content of the records.
- Archival description is multilevel, encompassing the whole of the collection, as well as each of its component parts. The same set of DACS data elements are available at any hierarchical level and, at any level, the core set will usually consist of name, title, date, and extent. Focusing on this core set helps to keep description lean and economical.

These considerations are the essential things to keep in front of us in our work as processing archivists. Understanding and applying them will keep our work manageable and also effective in terms of user outcomes. One final consideration to emphasize is that arrangement and description—and especially the latter—are rapidly changing functions. New technologies, as well as changing perceptions of the nature and purpose of archives, will no doubt affect the approaches and recommendations expressed in this work. Practitioners must pay close attention to evolving descriptive standards, as well as to the archival literature relating to arrangement and description. Change, in the form of challenges and opportunities alike, will continuously affect the practice of arrangement and description in the years ahead. Stay tuned!

APPENDIX A

Glossary of Arrangement and Description Terminology

Access. n. ~ 1. The ability to locate relevant information through the use of catalogs, indexes, finding aids, or other tools. - 2. The permission to locate and retrieve information for use (consultation or reference) within legally established restrictions of privacy, confidentiality, and security clearance.

Accession. - v. ~ 2. To take legal and physical custody of a group of records or other materials and to formally document their receipt. - 3. To document the transfer of records or materials in a register, database, or other log of the repository's holdings.

Access point. n. ~ 1. A category of headings in a catalog that serve a similar function. - 2. A name, term, phrase, or code used as a heading in a catalog, especially to group-related information under that heading.

Accrual. n. ~ Materials added to an existing collection; an accretion.

Administrative control. n. ~ The responsibility for management of materials in a repository's custody, including the documentation of actions taken on those materials.

Administrative history. n. ~ That portion of a finding aid or catalog record that provides context for the materials described by noting essential information about the organization that created or accumulated the materials.

Archival authority record. n. *From DACS* ~ An archival authority record identifies and describes a personal, family, or corporate entity associated with a body of archival materials; documents relationships between records creators, the records created by them, and/or other resources about them; and may control the creation and use of access points in archival descriptions.

Archival description. n. ~ 1. The process of analyzing, organizing, and recording details about the formal elements of a record or collection of records, such as creator, title, dates, extent, and contents, to facilitate the work's identification, management, and understanding. - 2. The product of such a process.

Archival processing. n. ~ 1. The arrangement, description, and housing of archival materials for storage and use by patrons.

Arrangement. n. ~ 1. The process of organizing materials with respect to their provenance and original order, to protect their context and to achieve physical or intellectual control over the materials. - 2. The organization and sequence of items within a collection.

Catalog record. n. ~ An entry describing a work within a catalog, especially in an automated catalog. Note: Such records are commonly encoded in the MARC21 format.

Collection. n. ~ 1. A group of materials with some unifying characteristic. - 2. Materials assembled by a person, organization, or repository from a variety of sources; an artificial collection.

Container list. n. ~ The part of a finding aid that indicates the range of materials in each box (or other container) in a collection.

Content. n. ~ The intellectual substance of a document, including text, data, symbols, numerals, images, and sound.

Content analysis. n. ~ CATALOGING The process of examining a work to determine its subjects, especially for purposes of writing an abstract or assigning access points.

Context. n. ~ 1. The organizational, functional, and operational circumstances surrounding materials' creation, receipt, storage, or use, and their relationship to other materials. - 2. The circumstances that a user may bring to a document that influences that user's understanding of the document.

Describing Archives: A Content Standard. n. (DACS, abbr.) ~ A standard for creating access tools for all forms of archival materials, including their archival creators and the forms of creator names.

Document. n. ~ 1. Any written or printed work; a writing. - 2. Information or data fixed in some media. - 3. Information or data fixed in some media, but which is not part of the official record; a nonrecord. - 4. A written or printed work of a legal or official nature that may be used as evidence or proof; a record

Electronic record. (also digital record; automated record, largely obsolete), n. ~ Data or information that has been captured and fixed for storage and manipulation in an automated system and that requires the use of the system to render it intelligible by a person.

Encoded Archival Context–Corporate Bodies, Persons, and Families. n. (EAC, abbr.) ~ A standard to mark up (encode) information relating to the circumstances of record creation and use, including the identification, characteristics, and interrelationships of the organizations, persons, and families who created, used, or were the subject of the records.

Encoded Archival Description. n. (EAD, abbr.) ~ A standard used to mark up (encode) finding aids that reflects the hierarchical nature of archival collections and that provides a structure for describing the whole of a collection, as well as its components.

Entity of origin. n. ~ The corporate body, administrative unit, family, or individual that creates, receives, or accumulates a body of records, personal papers, or objects.

Extensible Markup Standard. n. (XML, abbr.) ~ A standard to promote sharing information over the internet by specifying ways to describe the information's semantic structure and to validate that the structure is well formed. Note: EAD and EAC-CPF are both XML-based languages.

File. n. ~ 1. A group of documents related by use or topic, typically housed in a folder (or a group of folders for a large file).

Finding aid. n. ~ 1. A tool that facilitates discovery of information within a collection of records. - 2. A description of records that gives the repository physical and intellectual control over the materials and that assists users to gain access to and understand the materials. Notes: "Finding aid" comprises a wide range of formats, including card indexes, calendars, guides, inventories, shelf and container lists, and registers.

Fonds. n. ~ The entire body of records of an organization, family, or individual that have been created and accumulated as the result of an organic process reflecting the functions of the creator.

General International Standard for Archival Description. n. (ISAD(G), abbr.) ~ A standard published by the International Council on Archives that establishes general rules for the description of archival materials, regardless of format, to promote consistent and sufficient descriptions, and to facilitate exchange and integration of those descriptions.

Graphic records. n. ~ A broad class of records that are primarily images, as distinguished from textual records.

Intellectual control. n. ~ The creation of tools such as catalogs, finding aids, or other guides that enable researchers to locate materials relevant to their interests.

International Standard for Archival Authority Records: Corporate, Personal, Families. n. (ISAAR (CPF), abbr.) ~ A standard published by the International Council on Archives to establish controls for the creation and use of access points in archival descriptions and to identify the kinds of information that should be used to describe a corporate body, person, or family.

Inventory. n. ~ 1. A list of things. - 2. DESCRIPTION A finding aid that includes, at a minimum, a list of the series in a collection. - 3. RECORDS MANAGEMENT The process of surveying the records in an office, typically at the series level.

Item. n. ~ A thing that can be distinguished from a group and that is complete in itself. Notes: An item may consist of several pieces but is treated as a whole. For example, a letter may have several physically discrete pages but is treated as an item because of its content. The boundaries of an item are sometimes ambiguous; a photograph album may be considered an item, and the individual photographs within the album may also be considered items. Items are generally considered to be the smallest archival unit.

Manuscript collection. n. ~ A collection of personal or family papers.

MARC. (also USMARC, MARC21), n. ~ A data communications format that specifies a data structure for bibliographic description, authority, classification, community information, and holdings data.

Medium. n. (media, pl.) ~ 1. The physical material that serves as the carrier for information.

Moving image. n. ~ A generic term for a visual work that has the appearance of movement.

Multilevel description. n. ~ DESCRIPTION A finding aid or other access tool that consists of separate, interrelated descriptions of the whole and its parts, reflecting the hierarchy of the materials being described.

Original order. (also registry principle, respect for original order, *l'ordre primitif, respect de l'ordre intérieur*), n. ~ The organization and sequence of records established by the creator of the records.

Personal papers. (also personal records, private papers), n. ~ 1. Documents created, acquired, or received by an individual in the course of his or her affairs and preserved in their original order (if such order exists). - 2. Nonofficial documents kept by an individual at a place of work.

Physical control. n. ~ The function of tracking the storage of records to ensure that they can be located.

Physical form. n. ~ The overall appearance, configuration, or shape, derived from material characteristics and independent of intellectual content.

Preliminary inventory. n. ~ A listing of the contents and condition of a collection made before processing.

Provenance. n. (provenancial, adj.) ~ 1. The origin or source of something. - 2. Information regarding the origins, custody, and ownership of an item or collection.

Record group. (also archive group), n. ~ A collection of records that share the same provenance and are of a convenient size for administration.

Reproduction. n. ~ 1. Something that is made in imitation of an earlier style; a facsimile. - 2. A duplicate made from an original; a copy.

Respect des fonds. *See: Provenance.*

Series. n. ~ 1. A group of similar records that are arranged according to a filing system and that are related as the result of being created, received, or used in the same activity; a file group; a record series.

Sound recording. (also audio recording), n. ~ Any medium capable of capturing and reproducing an audible signal.

Subgroup. n. ~ A body of related records within a record group or collection, each corresponding to an administrative subdivision in the originating organization.

Subseries. n. ~ A body of documents within a series readily distinguished from the whole by filing arrangement, type, form, or content.

Textual records. n. ~ A general classification of records with content that is principally written words.

Most of the definitions are taken in whole or in part from Richard Pearce-Moses, *A Glossary of Archival and Records Terminology* (Chicago: Society of American Archivists, 2005), https://www2.archivists.org/glossary.

APPENDIX B

Examples of Institutional Processing Levels

In defining any processing project, repository staff must determine the granularity or intensity of the processing they will perform on the collection in question. Will we process the materials only to the series level (the MPLP-recommended baseline level), or will we perform work at a finer level? If we target a particular processing level, what does that mean in terms of the specific arrangement, conservation, and description actions we will perform?

Some archival repositories approach the problem of processing granularity by establishing a range of predefined levels of work that may be applied to any given project. Articulating these levels—usually published in a processing manual—helps to make clear what types of work will be applied to a collection and also removes the necessity of spelling out the specific actions that will be permitted for each and every project.

Following are examples of processing levels established in one of a few repositories that were pioneers in this sort of levels-based approach to developing project workplans.

Beinecke Rare Book & Manuscript Library. Processing Manual (2015)[1]
Chapter 2.4 Processing Levels

Collections may be processed to any of several levels of physical and intellectual control. All collections receive at least a "baseline" level of control, usually at the point of accessioning, which provides a collection-level description and at least a box-level inventory. A finer level of processing is carried out when research interest, preservation concerns, and/or security concerns warrant further work on a collection. Archivists determine the appropriate level of control for a collection, based on value of the material, its physical condition, and anticipated use.

> *Baseline processing standard*
> *Full MARC record*
> *Finding aid with a collection-level description*
> *Physical stabilization and identification of preservation concerns*
> *Container-level list*

Different components of a single collection may be processed to different levels. A writings or correspondence component, for example, may merit folder-level arrangement and description, but a component of financial records may be sufficiently served by a container-level arrangement and description.

A single component of a collection might be arranged at one level but described at another. Financial records, for example, may be arranged at the file level for ease of use, but described at the container level, which is sufficient to facilitate retrieval.

Definition of Levels

Level of Control	Arrangement	Description	Preservation
Collection Level	Rarely done. Most if not all collections are arranged at least at the series level within a short time of acquisition by the library.	Upon acquisition, every collection receives an accession record and a MARC record. The finding aid contains a collection-level scope and content note, comparable to the 520 field in MARC.	Blast freeze upon acquisition. Possibly microfilm, scan, reformat, or mass deacidify. Special media are separated for storage if necessary.
Series Level	During accessioning, papers are sometimes roughly organized into series based on subject or format.	Scope and content note for each series, in addition to at least a box-level description to facilitate retrieval. At least "circa" dates included.	Format-driven series or sub-series may receive treatment such as reformatting or mass deacidification.
Box Level	Boxes are arranged within a series structure or in a single run.	Material is listed at the container level. Dates may or may not be included.	Material is rehoused into standard-size acid-free containers.
File Level	Files and folders are arranged, but material is not sorted or identified within folders.	Material is listed at the file level. Dates may or may not be included. This level of description may include cross references between files and brief scope and content notes at the file level.	Material is rehoused into acid-free folders.
Item Level	Material is sorted and arranged within folders.	Rarely done. A calendar or item-level list is created only in exceptional cases where the need for security or considerations of access and retrieval necessitate such control. This level of control may also occur as the result of retrospective conversion of existing, item-level cards from the manuscript catalog, or the existence of a useful item-level donor- or dealer-supplied list.	Each item is evaluated, and sleeved, interleaved, or reformatted as appropriate. Hardware is removed.

NOTE

[1] Beinecke Rare Book & Manuscript Library, *Processing Manual* (2015), http://beinecke.library.yale.edu/processing-manual. For a guided explanation of how to use standard processing levels to create effective project workplans, see this excellent webcast by Jennifer O'Neal, University of Oregon, one of many rich resources for archivists and cultural resource administrators created by the Sustainable Heritage Network, managed by the Center for Digital Scholarship and Curation at Washington State University, and funded in part by the Institute of Museum and Library Services, https://sustainableheritagenetwork.org/digital-heritage/creating-processing-plan-tutorial.

APPENDIX C

Finding Aid Examples

This appendix includes examples drawn from a variety of full archival finding aids. None of the examples reproduce the complete finding aid; rather, they are segments illustrating particular arrangement and description scenarios that occur routinely and how repositories have dealt with them in their finding aids.

Example 1. Single-Level Control

Here is an example of a collection described under single-level control. This EAD-encoded full finding aid offers a small expansion of the information contained in its MARC record, but it refrains from including a container list. In a small, flat collection like this one, exhibiting no structural complexity whatsoever, a single-level description suffices in all respects.

(Source: University of California, Santa Barbara. Library.
Dept. of Special Collections, Santa Barbara, CA 93106)

GUIDE TO WOMEN'S RIGHTS SCRAPBOOKS, CA. 1868–1880

DESCRIPTIVE SUMMARY

Title:	Women's Rights Scrapbooks
Dates:	ca. 1868–1880
Collection number:	Mss 260
Collection Size:	0.6 linear feet (2 pamphlet boxes)
Abstract:	The collection contains volumes 1, 3 and 4 of a set of scrapbooks assembled by an unidentified San Francisco area woman, with mounted clippings pertaining to issues such as women's suffrage, property rights, education, marriage and divorce, women in professions such as medicine and law, and women in other cultures.
Physical location:	Del Sur.
Languages:	English
Access Restrictions:	None.
Publication Rights:	Copyright has not been assigned to the Department of Special Collections, UCSB. All requests for permission to publish or quote from manuscripts must be submitted in writing to the Head of Special Collections. Permission for publication is given on behalf of the Department of Special Collections as the owner of the physical items and is not intended to include or imply permission of the copyright holder, which also must be obtained.

Preferred Citation: Women's Rights Scrapbooks. Mss 260. Department of Special Collections, Davidson Library, University of California, Santa Barbara.

Acquisition Information: Purchase, 2009.

SCOPE AND CONTENT OF COLLECTION

The collection contains volumes 1, 3 and 4 of a set of scrapbooks assembled by an unidentified San Francisco area woman, with mounted clippings pertaining to issues such as women's suffrage, property rights, education, marriage and divorce, women in professions such as medicine and law, and women in other cultures. Some clippings are dated but sources generally are not indicated.

Titles of articles include: "Women in Turkey," "Our Women Workers," "Female Suffrage Refused," "Too Much Marrying," "Woman Suffrage in England," "Homes, not Votes," "Lady School Commissioners," "Age for Legal Marriages," "Why Women Should Read," and "Reform in Divorce Law."

There is no container list for this collection.

Indexing Terms

The following terms have been used to index the description of this collection in the library's online public access catalog.

> Women's rights—United States.

Example 2. Multilevel Control at the Container Level

This example illustrates how economical a finding aid might be while still providing all of the descriptive information that is truly required to explain the context of the materials' creation, as well as their informational content. All of the required DACS fields are included in the collection-level description, and the multilevel container list provides the minimum amount of information necessary for users to request access to the correct containers.

This efficient description is rendered more possible by the fact that the collection consists of two distinct series—and two distinct record types—each of which can be characterized quite simply, without requiring additional scope and content notes at the file level. This is clearly a case in which the physical order of the materials matches the intellectual order of the content.

Note that boldface headings are used to bundle, and sometimes distinguish, the significant DACS elements so that the finding aid is fairly simple to navigate and understand. The multilevel description elements are arranged in straightforward labeled columns for the same reasons.

A list of controlled access terms was removed for brevity's sake, but the remainder of the finding aid is presented intact.

(Source: Minnesota State Archives)

OVERVIEW OF THE RECORDS

Agency: Minnesota State Training School for Boys.
Series Title: Youth Vocational Center files.
Dates: 1960–1969.
Quantity: 12.5 cu. ft. (13 boxes).
Location: See Detailed Description section for box locations.

HISTORY OF THE YOUTH VOCATIONAL CENTER

Located near Rochester, Minnesota, the Youth Vocational Center was established in 1961 as a vocational training facility for approximately 50 boys, ages 16 through 18, transferred from the State Training School in Red Wing. The center was to both prepare the boys for future employment through vocational training and counseling in the areas of automotive mechanics, cooking, and small engine repair and provide academic tutoring in tenth through twelfth grade subjects applicable towards credits for a diploma from their home school. Additionally, the boys received training in such functionally related classes as remedial reading and mathematics and social living. Counseling, where the boys met both individually with caseworkers and attended group sessions, and leisure time, which provided opportunity to become acquainted with many meaningful activities, associations, and individuals, were also important components to the center's training. The center ceased operation in 1969.

SCOPE AND CONTENTS OF THE RECORDS

Case files of youths transferred to the Youth Vocational Center. The files include personal, academic, and correctional information from both prior to and during each boy's stay at the center.

There are also informational cards which include the same type of information, plus a chronology of each boy's stay at both the Red Wing Training School and the Youth Vocational Center. The cards are divided into sections for each year, including admissions, parole success, parole failures, and AWOL (absent without leave).

ARRANGEMENT OF THE RECORDS

The records are divided into two series: case files arranged alphabetically by surname and chronological information cards.

ADMINISTRATIVE INFORMATION

Restrictions:
Includes private information about individuals. Records with private information are closed for 75 years from date of last entry in the record. Researchers must apply for permission to use these records. Please consult library staff for more information.

Preferred Citation:
[Indicate the cited item and folder title here]. Minnesota State Training School for Boys. Youth Vocational Center Files. Minnesota Historical Society. State Archives.
See the Chicago Manual of Style for additional examples.

Accession Information:
Accession number(s): 2001-57

Processing Information:
Processed by: Mike Ehlert, March 2001
MNPALS ID No.: 1737363

DETAILED DESCRIPTION OF THE RECORDS

Note to Researchers: To request materials, please note both the location and box numbers shown below.

Case files, 1960–1969:

Location	Box	Contents
113.K.19.4F	1	A-Bri.
113.K.19.5B	2	Bro-Daniels.
113.K.19.6F	3	Danielson-Fol.
113.K.19.7B	4	Fos-Har.
113.K.19.8F	5	He-Ka.
113.K.20.1B	6	Kno-Lei.
113.K.20.2F	7	Ler-Mis.
113.K.20.3B	8	Mo-Ol.
113.K.20.4F	9	Os-Ross.
113.K.20.5B	10	Roy-Sob.
113.K.20.6F	11	Sor-Tuf.
113.K.20.7B	12	Tun-Zim.

YVC Information Cards:

Cards are divided into sections for each year, which include admissions, parole success, parole failures, and AWOL. They contain biographical information on one side and a timeline on the reverse, including arrival date at Red Wing Training School, transfer date to YVC, and parole date.

Location	Box	Contents
113.K.20.8F	13	1961–1969

Example 3. Multilevel Control at the Series Level

This example includes the descriptive summary and the container list portions of a finding aid for a collection arranged and described at the series level. Note that the description for each series in this multilevel finding aid contains three separate notes: physical description, arrangement, and scope and content. Also note that there is no description whatsoever for any levels below the series level, although the arrangement note does indicate how the materials at the file level are sequenced. The user will probably request all the materials in a given series to use them effectively. The relatively small size of the entire collection makes this descriptive strategy workable. Had the collection been significantly larger, it might be advisable to bring description down to the file level, resources permitting.

(Source: California State Archives)

DESCRIPTIVE SUMMARY

Title:	California State Heritage Task Force Records
Dates:	1979–1984
Collection number:	R294
Creator:	California State Heritage Task Force
Collection Size:	2.75 cubic feet of textual records
Abstract:	Senate Concurrent Resolution 4 created the Heritage Task Force (HTF) in 1981 to study and recommend policies, programs, and legislation to preserve and enhance California's architectural, cultural, and historic resources. The Heritage Task Force (HTF) records consist of 2.75 cubic feet of textual material covering the period of 1978–1984. The records reflect background information, working correspondence, and the development of the final reports produced for the State Legislature regarding the status of California's cultural heritage.

SERIES DESCRIPTIONS

Series 1. Out-of-State Historic Preservation Office Files 1982 (ID R294.1, Box 1, Folders 1–14)

Physical Description:	14 file folders
Arrangement:	Arranged alphabetically by state.
Scope and Content Note:	The State Historic Preservation Office Material Files contain information sent to the HTF from out-of-state Historic Preservation Offices regarding their own heritage programs or plans in response to a HTF request. Some states also sent information from their state tourism departments or commissions. The material retained in these files represents established or proposed programs in other states to attract interest in heritage sites as part of a tourist experience. Hawaii, Nevada, and Pennsylvania offered established and thorough examples of cultural resource and tourism studies. Louisiana and Oregon also submitted substantial examples of legislative work to protect heritage sites.

Series 2. Organizational Committee Files 1981–1984 (ID R294.2, Box 2, Folders 1–7)

Physical Description:	7 file folders
Arrangement:	Arranged alphabetically by subject.
Scope and Content Note:	The organizational files contain detailed information on the establishment of the HTF, their purpose, their working structure, and their main issues of study. The Organizational Committee's Analysis provides a concise overview of most of these functions. One point of interest in these files is the official federal and state requests for California to conduct a formal investigation into the status of heritage sites. The large volume of responses to questionnaires sent by the HTF confirmed that there were many issues that needed attention.

Series 3. State and Local Policy Committee Files 1981–1984 (ID R294.3, Box 2, Folders 8–15)

Physical Description:	8 file folders
Arrangement:	Arranged alphabetically by subject.
Scope and Content Note:	The State and Local Policy Committee files contain correspondence, reports, and background information used to assist the HTF with their legal recommendations to encourage preservation. Files that may be of interest refer to the California Environmental Quality Act (CEQA), the Historic Building Code, and Redevelopment Law as well as the Legislative files representing legislation introduced. This committee also proposed policy that affected underwater archeology as well as reclassifying cultural resource management positions within the State Personnel Board.

Series 4. Financial Incentives Committee Files 1980–1984 (ID R294.4, Box 2, Folders 16–20)

Physical Description:	5 file folders
Arrangement:	Arranged alphabetically by subject.
Scope and Content Note:	The Financial Incentive Committee files contain information on the legality of financial incentives the HTF proposed to encourage preservation of historic structures. Some background information on the Marks Historical Rehabilitation Act and the Mills Act is also included. Information on funding the task force from a combination of public/private sources such as grants and donations is also included.

Series 5. Press and Publications 1979–1984 (ID R294.5, Box 2, Folders 21–24)

Physical Description:	4 file folders
Arrangement:	Arranged alphabetically by subject.
Scope and Content Note:	The Press and Publication files include information received by the HTF from local governments regarding their preservation concerns, numerous press-clippings, and publications. Some of the publications received are newsletters from affiliated preservation groups or professional organizations. The press-clippings include newspaper articles related to preservation, cultural resources, and government action. Also included in the press-clipping file are press statements made by Senator Marks office or the Task Force.

Series 6. Reports 1979–1984 (ID R294.6, Box 3, Folders 1–15)

Physical Description:	15 file folders
Arrangement:	Arranged alphabetically by subject.
Scope and Content Note:	The Report files include draft and final reports of the four official reports produced by the HTF. These include: Heritage Task Force Final Report; California Historical and Cultural Resource Report; Heritage and Tourism in California Report; and Executive Summary. Other files include the numerous public comments to the proposals.

Example 4. Multilevel Control at the File Level

This example illustrates arrangement and description work performed down through the file level. This segment of a much larger finding aid shows the description of the files that comprise several subseries—minutes, correspondence, reports—within a large series of Labor Relations Board records. What distinguishes this level of descriptive control from the series-level control above is that each of the files is described with its own scope and content note. For example, within the subseries of *Correspondence*, each of the correspondence files is uniquely described. This results in much more granular, and helpful, content description and, of course, more intensive and time-consuming arrangement and description work.

(Source: Kheel Center for Labor-Management Documentation and Archives, Cornell University Library)

DESCRIPTIVE SUMMARY

Title: James Gross NLRB Files, 1933–1977
Collection Number: /4057
Creator: Gross, James
Quantity: 15 linear ft.
Forms of Material: Records (documents).
Language: Collection material in English

BIOGRAPHICAL NOTE

Professor Gross teaches Labor Law, Labor Arbitration, and a course entitled Values, Rights and Justice in Economics, Law, and Industrial Relations. He received his B.S. from LaSalle College, M.A. from Temple University, and Ph.D. from University of Wisconsin.

Professor Gross is a member of National Academy of Arbitrators and on the labor arbitration panels of the American Arbitration Association, Federal Mediation and Conciliation Service and New York State Public Employment Relations Board, as well as being a panelist named in several contracts. [www.ilr.cornell.edu/directory/jag28/biography.htm]

| CONTAINER LIST ||||
Date	Description	Container	
	Series I. NATIONAL LABOR BOARD, 1933–1934 (JUNE) *Sub-Series A. REGIONAL LABOR MEDIATION BOARD* MINUTES		
1933	Minutes 12/8/33; includes William Leiserson's, (Secretary, National Labor Board—NLB) discussion of the purpose, functions, powers and jurisdiction of the Regional Labor Mediation Board. Also includes rules for deciding cases and explanations of procedures	Box 1	Folder 1
	Sub-Series B. NATIONAL LABOR BOARD RECORDS *Sub-Series 1. CORRESPONDENCE. 8/5/33–6/16/34*		
1933	Correspondence 8/5/33–11/18/33; Letter of appointment from President Franklin Delano Roosevelt to Senator Robert F. Wagner as chairman of the National Labor Board (NLB); from Gerald Swope, (President, General Electric Co., NLB member) and Louis E. Kirstein, (General Manager, William Filene Sons Co. NLB member) to Wagner regarding the Brockton (?) Shoe Manufacturers' case, recommending representation elections; William Leiserson's discussion of the Board's role as a mediation and arbitration board (Philadelphia Bakers' case, the Tool and Die Makers' Strike in Detroit and Flint, Jameston Art Metal Co. case), recommending that the Board remain an arbitration tribunal (Berkeley Woolen Mills case); Leiserson's resignation as Secretary; from the NLB to the Brockton Central Labor Union, includes essay "Manufacturer Fighting to Keep Closed Shop"; James O'Connel's, (President, Brockton Central Labor Union) and Frank W. Gifford's (Secretary) demand that the ruling (Douglas Shoe Co.) be rescinded; Campbell MacCulloch's, (Secretary, Los Angeles Regional Labor Board) inquiry about the power and authority of regional boards as well as organizational structure and procedures; from MacCulloch to Creel concerning the selection of members to the Regional Labor Board (Byron Campbell, A. Schleicher, Tibbetts, John C. Austin, W.L. Stevens), objecting to labor appointees.	Box 1	Folder 2
1933	Correspondence 12/3/33–12/22/33; Letter from Elinore Herrick (Director, New York Regional Office) in regard to action the regional board intends to take in case no. 104; from L.L. Balleisen, (Secretary, Industrial Division, Brooklyn Chamber of Commerce) to Edward C. Blum, (President, Abraham & Straus, Inc. and Regional Board Member) about case no.104; Milton Handler's (General Counsel, NLB) explanation of the functions of regional labor boards; Daniel B. Shortal's (Buffalo Regional Labor Board) request for a copy of the decision handed down in the Philadelphia Bakery Drivers case because of its possible affect on the Hall Baking Co. and the Bakery Drivers Union no. 264 dispute; Benedict Wolf's (Executive Officer, NLB) recommendation to begin negotiations in the Stone Knitting Co. (case no. 25-25A); from G.W. Ramaker, (Secretary, Atlanta Regional Board) to Republic Steel Corp., Birmingham, Ala. in regard to a written complaint filed by employees concerning working conditions.	Box 1	Folder 3

(cont.)

CONTAINER LIST				
Date	Description		Container	
1933	Correspondence		Box 1	Folder 4
	1/2/34–2/20/34; Letter from MacCulloch to Creel in regard to the Greyhound and Wilson Packing Co. cases and company unions; from Wolf to Charles W. Hope (Seattle Regional Labor Board) affirming majority rule is law (Willopa Harbor Mills case); Wolf's confirmation that a union is not required to submit membership lists to a company (Houde Engineering Corporation); from the Chairman (Atlanta Regional Labor Board)(?) about Board's authority to issue binding orders (Republic Steel Corporation); Executive Order no. 6550, regulating the further allocation and obligation of emergency funds; from George L. Berry (Division Administrator, NLB and President, International Pressmen's and Assistants' Union) to Walter C. Teagle (Chairman, Industrial Advisory Board and President, Standard Oil Company) in regard to Teagle's paper "Employee Representation and Collective Bargaining", and the passage of the National Industrial Recovery Act (NIRA); Wagner's demand for a written agreement in the Pierson Manufacturing Company case; Houde Engineering Corporation's refusal to meet the United Automobile Workers Federal Labor Union (UAW) no. 18839 representatives; from the Chicago Regional Labor Board to the NLB concerning Communist controlled unions and majority rule; from Wolf to the Chicago Regional Labor Board on the representation election process, and majority rule; from Milton Handler to the Chicago Regional Labor Board in regard to collective bargaining, written agreements (Harriman Case), and union recognition; from Wagner to the Regional Labor Boards announcing members of the State Directors of the National Emergency Council and their relation to regional boards; from the Attorney General to the President about Executive Order no. 6580; from Swope to Wagner in regard to state directors' report "Public Attitude toward the NRA Program."			
	Sub-Series 2. REPORTS AND OFFICIAL DOCUMENTS 1934-35			
1935	Radio reports; General Instructions for Regional Labor Boards; summary of NLB activities		Box 1	Folder 8
1933–1934	Reports		Box 1	Folder 9
	National Recovery Administration (NRA) release no.2678, NLB transmits Budd case to compliance director; 4th draft of the Wagner Act by Leon Keyserling; confidential advice from William Leiserson to regional boards; 6th draft of the Wagner Act; 1st draft of the procedural section of the Wagner Bill by Charles Wyzanski (Counsel for the Dept. of Labor); NRA release no. 3414, NLB reports to the President; NRA release no. 4118, NLB issues election regulations; statement of jurisdiction and powers of the NLB and regional labor boards; preliminary report on Board's handling 7a cases; 4 part report by Emily C. Brown on elections conducted by the NLB and regional boards 8/5/33–7/9/34; NLB principles with applicable cases 8/5/33–7/9/34.			
	The Labor Disputes Act no. S.2926, undated.		Box 1	Folder 10

Example 5. Multilevel Control at the Item Level

This example illustrates description at the item level, which tends to be most frequently employed in small collections consisting of items that are all esteemed to have high value, whether informational or monetary. In some applications of item-level description, individual item entries might also include bioghist, scope and content, or access and use notes.

Item-level description often makes sense also in small collections that have no apparent hierarchical structure, often referred to as "flat" collections. In such cases, the collection may be best described simply as an arbitrary sequence of individually described items with no attempt at grouping the materials intellectually. This example diverges from that category in that the items are divided into a few files based on material types.

(Source: UCLA Chicano Studies Research Center)

Title:	Ester Hernandez Papers
Identifier/Call Number:	CSRC.0047
Language of Material:	English
Physical Description:	0.4 linear feet (1 box)
Date (inclusive):	1972–2005
Abstract:	Collection of articles about Ester Hernandez and her artwork. Collection includes various post cards, gallery cards and other Illustrations of Hernandez's art.
Creator:	Hernandez, Ester 1944–

BIOGRAPHY

Ester Hernandez is one of the pioneers of the Chicano art movement. She grew up in the migrant farm-working community of the central San Joaquin Valley of California and she experienced firsthand the farm-worker's struggle. She was surrounded by artisans within her family: her mother continued the family tradition of embroidery from Central Mexico; her grandfather was a master carpenter and made religious sculpture in his spare time; Ester's father was an amateur photographer and visual artist. Through her personal involvement with the farm-worker community, Ester developed a great interest in community arts, committing herself to "visually depict the dignity, strength, experiences and dreams of Latina women through printmaking and pastels." (E.H.) Ester Hernandez has created art relating to farm-workers, pesticides, laborers, women's issues, civil rights and social justice. Her work has been exhibited at the Smithsonian Institution in Washington D.C., UCLA, Los Angeles County Museum of Art, The Mexican Museum, Galería de la Raza and Internationally. As of this writing in 2006, Ester Hernandez teaches and manages at Creativity Explored, a San Francisco art production and education center for developmentally-challenged adults.

SCOPE AND CONTENT

This collection of articles, press reviews, exhibition catalog excerpts, and illustrations about Ester Hernandez and her artwork was compiled by the artist herself.

Box 1, Folder 1. Articles on Ester Hernandez 1990–2004

"Sun Mad" from *Mixed Blessings* by Lucy Lippard, 1990

Ester Hernandez, Chicana, brief description

Revista Literaria de el Tecolote, cover art Malathion Spraying, vol 3, no. 3

Ester Hernandez, brief bio from Hispanic Research Center, 2000

"Ester Hernandez, Frida and Me," brief introduction from unknown source

"Decontaminating Amerika: The Art of Ester Hernandez" by Juan Felipe Herrera

"Chicanas Speak Out, " by Betty A. Brown, *Artweek*, Jan 14, 1984

Ester Hernandez brief intro from SAIIC, vol. 2, no. 3 Spring 1986

"Chicana Artist Ester M. Hernandez: Her Art Stirs Feeling for the Plight of Humanity," *La Ventana* vol. 1, no. 2 May 1987

"The Power of Feminist Art" by Harry Adams from *Challenging Modernism: Facets of Feminist Art*, 1994

"Movement Graphics and Murals" brief article on Las Mujeres Muralistas

"The Art of Provocation, or in Other Words, Ester Hernandez" in *Chicano Visions: American Painters on the Verge* by Cheech Marin, 2002

At Work: The Art of California Labor, Mark Dean Johnson, ed. 2003

"Chicano Art for Our Millenium: Collected Works from the Arizona State University" by Gary Keller, 2004.

Box 1, Folder 2. Press reviews 1974–2001

"Walls with Tongue: Chicano Mural, " Amsterdam (in Dutch),1979

"Women, " *SF Chronicle*, 1974

"An Inside Look at Four Outdoor Murals" by Al Morch, *SF Examiner*, Nov. 1986

"Mural, Mural on the Wall" by Steve Jenkins, *Daily Californian*, Nov. 21, 1986

"Waiting for Eternity" by Mark Leonhart, *Chicago Reader*, July 3, 1987

(Numerous item entries removed for sake of brevity)

Box 1, Folder 3. Exhibitions and events 1992–1997

Heroes and Saints, flyer and postcard copy, 1992.

postcard: The Defiant Eye: Works by Ester Hernandez

postcard: Brava! Women for the Arts Calendar

The Art of Provocation: Ester Hernandez 1995

Mexican Museum membership application

postcard copy: Opening the Window: Examining the Border

Talk Back! The Community Responds to the Permanent Collection Part II, Bronx Museum of the Arts, 1997

exhibition brochure mailer: Ghosts of Little Boy.

APPENDIX D

Example of Full Finding Aid Encoded in EAD

This appendix conveys a full EAD finding aid for a small collection—the Penumbra Theatre Company Records—in two versions. The first version demonstrates the finding aid in its native XML encoding. The second shows it after it has been transformed, utilizing an XSLT stylesheet, into a user-friendly text document.

Note that this example is encoded in EAD2002, rather than the current version, EAD3. It is intended to be illustrative, rather than prescriptive.

(Source: Minnesota Historical Society Manuscript Collections)

Version 1. Raw EAD encoding

```xml
<?xml version="1.0" encoding="UTF-8"?>
<?xml-stylesheet type="text/xsl" href="webead.xsl"?>
<!DOCTYPE ead PUBLIC "+//ISBN 1-931666-00-8//DTD ead.dtd (Encoded Archival
    Description (EAD) Version 2002)//EN" "ead.dtd">

<ead audience="external" relatedencoding="USMARC">
    <eadheader findaidstatus="edited-full-draft" scriptencoding="iso15924"
    dateencoding="iso8601" countryencoding="iso3166-1"
    repositoryencoding="iso15511" langencoding="iso639-2">
        <eadid countrycode="us" mainagencycode="MnHi">P2319</eadid>
        <filedesc>
            <titlestmt>
                <titleproper>PENUMBRA THEATRE:</titleproper>
                <subtitle>An Inventory of Its Records at the Minnesota Historical
                    Society</subtitle>
                <author>Finding aid prepared by Lara D. Friedman~Shedlov.
                    </author>
            </titlestmt>
            <publicationstmt><publisher encodinganalog="Publisher">Minnesota
                Historical Society</publisher><address><addressline>St. Paul
                MN.</addressline></address>
            </publicationstmt>
            <seriesstmt><p>Manuscripts Collection</p></seriesstmt>
        </filedesc>
        <profiledesc>
            <creation>Finding aid encoded by Stephanie Grabowski,
                <date era="ce" calendar="gregorian">April 2, 1999.</date>
            </creation>
            <langusage>Finding aid written in
                <language langcode="eng">English</language>
```

```
        </langusage>
    </profiledesc>
    <revisiondesc><change><date>August 2008</date><item>Converted from EAD
        Version 1.0 to Version 2002 by Monica Manny Ralston, Daniel Sher, and
        Joyce Chapman.</item></change>
    </revisiondesc></eadheader>

<archdesc relatedencoding="MARC" type="inventory" level="collection">
    <did id="a1">
        <head>OVERVIEW</head>
        <repository label="Repository:">Minnesota Historical Society
            </repository>
        <origination label="Creator:" encodinganalog="110">
            <corpname encodinganalog="110" role="creator"> Penumbra Theatre
                Company (Saint Paul, Minn.).
            </corpname>
        </origination>
        <unittitle label="Title:">Theater records.</unittitle>
        <unitdate label="Date:" era="ce" calendar="gregorian"
            normal="1990/1997">1990-1997.</unitdate>
        <abstract label="Abstract:">Minutes, financial statements, and
            other records from the board of the Penumbra Theatre Company, a
            professional African American theater company based in St. Paul,
            Minnesota.</abstract>
        <physdesc label="Quantity:">0.4 cubic feet (1 box).</physdesc>
        <physloc label="Location:">P2319: See <ref target="a9">Detailed
            Description</ref> section for shelf location.</physloc>
    </did>
    <bioghist>
        <head id="a2" altrender="history">HISTORICAL NOTE</head>
        <p>The Penumbra Theatre Company was founded in 1976 by Lou Bellamy,
            a St. Paul resident and a professor in the University of
            Minnesota's theater and dance department. Bellamy was prompted
            to found the theater in large part because of the paucity of
            work available in the Twin Cities area for African American
            performers. Perhaps best known for launching the career of
            Pulitzer Prize-winning playwright August Wilson, the theater's
            mission is to present productions from an African American
            perspective and increase awareness of the contributions of
            African Americans to the American theater tradition. Since its
            inception, the theater has been located in the heart of St.
            Paul's Black community, the Rondo neighborhood, and has hired
            only Black directors, though as much as eighty percent of its
            audience is white.</p>
    </bioghist>
    <relatedmaterial>
        <head id="a5">RELATED MATERIALS</head>
        <p>Programs from several Penumbra Theatre Company productions are
            separately cataloged in the Minnesota Historical Society book
            collection.</p>
    </relatedmaterial>
```

```
<controlaccess>
    <head id="a7">CATALOG HEADINGS</head>
    <p>This collection is indexed under the following headings in the
        catalog of the Minnesota Historical Society. Researchers desiring
        materials about related topics, persons or places should <extref
        linktype="simple" show="new" href="http://mnhs.mnpals.net">search
        the catalog</extref> using these headings.</p>
<controlaccess>
    <head>Topics:</head>
    <subject>African American theater -- Minnesota -- Saint Paul.
        </subject>
    <subject>Theater -- Minnesota -- Saint Paul -- Finance.</subject>
    <subject>Theater audiences -- Minnesota -- Saint Paul.</subject>
    <subject>Theater management -- Minnesota -- Saint Paul.</subject>
</controlaccess>
<controlaccess>
    <head>Person:</head>
    <persname>Bellamy, Lou.</persname>
</controlaccess>
</controlaccess>
<descgrp type="admininfo">
    <head id="a8">ADMINISTRATIVE INFORMATION</head>
    <prefercite>
        <head>Preferred Citation:</head>
        <p><emph render="italic">[Indicate the cited item and/or series
            here].</emph> Penumbra Theatre Company Records. Minnesota
            Historical Society.</p>
        <p><emph render="italic">See the Chicago Manual of Style for
            additional examples.</emph></p>
    </prefercite>
    <acqinfo>
        <head>Accession Information:</head>
        <p>Accession Number: 15,344</p>
    </acqinfo>
    <processinfo>
        <head>Processing Information:</head>
        <p>Processed by: Lara D. Friedman~Shedlov, September 1998</p>
        <p>Catalog ID number: 09-00320304</p>
    </processinfo>
</descgrp>

<dsc type="combined">
    <head id="a9">DETAILED DESCRIPTION</head>
    <c01>
        <did>
            <physloc>P2319</physloc>
            <container>1</container>
            <unittitle>Background information.</unittitle>
        </did>
    </c01>
```

```
            <c01>
               <did>
                  <unittitle>Bylaws, undated.</unittitle>
               </did>
            </c01>
            <c01>
               <did>
                  <unittitle>Annual report, </unittitle>
                  <unitdate era="ce" calendar="gregorian">1996-97.</unitdate>
               </did>
            </c01>
            <c01>
               <did>
                  <unittitle>Board of directors rosters, undated and 1990-
                     1992.</unittitle>
               </did>
            </c01>
            <c01>
               <did>
                  <unittitle>Minutes and related documents, October
                     1990-October 1992, March 1993-October 1993. </unittitle>
                  <physdesc>6 folders</physdesc>
               </did>
               <scopecontent>
                  <p>Includes minutes, financial statements, memoranda,
                     correspondence, reports, and other materials. Minutes
                     document the theater's study and analysis of its audience,
                     funding efforts, and marketing strategies. They also
                     include information on the theater's expansion and
                     reorganization in 1990.</p>
               </scopecontent>
            </c01>
            <c01>
               <did>
                  <unittitle>Newsletters, Summer/Fall 1995.</unittitle>
               </did>
            </c01>
            <c01>
               <did>
                  <unittitle>Audience Survey, Fall 1991.</unittitle>
               </did>
            </c01>
         </dsc>
      </archdesc>
</ead>
```

Version 2. Transformation into Text Document

Penumbra Theatre Company (Saint Paul, Minn.).
An Inventory of Its Records at the Minnesota Historical Society

OVERVIEW

Creator: Penumbra Theatre Company (Saint Paul, Minn.).
Title: Theater records.
Dates: 1990–1997.
Abstract: Minutes, financial statements, and other records from the board of the Penumbra Theatre Company, a professional African American theater company based in St. Paul, Minnesota.
Quantity: 0.4 cubic feet (1 box).
Location: P2319: See Detailed Description section for shelf location.

HISTORICAL NOTE

The Penumbra Theatre Company was founded in 1976 by Lou Bellamy, a St. Paul resident and a professor in the University of Minnesota's theater and dance department. Bellamy was prompted to found the theater in large part because of the paucity of work available in the Twin Cities area for African American performers. Perhaps best known for launching the career of Pulitzer Prize-winning playwright August Wilson, the theater's mission is to present productions from an African American perspective and increase awareness of the contributions of African Americans to the American theater tradition. Since its inception, the theater has been located in the heart of St. Paul's Black community, the Rondo neighborhood, and has hired only Black directors, though as much as eighty percent of its audience is white.

ADMINISTRATIVE INFORMATION

Preferred Citation:

[Indicate the cited item and/or series here]. Penumbra Theatre Company Records. Minnesota Historical Society.
See the Chicago Manual of Style for additional examples.

Accession Information:

Accession Number: 15,344

Processing Information:

Processed by: Lara D. Friedman-Shedlov, September 1998
Catalog ID number: 09-00320304

DETAILED DESCRIPTION

Location	Box	
P2319	1	Background information. Bylaws, undated. Annual report, 1996–97. Board of directors rosters, undated and 1990–1992.

Minutes and related documents, October 1990–
October 1992, March 1993–October 1993. 6 folders
Includes minutes, financial statements, memoranda, correspondence, reports, and other materials. Minutes document the theater's study and analysis of its audience, funding efforts, and marketing strategies. They also include information on the theater's expansion and reorganization in 1990.
Newsletters, Summer/Fall 1995.
Audience Survey, Fall 1991.

RELATED MATERIALS

Programs from several Penumbra Theatre Company productions are separately cataloged in the Minnesota Historical Society book collection.

CATALOG HEADINGS

This collection is indexed under the following headings in the catalog of the Minnesota Historical Society. Researchers desiring materials about related topics, persons or places should search the catalog using these headings.

Topics:
African American theater—Minnesota—Saint Paul.
Theater—Minnesota—Saint Paul—Finance.
Theater audiences—Minnesota—Saint Paul.
Theater management—Minnesota—Saint Paul.

Persons:
Bellamy, Lou.

APPENDIX E

Example of MARC21 Record

Following are two expressions of the same collection-level catalog record for a large manuscript collection of organizational records, the first in its machine-readable form and the second in a human-readable form. Note that, even for a sizable collection, a collection-level record can be very brief and still achieve its discovery and identification objectives. This catalog record is the discovery layer of a typical two-stage description system in which the collection is discovered, via the MARC record, presumably in an OPAC, which then links out to the EAD finding aid for rich, text-searchable descriptions of its component parts.

All of the DACS-supported data elements in the MARC record can be repurposed to form the collection-level (<archdesc>) portion of an EAD finding aid for the collection. The EAD finding aid for the collection is available at http://www2.mnhs.org/library/findaids/00229.xml.

MARC21 Record in Native Encoded Format

FMT	MX
LDR	cpca 2200997 i 4500
001	001732914
005	20100127103352.0
008	960320i19661990mnu eng d
0359	$a 313844796
035	$a ocn313844796
040	$a MHS $e dacs $c MHS $d OCLCQ $d MHS
043	$a n-us-mn $a n-us-sd
049	$a MHSQ
052	$a 4144 $b S4
099	$a See Finding Aid
110 2	$a Wounded Knee Legal Defense/Offense Committee, $e creator.
245 10	$a Wounded Knee Legal Defense/Offense Committee records, $f 1966–1990 $g (bulk 1973–1976).
300	$a 142.0 cubic feet (149 boxes).
351	$a These documents are organized into the following sections: Events and Legal Proceedings; WKLD/OC Administration; Press Coverage; Audiovisual Materials; Newspaper Clippings; Transcripts.
506 1	$a Masters and submasters of certain audio and visual recordings are closed to general use. User copies of most of those materials are available in the collection's Audio-visual Materials section.
520	$a Records documenting the history, internal operation, and legal practice of a committee established by lawyers, legal workers, and others dedicated to the

	defense of activists involved in the American Indian protest movement of the 1970s.
520 8	$b The records include correspondence, legal documents, evidentiary material, indexes, minutes, financial records, press releases, newspaper clippings, audiovisual materials, and printed matter.
520 8	$b The bulk of the records relate to the occupation of Wounded Knee (S.D.) by American Indian activists (February–May 1973) and to the massive and complex legal proceedings that followed (1973–1976). Events leading up to and following the occupation are also documented, including a protest riot in Custer, S.D. (February 6, 1973), the widespread harassment and violence on the Pine Ridge Reservation after the occupation, a shoot-out at Oglala, S.D. (June 26, 1975), which resulted in the death of two FBI agents, and the legal actions taken in order to prohibit the publication of author Peter Matthiessen's account of the Oglala incident.
555 0	$a Finding aid available in the repository and on the web $u http://www.mnhs.org/library/findaids/00229.xml
541	$e Many $3 Records $a See accession file 11,994
600 10	$a Banks, Dennis.
600 10	$a Means, Russell, $d 1939–
600 10	$a Crow Dog, Leonard, $d 1942–
600 10	$a Camp, Carter.
600 10	$a Holder, Stanley.
600 10	$a Bellecourt, Clyde H. $q (Clyde Howard), $d 1936–
600 10	$a Bellecourt, Vernon.
600 10	$a Bissonette, Pedro.
600 10	$a Bad Heart Bull, Sarah $x Trials, litigation, etc.
600 10	$a Peltier, Leonard $x Trials, litigation, etc.
600 10	$a Aquash, Anna Mae, $d 1945–1976.
600 10	$a Robideau, Robert E. $x Trials, litigation, etc.
600 10	$a Marshall, Richard $x Trials, litigation, etc.
600 10	$a Matthiessen, Peter $x Trials, litigation, etc.
600 10	$a Ellison, Bruce $x Trials, litigation, etc.
600 10	$a Wilson, Dick.
600 10	$a Janklow, William.
610 20	$a American Indian Movement.
610 20	$a Oglala Sioux Civil Rights Organization.
610 10	$a United States. $b Bureau of Indian Affairs.
610 10	$a United States. $b Federal Bureau of Investigation.
650 0	$a Indians of North America $x Government relations $y 1934–
650 0	$a Indians of North America $x Civil rights.
650 0	$a Oglala Indians $x Government relations.

MARC21 Record Output as Text Document

Location: Minnesota Historical Society Manuscripts
Author: Wounded Knee Legal Defense/Offense Committee, *creator*.
Title: Wounded Knee Legal Defense/Offense Committee records, 1966–1990 (bulk 1973–1976).
Physical Details: 142.0 cubic feet (149 boxes).

ARRANGEMENT

These documents are organized into the following sections: Events and Legal Proceedings; WKLD/OC Administration; Press Coverage; Audiovisual Materials; Newspaper Clippings; Transcripts.

ACCESS RESTRICTIONS

Masters and submasters of certain audio and visual recordings are closed to general use. User copies of most of those materials are available in the collection's Audio-visual Materials section.

SUMMARY

Records documenting the history, internal operation, and legal practice of a committee established by lawyers, legal workers, and others dedicated to the defense of activists involved in the American Indian protest movement of the 1970s.

The records include correspondence, legal documents, evidentiary material, indexes, minutes, financial records, press releases, newspaper clippings, audiovisual materials, and printed matter.

The bulk of the records relate to the occupation of Wounded Knee (S.D.) by American Indian activists (February–May 1973) and to the massive and complex legal proceedings that followed (1973–1976). Events leading up to and following the occupation are also documented, including a protest riot in Custer, S.D. (February 6, 1973), the widespread harassment and violence on the Pine Ridge Reservation after the occupation, a shoot-out at Oglala, S.D. (June 26, 1975), which resulted in the death of two FBI agents, and the legal actions taken in order to prohibit the publication of author Peter Matthiessen's account of the Oglala incident.

FINDING AIDS

Finding aid available in the repository (filed under Wounded Knee Legal Defense/Offense Committee) and on the web http://www.mnhs.org/library/findaids/00229.xml

NAME SUBJECTS

Banks, Dennis.
Means, Russell, 1939–
Crow Dog, Leonard, 1942–
Camp, Carter.
Holder, Stanley.
Bellecourt, Clyde H. (Clyde Howard), 1936–
Bellecourt, Vernon.
Bissonette, Pedro.

Bad Heart Bull, Sarah—Trials, litigation, etc.
Peltier, Leonard—Trials, litigation, etc.
Aquash, Anna Mae, 1945–1976.
Robideau, Robert E.—Trials, litigation, etc.
Marshall, Richard—Trials, litigation, etc.
Matthiessen, Peter—Trials, litigation, etc.
Ellison, Bruce—Trials, litigation, etc.
Wilson, Dick.
Janklow, William.

TOPICAL SUBJECTS

American Indian Movement.
Oglala Sioux Civil Rights Organization.
United States. Bureau of Indian Affairs.
United States. Federal Bureau of Investigation.
United States. Marshals Service.
Indians of North America—Government relations—1934–
Indians of North America—Civil rights.
Oglala Indians—Government relations.
Oglala Indians—Claims.
Oglala Indians—Criminal justice, Administration of.
Oglala Indians—Public opinion.
Tribal government—South Dakota—Pine Ridge Indian Reservation.
Government, Resistance to—United States.
Trials (Conspiracy)
Trials (Political crimes and offenses)
Political crimes and offenses—Investigation.
Defense (Criminal procedure)
Jury selection.
Riots—South Dakota—Custer.
Riots—South Dakota—Sioux Falls.
Justice, Administration of—Political aspects—United States.
Political persecution—South Dakota—Pine Ridge Indian Reservation.
Civil-military relations—United States.
Trials (Riots)

GEOGRAPHICAL LOCATIONS

Pine Ridge Indian Reservation (S.D.)
Rosebud Indian Reservation (S.D.)
Wounded Knee (S.D.) – History—Indian occupation, 1973.
Oglala (S.D.)
South Dakota—Race relations.

FORM/GENRE HEADINGS

Photographs.
Sound recordings.
Video recordings.

AUTHORS

Tilsen, Kenneth E., 1927–
Kunstler, William Moses, 1919–.
Leventhal, Larry B.
Thorne, John.
Robideau, Ramon A., 1924–.
Lane, Mark.
Beeler, Joseph.

Uniform Title: Voices from Wounded Knee, 1973, in the words of the participants.
System Number: 313844796

APPENDIX F

Crosswalks between Descriptive Standards

This set of crosswalks, which is borrowed from the current DACS standard, represents the relationships between DACS information elements and the analogous elements in ISAAR(CPF), EAC-CPF, EAD, MARC21, and ISAD(G). It is intended to help you understand the relationships between these standards and to visualize how to encode DACS information in a structured finding aid. Although these crosswalks were accurate in January 2018, standards are in continuous maintenance. Therefore, you should consult the latest version of DACS at https://github.com/saa-ts-dacs/dacs.

DACS	ISAAR(CPF)	EAC-CPF
Chapter 2 Identity Elements		
2.6 Name of Creator(s)	5.1 Identity area	<identity>
2.7 Administrative/Biographical History	5.2.2 History	<biogHist>
2.7.13 Names	5.1.2 Authorized form(s) of name	<nameEntry> or <nameEntryParallel> with <authorizedForm>
2.7.14 Family information	5.2.7 Internal structure/Genealogy	<structureOrGenealogy>
2.7.15 Dates	5.2.1 Dates of existence	<existDates>
2.7.16 Place of residence	5.2.3 Places	<place> or <places>
2.7.17 Education	5.2.2 History	<biogHist>
2.7.18 Occupation, life, and activities	5.2.5 Functions, occupations, and activities	<biogHist>
2.7.19 Other relationships	5.2.8 General context	<relations>
2.7.20 Family relationships	5.2.7 Internal structure/Genealogy	<cpfRelation cpfRelationType="family">
2.7.21 Other significant information	5.2.9 Other significant information	<generalContext>
2.7.22–23 Administrative history	5.2.2 History	<biogHist>
2.7.24 Dates of founding and/or dissolution	5.2.1 Dates of existence	<existDates>
2.7.25 Geographical areas	5.2.3 Places	<place> or <places>
2.7.26 Mandate	5.2.6 Mandates/Sources of authority	<mandate> or <mandates>
2.7.27 Functions	5.2.5 Functions, occupations, and activities	<function> or <functions>,<occupation> or <occupations>
2.7.28 Administrative structure	5.2.7 Internal structure/Genealogy	<structureOrGenealogy>
2.7.29 Predecessor and successor bodies	5.2.2 History	<cpfRelation cpfRelationType="temporal-earlier"> or "temporallater">
2.7.30 Amalgamations and mergers	5.2.2 History	<cpfRelation cpfRelationType="[value]">

(cont.)

DACS	ISAAR(CPF)	EAC-CPF
2.7.31 Name changes	5.2.2 History	<cpfRelation cpfRelationType="[value]">
2.7.32 Names of officers	5.2.2 History	
2.7.33 Other significant information	5.2.8 General context	<generalContext>
Part II: Chapter 9 Archival Authority Records / Chapter 10 Form of the Name		
10.1 Authorized Form of the Name	5.1.2 Authorized form(s) of name	<nameEntry> or <nameEntryParallel> with<authorizedForm>
10.2 Type of Entity	5.1.1 Type of entity	<entityType>
10.3 Variant Forms of Names	5.1.3 Parallel forms of name	<nameEntryParallel>
10.3.2 Standardized form of the name according to other rules	5.1.4 Standardized forms of name according to other rules	<nameEntry> or <nameEntryParallel> with<authorizedForm>
10.3.3 Other forms of name	5.1.5 Other forms of name	<nameEntry> or <nameEntryParallel> with<alternativeForm>
10.4 Identifiers for Corporate Bodies	5.1.6 Identifiers for corporate bodies	<entityID>
Chapter 11 Description of the Person, Family, or Corporate Body		
11.1 Dates of Existence	5.2.1 Dates of existence	<existDate>
11.2 Historical Summary	5.2.2 History	<biogHist>
11.3 Places	5.2.3 Places	<place> or <places>
11.4 Legal Status	5.2.4 Legal Status	<legalStatus> or <legalStatuses>
11.5 Functions, Occupations, and Activities	5.2.5 Functions, occupations, and activities	<function> or <functions>,<occupation> or <occupations>
11.6 Mandates/Source of Authority	5.2.6 Mandates/Sources of authority	<mandate> or <mandates>
11.7 Internal Structure/ Genealogy	5.2.7 Internal structure/Genealogy	<structureOrGenealogy>
Chapter 12 Related Corporate Bodies, Persons, and Families		
12.1–12.2 Names/Identifiers of Related Corporate Bodies, Persons, or Families and Type of Related Entity	5.3.1 Names/identifiers of related corporate bodies, persons or families	<cpfRelation> and <entityType>
12.3 Nature of Relationship	5.3.2 Category of relationship	<cpfRelation cpfRelationType="[value]">
12.3 Nature of Relationship	5.3.3 Description of the relationship	<objectXMLWrap> or <objectBinWrap> or <relationEntry>
12.4 Dates of the Relationship	5.3.4 Dates of the relationship	<cpfRelation>/<date> or <dateRange> or <dateSet>
Chapter 13 Authority Record Management		
13.1 Repository Code	5.4.2 Institution identifiers	<maintenanceAgency/agencyCode and/or agencyName>
13.2 Authority Record Identifier	5.4.1 Authority record identifier	<recordId>
13.3 Rules or Conventions	5.4.3 Rules and/or conventions	<conventionDeclaration>
13.4 Status	5.4.4 Status	<maintenanceStatus>
13.5 Level of Detail	5.4.5 Level of detail	<localControl>
13.6 Date(s) of Authority Record Creation and Revision	5.4.6 Dates of creation, revision, or deletion	<maintenanceEvent>/<eventDateTime>

(cont.)

DACS	ISAAR(CPF)	EAC-CPF
13.7 Languages or Scripts	5.4.7 Languages and scripts	<languageDeclaration>
13.8 Sources	5.4.8 Sources	<sources>
13.9 Maintenance Information	5.4.9 Maintenance notes	<maintenanceEvent>/ <maintenanceDescription>
Chapter 14 Related Archival Materials and Other Resources		
14.1 Identifiers and Titles of Related Resources	6.1 Identifiers and titles of related resources	<objectXMLWrap> or <objectBinWrap> or <relationEntry>
14.2 Types of Related Resources	6.2 Types of related resources	<resourceRelation xlink:role="[value]">
14.3 Nature of Relationship to Related Resources	6.3 Nature of relationships	<resourceRelation resourceRelationType="[value]">
14.4 Dates of Related Resources and/or Relationships	6.4 Dates of related resources and/or relationships	<resourceRelation>/<date> or <dateRange> or <dateSet>

DACS	EAD	MARC21
1 Level of Description	<archdesc> and <c> LEVEL attribute	351$c
2 Identity Elements		
2.1.3 Local identifier	<unitid>	099, 090
2.1.4 Repository identifier	<unitid> REPOSITORYCODE attribute	040$a
2.1.5 Country identifier	<unitid> COUNTRYCODE attribute	The MARC21 format does not contain a straightforward mapping for this DACS subelement value.
2.2 Name and Location of Repository	<repository>	852, 524 (if the preferred citation indicates both the name and location of the repository)
2.3 Title	<unittitle>	245$a
2.4 Date	<unitdate>	245$f, 245$g
2.5 Extent	<physdesc> and subelements<extent>, <dimensions>, <genreform>, <physfacet>	300$a and potentially other subfields
3 Content and Structure Elements		
3.1 Scope and Content	<scopecontent>	520
3.2 System of Arrangement	<arrangement>	351
4 Access Elements		
4.1 Conditions Governing Access	<accessrestrict>	506
4.2 Physical Access	<accessrestrict>, <phystech>,<physloc>	340, 506
4.3 Technical Access	<phystech>	340, 538
4.4 Conditions Governing Reproduction and Use	<userestrict>	540
4.5 Languages and Scripts of the Material	<langmaterial>	546
4.6 Finding Aids	<otherfindaid>	555
5 Acquisition and Appraisal Elements		
5.1 Custodial History	<custodhist>	561
5.2 Immediate Source of Acquisition	<acqinfo>	541
5.3 Appraisal, Destruction, and Scheduling Information	<appraisal>	583
5.4 Accruals	<accruals>	584
6 Related Materials Elements		
6.1 Existence and Location of Originals	<originalsloc>	535
6.2 Existence and Location of Copies	<altformavail>	530, 533
6.3 Related Archival Materials	<relatedmaterial> <separatedmaterial>	544
6.4 Publication Note	<p> or<bibref>	581
7 Notes[1]	<odd>, <note>	500
8 Description Control	<processinfo>	583
8.1.4 Rules or conventions	<descrules>	040$e
8.1.5 Archivist and date	<processinfo><p><date>	583

DACS	ISAD(G)
1 Levels of Description	3.1.4 Level of description
2 Identity Elements	
2.1 Reference Code	3.1.1 Reference code(s)
2.3 Title	3.1.2 Title
2.4 Date	3.1.3 Dates
2.5 Extent	3.1.5 Extent and medium of the unit
2.6 Name of Creator(s)	3.2.1 Name of creator
2.7 Administrative/Biographical History	3.2.2 Administrative/Biographical history
3 Content and Structure Elements	
3.1 Scope and Content	3.3.1 Scope and content
3.2 System of Arrangement	3.3.4 System of arrangement
4 Access Elements	
4.1 Conditions Governing Access	3.4.1 Conditions governing access
4.2 Physical Access	3.4.4 Physical characteristics and technical requirements
4.3 Technical Access	3.4.4 Physical char. and technical req.
4.4 Conditions Governing Reproduction and Use	3.4.2 Conditions governing reproduction
4.5 Languages and Scripts of the Material	3.4.3 Language/scripts of material
4.6 Finding Aids	3.4.5 Finding aids
5 Acquisition and Appraisal Elements	
5.1 Custodial History	3.2.3 Archival history
5.2 Immediate Source of Acquisition	3.2.4 Immediate source of acquisition
5.3 Appraisal, Destruction, and Scheduling Information	3.3.2 Appraisal, destruction, scheduling
5.4 Accruals	3.3.3 Accruals
6 Related Materials Elements	
6.1 Existence and Location of Originals	3.5.1 Existence and location of originals
6.2 Existence and Location of Copies	3.5.2 Existence and location of copies
6.3 Related Archival Materials	3.5.3 Related units of description
6.4 Publication Note	3.5.4 Publication note
7 Notes	3.6.1 Note
8 Description Control	3.7.1 Archivist's note
8.1.4 Rules or conventions	3.7.2 Rules or conventions
8.1.5 Archivist and date	3.7.3 Date(s) of descriptions
Part II: Introduction to Describing Creators	
10 Form of the Name	
11 Description of the Person, Family, or Corporate Body	3.2.1 Name of creator
12 Related Corporate Bodies, Persons, and Families	3.2.2 Administrative/Biographical history
13 Authority Record Management	
14 Related Archival Materials and Other Resources	

NOTE

[1] Notes should only be encoded using the more generic <odd> and <note> elements (EAD) or 500 field (MARC21) when they do not correspond to a more specific EAD element or MARC21 field.

APPENDIX G

Recommended Reading: Archival Arrangement and Description

General Works

Berner, Richard C. *Archival Theory and Practice in the United States: A Historical Analysis.* Seattle: University of Washington Press, 1983.
Berner delivers a thorough summary of the historical evolution of archival description in the United States up to the point when the pace and direction of change became dramatically influenced by both standards development and technology.

Gracy, David B. II, *An Introduction to Archives and Manuscripts.* New York, [c. 1981].
A brief, solid overview of archives and their management, including practical processing advice.

O'Toole, James M., and Richard J. Cox, *Understanding Archives and Manuscripts.* Chicago: Society of American Archivists, 2006.
A fundamental work whose primary purpose is to explain archives and archivists to external stakeholders, students, and new professionals. Its treatment of arrangement and description is minimal, but it provides deep and articulate discussions of the core values and principles undergirding this work.

Schellenberg, T. R. *The Management of Archives.* New York: Columbia University Press, 1965.
The assistant archivist of the United States and a leading archival theorist offers historical and conceptual background about American archives, devoting considerable attention to archival processing. Although some of the practical steps and products are dated, he thoroughly grounds his prescriptions in archival theory.

Yakel, Elizabeth. *Starting an Archives.* Chicago: Society of American Archivists and Scarecrow Press, 1994.
In this general manual for novice archivists initiating practice in a new archives administrative unit, chapter 6 guides the practitioner in understanding the essentials of arrangement and description and in establishing a processing regimen.

Theoretical Works

Abraham, Terry. "Oliver W. Holmes Revisited: Five Levels of Arrangement and Description in Practice." *American Archivist* 54, no. 3 (1991): 370–77.
Abraham notes that Holmes's five levels have failed to impact modern descriptive practices, and he especially points to the failure of automated systems to produce truly hierarchical description systems within the structure afforded by institutional and consortial databases.

Bailey, Jefferson. "Disrespect Des Fonds: Rethinking Arrangement and Description in Born-Digital Archives." *Archive Journal*, no. 3 (2013). http://www.archivejournal.net/essays/disrespect-des-fonds-rethinking-arrangement-and-description-in-born-digital-archives.

In a thought-provoking piece, Bailey details the social and material conditions that produced the theory of *respect des fonds* and analyzes the theory's complex practical implementations, the emergence of alternate models, and how born-digital materials expose the theory's analog origins and limitations. He concludes, among other things, that *respect des fonds* was a practical creature of its times—a solution to an immediate and pressing problem—and perhaps does not need to be treated with reverence in a digital age.

Duff, Wendy, and Verne Harris. "Stories and Names: Archival Description as Narrating Records and Constructing Meanings." *Archival Science* 2, no. 3 (2002): 263–85.

The authors examine the function of archival description as an activity that creates meaning, rather than simply relating meaning that intrinsically exists in the archival records being described.

Eastwood, Terry. "Putting the Parts of the Whole Together: Systematic Arrangement of Archives." *Archivaria* 50 (Fall 2000). http://archivaria.ca/index.php/archivaria/article/view/12767/13959, captured at https://perma.cc/J23R-B6G4.

Eastwood reexamines the principle-based rules that produce systematic arrangement, distinguishing between external structures (activities) and internal structures (documents). He emphasizes that arrangement is fundamentally a process of identifying relationships, not one of physically sequencing documents. He also examines the problem of *fonds*-level control as opposed to series-level control.

Gilliland, Anne J. *Conceptualizing 21st-Century Archives.* Chicago: Society of American Archivists, 2014.

An archival educator examines how archival paradigms are changing in the face of societal and technological disruptions. Chapters 4 and 5, specifically, treat archival description, including the evolution of standards, impacts of automation, and descriptive metadata in a networked world.

Holmes, Oliver W. "Archival Arrangement—Five Different Options at Five Different Levels." In *A Modern Archives Reader*, edited by Maygene F. Daniels and Timothy Walch, 162–80. Washington, DC: National Archives Trust Fund Board, 1984). Originally published in *American Archivist* 27, no. 1 (1964).

Holmes's classic explanation of the five levels of arrangement—repository, record group, series, file, item—as practiced at the US National Archives, which established it as an important element in arrangement theory.

Light, Michelle, and Tom Hyry. "Colophons and Annotations: New Directions for the Finding Aid." *American Archivist* 65, no. 2 (2002): 216–30.

Grappling with the problem of perspective in archival finding aids (i.e., finding aids tend to represent one perspective on the collection developed by the original processor), the authors argue the need for accommodating multiple perspectives that might result from later interactions with the materials by users and other archivists. They make a case for the use of colophons and annotations as tools to capture and present additional perspectives.

Lyons, Bertram. *Writing Archives/Crafting Order: A Critique on the Longstanding Archival Practices of Arrangement and Description.* MA thesis, University of Kansas, 2009. 145 pp.

Lyons analyzes traditional assumptions about archives and the long-standing archival descriptive practices that resulted. In so doing, he interrogates such notions as our ability to establish a "neutral voice" in archival description, the preferencing of written over oral sources, and "authority" in archives as representing a distinctly Western and hegemonic set of assumptions. The author's objective "is to illuminate the ambiguities, the complexities, the practices, the standards and the layers of interpretation related to processing archival collections—writing archives and creating order."

MacNeil, Heather. "Picking Our Text: Archival Description, Authenticity, and the Archivist as Editor." *American Archivist* 68, no. 2 (2005): 264–78.

MacNeil provides a critical examination of the relationship between archival description and the archival concept of authenticity, comparing along the way the authenticating function of archival description with that of textual criticism.

Meehan, Jennifer. "Making the Leap from Parts to Whole: Evidence and Inference in Archival Arrangement and Description." *American Archivist* 72, no. 1 (2009): 72–90.

The author considers the extent to which the archivist's description of records is based on evidence and to what extent it is based on inference. She assesses the resulting speculative nature of the analytical process in description and the active role of the archivist in shaping the records.

Riley, Jenn, and Kelcy Shepherd. "A Brave New World: Archivists and Shareable Descriptive Metadata." *American Archivist* 72, no. 1 (2009): 91–112.

The authors argue for the value of truly sharable archival metadata and also outline recommendations for action by the archival community to make it a reality.

Schellenberg, T. R. "Archival Principles of Arrangement." In *A Modern Archives Reader*, edited by Maygene F. Daniels and Timothy Walch, 149–61. Washington, DC: National Archives Trust Fund Board, 1984. Originally published in *American Archivist* 24, no. 1 (January 1961).

In this article, Schellenberg distills the arrangement principles set forth in greater detail in his monographs on archives management.

———. *Modern Archives: Principles and Techniques.* Chicago: University of Chicago Press, 1956.

A series of lectures presented to Australian archivists encapsulate Schellenberg's thinking about the nature and management of archives, as well as modern records management. Chapters 14 and 15 describe principles of archival arrangement and description as practiced in Europe and the United States.

Scott, Peter. "The Record Group Concept: A Case for Abandonment." *American Archivist* 29, no. 4 (1966): 493–504.

Scott here presents the provocative idea that the *fonds*-based system of arrangement has become an impediment in arranging archives, the essential problem being that the activities that form the documentary focus in archives migrate from entity to entity over the course of their existence. In effect, they may belong to multiples *fonds* over time. The solution is to treat the series, which is coterminous with the activity, as the essential building block of archival arrangement. This notion became a guiding principle in Australian government archives and influenced American archival thought.

Descriptive Standards and Practices

Chapman, Joyce Celeste. "Observing Users: An Empirical Analysis of User Interaction with Online Finding Aids." *Journal of Archival Organization* 8 (2010).
The author conducts a rigorous study of real-time user interactions with online finding aids, pointing out the areas in which the finding aids succeed and fail in their goals of explaining the content and context of archival collections and enabling user access.

Combs Michele, Mark A. Matienzo, Merrilee Proffitt, and Lisa Spiro. *Over, Under, Around, and Through: Getting around Barriers to EAD Implementation.* Dublin, OH: OCLC Research, 2010. http://www.oclc.org/content/dam/research/publications/library/2010/2010-04.pdf, captured at https://perma.cc/NAH7-Z936.
Archivists attempting to begin encoding and publishing their finding aids in EAD can face a number of hurdles, some of them political and some technical. This brief report identifies practical strategies for overcoming resistance and moving EAD efforts forward.

Describing Archives: A Content Standard, 2nd. ed. Chicago: Society of American Archivists, 2013, xxiv. 172 pp. https://www2.archivists.org/standards/DACS.
This is the most recent version of the content standard originally adopted by the Society of American Archivists in 2004 and now under continuous maintenance by its Technical Subcommittee on *Describing Archives: A Content Standard.*

Dooley, Jackie M, ed. *Encoded Archival Description: Context, Theory, and Case Studies.* Chicago: Society of American Archivists, 1998.
This very helpful work reprints the twelve articles that comprise volume 60, numbers 3 and 4 of *American Archivist,* which was devoted to familiarizing archivists with the newly adopted EAD standard. The first six articles explore the context and theory underlying EAD as a descriptive standard, and the rest consist of case studies showing the standard in practice among early adopters.

Encoded Archival Working Group of the Society of American Archivists. *Encoded Archival Description: Application Guidelines*, ver. 1.0. Chicago: Society of American Archivists, 1999. 308 pp.
As the title suggests, this work is essentially a manual of practice to help archivists put the EAD standard into practice. It explains the SGML/XML encoding standard behind EAD, the EAD elements in practice, how to author and publish EAD finding aids, examples of encoded finding aids, and crosswalks between EAD and other descriptive standards. It is somewhat dated, focusing as it does on version 1.0, and much of its relevant content has since migrated into the EAD resources section of the SAA Standards Portal.

Evans, Max. "Archives of the People, By the People, and For the People." *American Archivist* 70, no. 2 (2007): 387–400.
Evans proposes a radical rethinking of how we perform arrangement and description in an emerging world where users expect on-demand access to collection materials. He proposes a "commons-based peer-production" model in which users and other entities actively participate in deciding what gets digitized or more aggressively processed and then in helping to get the work done.

Fox, Michael J. "Descriptive Cataloging for Archival Materials." *Cataloging & Classification Quarterly* 11 (1990): 17–34.

> Fox, in a work intended to introduce archivists and librarians to the requirements for catalog records for archival holdings, discusses the nature and descriptive needs of archives and manuscripts, the value created by the new APPM cataloging standard, and the relationship of catalog records to other archival findings aids.

Hensen, Steven L. *Archives, Personal Papers, and Manuscripts: A Cataloging Manual for Archival Repositories, Historical Societies, and Manuscript Libraries,* 2nd ed. Chicago: Society of American Archivists, 1989.

> APPM was a pioneering effort that resulted in rules and practices for preparing catalog records for manuscript collections. As the first descriptive standard purpose-built for archival materials, it was the direct precursor to DACS and articulates the reasons for a truly archival approach to descriptive cataloging.

Nimer, Cory L. "Implementing DACS: A Guide to the Archival Content Standard." Module 17 in *Trends in Archival Practice: Putting Standards to Work*, edited by Kris Kiesling and Christopher J. Prom. Chicago: Society of American Archivists, 2017, 7–154.

> The author has created a comprehensive guide aimed at applying the DACS rules to the practical work of creating finding aids. The work provides some useful background on the development of DACS and marches sequentially through the DACS descriptive elements, explaining how to use them in creating EAD, EAC-CPF, or MARC finding aids, and then providing brief encoded examples. An exhaustive bibliography further strengthens the work.

Pitti, Daniel V. "Creator Description: Encoded Archival Context." *Cataloging & Classification Quarterly* 38, nos. 3–4 (2004): 201–26.

> In this articulation of the principles and mechanics behind the initial version of EAC, Pitti discusses the project's evolution and makes the case for the need to describe creators and context as an essential part of archival description.

———, and Wendy M. Duff, eds. *Encoded Archival Description on the Internet.* New York: Haworth Press, 2001.

> The editors include a range of articles on the development and implementation of EAD in varying types of repositories, in consortial projects, and in museums.

Rubenstein, Aaron. "Sharing Archival Metadata." Module 20 in *Trends in Archival Practice: Putting Standards to Work*, edited by Kris Kiesling and Christopher J. Prom. Chicago: Society of American Archivists, 2017, 297–352.

> The author engagingly walks the reader through concepts of structured metadata and how to share it in the current information landscape. He emphasizes the wealth and possibilities of the archival metadata bound up in our finding aids, discusses best practices for sharing it, explains emerging metadata standards like RDF and linked open data, and makes recommendations. It is supplemented with a bibliography and a couple of case studies.

Schaefer, Sibyl, and Janet M. Bunde. "Standards for Archival Description." In *Trends in Archival Practice: Archival Arrangement and Description*, edited and with an introduction by Christopher J. Prom and Thomas J. Frusciano. Chicago: Society of American Archivists, 2013, 9–86.

A thorough and nicely presented introduction to the full suite of archival descriptive standards, as well as some of the most commonly used companion standards. Any reader interested in a deeper understanding of current standards should begin here.

Schaffner, Jennifer. *The Metadata Is the Interface: Better Description for Better Discovery of Archives and Special Collections, Synthesized from User Studies*. Report produced by OCLC Research, 2009, http://www.oclc.org/research/publications/library/2009/2009-06.pdf, captured at https://perma.cc/G48C-QXF8.

The author argues that the structured metadata that currently characterizes our networked description of archival resources does not necessarily help researchers discover those resources in web searches. Her report attempts to synthesize evidence about the descriptive information users say they need for their research.

Shepherd, Kelcy. "Using EAD3." Module 18 in *Trends in Archival Practice: Putting Standards to Work*, edited by Kris Kiesling and Christopher J. Prom. Chicago: Society of American Archivists, 2017, 155–238.

The author contextualizes EAD as a standard, explains the third version and how to migrate finding aids to it from earlier versions, and then walks thoroughly through the important steps of implementation: planning, creating finding aids, transforming and publishing them, and assessing their usability. The work includes helpful case studies, examples of encoded finding aids illustrating the full suite of EAD elements, and a comprehensive list of further readings organized by topic.

Wisser, Katherine M. "Describing Entities and Identities: The Development and Structure of Encoded Archival Context—Corporate Bodies, Persons, and Families." *Journal of Library Metadata* 11 (2011): 166–75.

The chair of SAA's EAC Working Group explains the recently approved standard, *Encoded Archival Context—Corporate Bodies, Persons, and Families*, its historical development, and its potential for expanding and structuring the description of creators in archival finding aids.

———. "Introducing EAC-CPF." Module 19 in *Trends in Archival Practice: Putting Standards to Work*, edited by Kris Kiesling and Christopher J. Prom. Chicago: Society of American Archivists, 2017, 239–96.

The author expands upon her earlier (2011) introduction of EAC-CPF, focusing on its development and its relationships to other archival standards. She explains in some detail the structure of EAC-CPF authority records, recent developments, and their use in current practice. The work is supplemented with a thorough bibliography, some encoded and published authority record examples, and some useful crosswalks between EAC-CPF and other metadata standards.

Methodology

Cocciolo, Anthony. *Moving Image and Sound Collections for Archivists.* Chicago: Society of American Archivists, 2017.

Cocciolo has written a comprehensive and authoritative reference for the management of sound and moving image materials in archives.

Faulder, Erin, Veronica Martzahl, and Eliot Wilczek. "More than a <bioghist> Note: Early Experiences with Implementing EAC-CPF." In *Description: Innovative Practices for Archives and Special Collections*, edited by Kate Theimer, 17–33. Lanham, MD: Rowman and Littlefield, 2014.

Archivists at Tufts University describe the implementation of EAC-CPF at their repository over a multiyear period. They relate their project planning, choice of a system to author and display records, conversion of <bioghist> notes in existing finding aids into full-blown EAC-CPF records, and the use of DACS rules to prepare records for individuals, families, and corporate bodies.

McShea, Megan. *Guidelines for Processing Collections with Audiovisual Material.* Washington, DC: Smithsonian Institution, Archives of American Art, 2015. https://www.aaa.si.edu/documentation/guidelines-for-processing-collections-with-audiovisual-material, captured at https://perma.cc/5JBZ-GD8L.

The author, in this very specialized and extremely useful institutional processing manual, provides a comprehensive guide to processing still images, sound recordings, and moving image materials in archival collections. Chapters treat holdings assessment, levels of processing, rehousing and storage, arrangement, and description. This is a recommended first stop for readers seeking advice on arranging and describing sound and moving image materials.

Santamaria, Daniel A. "Designing Descriptive and Access Systems." In *Trends in Archival Practice: Archival Arrangement and Description*, edited and with an introduction by Christopher J. Prom and Thomas J. Frusciano, 145–215. Chicago: Society of American Archivists, 2013.

Santamaria provides very thorough and helpful guidance on developing local systems to author, manage, and publish archival descriptions. He discusses tools, software applications, and collection management systems in a very accessible way, and he also categorizes the approaches that a repository can take on a scale of low, medium, and high cost and difficulty.

———. *Extensible Processing for Archives and Special Collections: Reducing Processing Backlogs.* Chicago: Neal-Schuman, an imprint of the American Library Association, 2015. 248 pp.

Santamaria argues persuasively (having amassed a great deal of supporting evidence) that archival processing is most successfully approached as an iterative activity in which we arrange and describe collections to an acceptable baseline level, with the understanding that we may perform more intensive remedial actions at any time as new understandings or changing circumstances dictate. He argues for establishing disciplined processing policies at the repository level, recommending workflows that preference creating standardized and structured description, managing archival materials in the aggregate, limiting physical processing, planning future iterative processing based on use statistics and research value, and managing processing holistically.

Southcott, Margaret, Roger Andre, and Neil Thomas. "Theory, Practice and Pragmatism: Arrangement and Description of Personal Papers in the Mortlock Library of South Australia." *Archives and Manuscripts* 24, no. 1 (1996): 102–15.
This case study of practice in an Australian repository emphasizes pragmatic approaches to arrangement and description.

Tansey, Eira. "Step by Step, Stage by Stage: Getting a Diverse Backlog of Legacy Finding Aids Online." In *Description: Innovative Practices for Archives and Special Collections*, edited by Kate Theimer, 53–67. Lanham, MD: Rowman and Littlefield, 2014.
This useful case study from Tulane University describes its project to migrate existing finding aids to an online format and to prepare finding aids for 375 collections lacking them entirely. It is a good study of how archivists planned and implemented their work, and the lessons learned from the project.

Administration and Management

Dean, Pam Hackbart, and Christine de Catanzaro. "The Strongest Link: The Management and Processing of Archival Collections." *Archival Issues* 27, no. 2 (2002): 125–36.
This article focuses on processing planning and management, rather than on the mechanics or "craft" of processing. The authors treat such topics as planning priorities for processing, determining levels of arrangement and description, establishing standards and procedures for processing, and working with accruals.

Handbooks and Manuals

Beinecke Rare Book and Manuscript Library, Yale University. *Processing Manual*. Yale University Libraries, 2015. http://beinecke.library.yale.edu/processing-manual.
A thorough and helpful repository manual of practice focused on advising staff and student workers on all aspects of arrangement and description work. It does a good job in explaining how processors should approach work at each hierarchical level of arrangement.

Brunton, Paul, and Tim Robinson. "Arrangement and Description." In *Keeping Archives*, edited by Judith Ellis, 2nd ed., 222–47. Port Melbourne, Vic.: DW Thorpe, 2000.
Comprehensive and practical guidance on all phases of archives processing from the perspective of the Australian Society of Archivists. Among the notable virtues of this chapter are the authors' use of several case studies to illustrate processing project approaches and decisions, as well as graphic representations of a number of common arrangement alternatives.

Carmicheal, David W. *Organizing Archival Records: A Practical Method of Arrangement and Description for Small Archives*. Lanham, MD: AltaMira Press, 2012.
In this manual copublished with the American Association for State and Local History, Carmicheal provides basic but thorough guidance for practitioners in small repositories. He walks the reader through all the mechanics of arrangement and description, keeping in mind the experience and resources of the small historical societies, local archives, museums, and public libraries that are the heart of his audience. A large section of examples submitted by repositories demonstrates various approaches to constructing finding aids.

Fox, Michael J., and Peter L. Wilkerson. *Introduction to Archival Organization and Description*, edited by Susanne R. Warren. Getty Information Institute, 1998. 58 pp. http://d2aohiyo3d3idm.cloudfront.net/publications/virtuallibrary/0892365455.pdf, captured at https://perma.cc/ZZK9-UGYL.

This brief guide to the basic concepts and approaches to archival arrangement and description is primarily aimed at nonarchival audiences, especially those in the library and museum communities. It presents and explains archival approaches, standards, and tools clearly and briefly and is therefore a helpful guide.

Gracy, David II. *Archives & Manuscripts: Arrangement & Description*. Chicago: Society of American Archivists, 1977.

Although now somewhat dated in its approaches, the initial SAA manual on arrangement and description is still helpful in very briefly explaining the essential parts and pieces of practical processing.

Hunter, Gregory S. *Developing & Maintaining Practical Archives: A How-to-do-it Manual*, 2nd ed., chapters 5, 6, pp. 97–132. New York: Neal-Schuman Publishers, 2003.

True to its title, this very practical guide walks the reader very quickly through principles, approaches, and examples of arrangement and description. Hunter focuses his guidance on the objectives of processing, a very useful and accessible starting place for neophytes.

Lynch, Karen T., and Helen W. Slotkin, with the assistance of Deborah A. Cozort, Mary Jane McCavitt, and Rowland Aertker. *Processing Manual for the Institute Archives and Special Collections, M.I.T. Libraries*. Massachusetts Institute of Technology Libraries, 1981. 61 pp.

This is an excellent local manual for processing archival collections. In addition to emphasizing a practical, sustainable approach to arrangement and description, it also provides an exemplary model for any repository desiring to produce a processing manual for its institution.

Miller, Fredric M., *Arranging and Describing Archives and Manuscripts*. Chicago: Society of American Archivists, 1990. 131 pp.

The second iteration of SAA's arrangement and description manual, like its predecessor by David Gracy, offers a view of approaches and practices of a previous generation, but is still a good source of practical advice on the nuts and bolts of archival processing.

Procter, Margaret, and Michael Cook. *Manual of Archival Description*. 3rd ed. Aldershot, UK: Gower, 2000.

This comprehensive work offers insights into archival description as practiced in the United Kingdom. Notable features include a breakdown of descriptive practice by formats of materials and a typology of archival descriptions.

Roe, Kathleen D. *Fundamentals of Arrangement and Description*. Chicago: Society of American Archivists, 2005.

Roe's manual, the third in SAA's series, remains an excellent manual of practice. It includes very thorough discussions of MARC cataloging and systems of finding aids within repositories, which the present work treats more lightly.

———. *Guidelines for Arrangement and Description of Archives and Manuscripts: A Manual for Historical Records Programs in New York State.* Albany: University of the State of New York, New York State Education Department, and New York State Archives and Records Administration, 1991.

This meticulous and concise manual guides processing practice within a statewide network of government archives. It is a good model for how to draft rules and guidelines to achieve standardization and robust practice within a multiple-repository confederation.

St. Johnsbury Athenaeum Archives, *Archives Processing Manual*, draft 2. May 2001. http://datadrivenarchives.pbworks.com/f/Processing+Manual+St.+Johnsbury+Athenaeum.pdf, captured at https://perma.cc/LS7F-UGZ7.

Taking the previously cited MIT processing manual as its baseline, this manual is also a thorough and practical guide to local practice. It provides a replicable model for repository processing manuals.

Seltzer, Sara, et al. *Archival Processing Manual.* Updated September 24, 2014. University of California, Irvine. Special Collections and Archives. https://staff.lib.uci.edu/departments/sca/docs/Processing_Manual.pdf, captured at https://perma.cc/HDY2-BP26.

This comprehensive and well-written repository processing manual is aimed at local practice, but has sound advice for all processing archivists. Includes (Appendix G) a sample processing workplan.

Performance and Metrics

Abraham, Terry, Stephen E. Balzarini, and Anne Frantilla. "What Is Backlog Is Prologue: A Measurement of Archival Processing." *American Archivist* 48, no. 1 (1985): 31–44.

The authors report the results of one of the earliest examinations of a repository's processing performance, which was conducted to establish baseline results that could be tested and applied to future processing results. They establish variables—collection size, collection era, material formats—against which to measure average processing time per volume of materials. They also preliminarily analyze the performance effect of using word processors, as opposed to typewriters, to record descriptive information.

Bachli, Kelley, James Eason, Michelle Light, Kelly McAnnaney, Daryl Morrison, and David Seubert. *Guidelines for Efficient Archival Processing in the University of California Libraries.* University of California Libraries, September 18, 2012. http://libraries.universityofcalifornia.edu/groups/files/hosc/docs/_Efficient_Archival_Processing_Guidelines_v3-1.pdf, captured at https://perma.cc/NG7X-CUTW.

Although this work might qualify as a repository processing manual, its intent is really to reshape a processing culture throughout the archival units of the University of California Libraries system. Influenced in part by MPLP, it articulates baseline levels for performing various phases of arrangement and description work and recommends conditions under which those baselines will be exceeded or otherwise varied from, all with a goal of increasing performance to reduce backlogs.

Desnoyers, Megan. "When Is It Processed?" In *A Modern Archives Reader*, edited by Maygene F. Daniels and Timothy Walch, 309–25. Washington, DC: National Archives Trust Fund Board, 1984). Originally published in *Midwestern Archivist* 7, no. 2 (1982).

> This frequently cited article is one of the earliest works that strongly encouraged archivists to think about the levels of arrangement and description that were really useful to researchers and therefore necessary for archivists to perform. Desnoyers makes a strong case for focusing work at the series level and above, rather than assuming that we are obliged to perform the more granular (and costly) work required at lower levels. She includes tables expressing a continuum of processing levels and the tasks associated with each—arrangement, description, preservation, and content screening—which is quite helpful.

Erickson, Paul, and Robert Schuster. "Beneficial Shocks: The Place of Processing-Cost Analysis in Archival Administration." *American Archivist* 58, no. 1 (1995): 32–53.

> Largely a literature review, the authors very helpfully gather and analyze case studies of processing performance at various repositories. They argue that the dollar costs that can be deduced from these studies provide a necessary wakeup call to force repositories to consider the real costs of all the actions that they perform on collections over the course of processing.

Greene, Mark A., and Dennis Meissner. "More Product, Less Process: Revamping Traditional Archival Processing." *American Archivist* 68, no. 2 (2005): 208–63.

> In this fairly exhaustive study of processing theory and practice in the United States, the authors argue that traditional processing methods and protocols are not sustainable, as evidenced by large and growing backlogs across the landscape of repositories. They argue for a user-focused approach to arrangement and description that deprecates work that adds costs while not directly improving outcomes for researchers. They contend that processing work at the series level and above is usually sufficient and achieves the greatest performance value.

Lynch, Karen Temple, and Thomas E. Lynch. "Rates of Processing Manuscripts and Archives." *Midwestern Archivist* 7 (1982): 25–34.

> The authors glean data from processing rates expressed in grant proposals to derive rough baseline processing performance figures for personal papers and for organizational records. Their goal is to help institutions conduct better planning in terms of matching processing resources to their acquisitions.

Maher, William J. "Measurement and Analysis of Processing Costs in Academic Archives." *College & Research Libraries* 43, no. 1 (1982): 59–7.

> Maher compiles processing performance data from the University of Illinois to ascertain the true costs of processing. His study provides much useful data and is notable in its attempt to factor in the full range of costs that ought to be applied to processing projects.

McCrea, Donna E. "Getting More for Less: Testing a New Processing Model at the University of Montana." *American Archivist* 69, no. 22 (2006): 284–90.

> The author produces a case study that is one of the earliest tests of applying an MPLP-influenced processing regimen in an academic archives. McCrea reports favorable results in terms of increased efficiency and satisfactory user outcomes.

Meissner, Dennis, and Mark A. Greene. "More Application while Less Appreciation: The Adopters and Antagonists of MPLP." *Journal of Archival Organization* 8, no. 3 (2010): 174–226.

Five years after the publication of MPLP, the authors examine the results of test applications in several repositories, as well as critical and supportive literature. They also attempt to correct some common misperceptions about MPLP and its recommendations.

Slotkin, Helen W., and Lynch Karen T. "An Analysis of Processing Procedures: The Adaptable Approach." *American Archivist* 45, no. 2 (1982): 155–63.
The authors of the MIT processing manual recommend an approach to processing intended to achieve basic objectives while containing costs. They argue that instead of processing every collection to the same level of granularity, it would be better to take a flexible approach that matches the needs of a particular collection to a certain level of processing.

Weideman, Christine. "Accessioning as Processing." *American Archivist* 69, no. 2 (2006): 274–83.
Weideman, a very early advocate for taking sustainable approaches to processing, explains an accessioning regimen at the Yale University Archives that identifies certain collections as being amenable to minimal processing and then performs that work at the point of accessioning. This approach avoids adding new materials to existing backlogs to the greatest extent possible.

Digital Archives

AIMS Work Group. *AIMS Born-Digital Collections: An Inter-Institutional Model for Stewardship.* 2012. https://dcs.library.virginia.edu/files/2013/02/AIMS_final_text.pdf, captured at https://perma.cc/P7QK-98AV.
The AIMS report was an important step in thinking through what accessioning and processing looks like for born-digital collections. It suggests policy and workflow processes for managing materials.

Daines, J. Gordon III. "Processing Digital Records and Manuscripts." In *Trends in Archival Practice: Archival Arrangement and Description*, edited and with an introduction by Christopher J. Prom and Thomas J. Frusciano, 87–143. Chicago: Society of American Archivists, 2013.
Daines provides a very thorough primer on arranging and describing digital archives. This is a highly recommended starting point for archivists processing any collection that includes digital content.

Dean, Jackie, and Meg Tuomala. "Business as Usual: Integrating Born-Digital Materials into Regular Workflows." In *Description: Innovative Practices for Archives and Special Collections*, edited by Kate Theimer, 149–61 (Lanham, MD: Rowman and Littlefield, 2014).
The authors present a case study of their arrangement of one particular collection to show how they have integrated hybrid collections containing born-digital materials into their normal processing procedures. They discuss how they deal with diverse software formats and media in the course of processing collections.

Gilliland-Swetland, Anne J. *Enduring Paradigm, New Opportunities: The Value of the Archival Perspective in the Digital Environment.* Washington, DC: Council on Library and Information Services, February 2000. https://clir.wordpress.clir.org/wp-content/uploads/sites/6/pub89.pdf, captured at https://perma.cc/XH4N-QTLV.

In considering how archivists manage digital holdings, the author stresses the value of the core archival principles of provenance and original order. It is a helpful counterweight to inclinations to see digital archives as completely novel entities.

Goldman, Ben. "Bridging the Gap: Taking Practical Steps Toward Managing Born-Digital Collections in Manuscript Repositories." *RBM: A Journal of Rare Books, Manuscripts, and Cultural Heritage* 12, no. 1 (2011): 11–24.

Goldman offers a wealth of very accessible practical advice for managing digital collections in archival settings.

Greene, Mark A. "MPLP: It Is Not Just for Processing Anymore." *American Archivist* 73, no. 1 (2010): 175–203.

The author argues for the applicability of More Product, Less Process approaches to nonprocessing archival functions, but also treats its relevance for arranging and describing digital records.

Niu, Jinfang. "Archival Intellectual Control in the Digital Age." *Journal of Archival Organization* 12, nos. 3–4 (2015): 186–97.

The author discusses numerous changes to our thinking about arrangement and description that have occurred as a result of our experiences with digital archives. He discusses new approaches to aggregate description, movements away from aggregate descriptions toward item-focused description, and even description at a subitem level.

Yeo, Geoffrey. "Contexts, Original Orders, and Item-Level Orientation: Responding Creatively to Users' Needs and Technological Change." *Journal of Archival Organization* 12, nos. 3–4 (2015): 170–85.

Yeo provocatively challenges the traditional notion that archival aggregations must be rigidly defined, arguing that new technologies allow users to re-aggregate content to suit their needs. Enabling this functionality requires archivists to shift their descriptive approach to the item level, rather than focusing on higher levels of aggregation.

Acknowledgments

It's always tempting to turn to that ancient and well-exercised trope—"I stand on the shoulders of giants"—to suggest our debt to our predecessors and colleagues. Although the giants are clearly out there, and well known to us all, I am especially indebted to all of those folks who I have directly leaned on and learned from along the road to becoming an archivist that the SAA Publications Board was eventually willing to gamble on to write this manual. I hope that gamble pays off.

I learned both the craft and the importance of archival arrangement and description from my bosses and mentors at the Minnesota Historical Society, especially Lydia Lucas and Michael Fox. I came to understand the power and necessity of descriptive tools and standards from the host of archivists who have led SAA's Description Section, its Standards Committee, and the many working groups and subcommittees that relentlessly carry those efforts forward. Too numerous to name here, the reader will find them noted in the Recommended Readings appendix. Much of what I know I learned from working with these fine archivists personally, and their writings form the extensive foundation upon which this brief manual rests. I certainly leaned heavily on Kathleen Roe's predecessor manual and have always valued her knowledge and support.

I am equally indebted to workplace colleagues and proteges, to workshop participants, and especially to the students in the Western Archives Institute, which I taught three times while planning and writing this manual. Any ability I acquired to explain, and to cultivate an appreciation for, the complicated work of arrangement and description, I achieved through teaching and coaching others who were newer to the endeavor.

I leaned on a few colleagues directly in preparing this manuscript. I am grateful to Monica Ralston and Meagan Kellom at the Minnesota Historical Society for sharing some examples of specific descriptive tools and approaches from that repository. And I am especially indebted to Maureen Callahan at Smith College, who generously read and critiqued a few parts of the manuscript in its later stages. This manual benefits materially from their help as it does from the recommendations of the peer reviewers, whose critiques were right on the mark. And I am grateful to the copy editor who made me look like a competent writer.

Finally, I am deeply indebted to my wife, Debi. She listened patiently to my problems and anxieties throughout the writing and offered helpful advice where she could. Most significantly, she tolerated this project's considerable encroachment into the first two years of our retirement.

DENNIS MEISSNER

Index

A
access points, 103–4, 116
access restrictions, 88, 104–5, 115–16, 117–18
accession file, 71–72
accession register, 71
accession report, 70, 71–72
accessioning
    about, 68–69
    administrative control, 71–72
    digital materials, 137–39
    intellectual control, 71
    physical control, 69–70
    as processing, 72–74
accidental order, 24
accruals, 90–91, 108
acquisition, 68, 107–8
acquisition notes, 116
activities, as access points, 103–4
administrative history, 99–100, 117
administrative order, 64
aggregators, 124
Alabama Department of History and Archives, 7
American Historical Association, 7
Anglo-American Cataloging Rules, Second Edition (AACR2), 46–47

annotations, 152
appraisal, 68, 77–78, 107–8
appraisal (DACS), 108
Archival Fundamental Series, 68
Archival Information Package (AIP), 136
archival methods, 13–14
ArchiveGrid, 124
archives, characteristics of, 12–13
Archives, Personal Papers, and Manuscripts (APPM), 47
Archives Nationales, 6
ArchivesSpace, 11, 52, 119–22, 125–26, 128n12
Archivists' Toolkit, 11
Archon, 11
arrangement
    about, 1–2
    of additions, 89–90
    assumptions, 3
    collection review, 76–78
    contextual research, 75–76
    description and, 39–40, 57, 93
    description of, 102–3
    of digital materials, 139–41, 193
    granularity of, 32–33
    history of, 5–11
    as intellectual exercise, 31, 156

labeling, 86–88
levels of, 81, 85–86, 164
methodology, 84–86
options for, 16–17
physical, 80–85
preparation, 74–75
processing plan, 78–80
reasons for, 4
recommended reading, 192–94
of unstructured material, 31–32
arrangement methodology, 84–86
arrangement notes, 102–3, 115, 118
Arranging and Describing Manuscripts (SAA), 68
Art and Architecture Thesaurus (AAT), 55–56
artificial levels, 30–31
AtoM, 11, 121, 122
audiovisual materials, 131–32, 198
authority records, 55, 63–64. *see also* EAC-CPF (*Encoded Archival Context*)

B
backlog, reducing, 198, 199
Barritt, Marjorie, 5
Beinecke Library, 163–64, 199
Berkeley Finding Aid Project, 51
bias, 152
bibliographic description, vs. archival, 46–47, 58, 63–64
biographical information, 63–64, 99–100, 117
born-digital material. *see* digital archives
Bunde, Janet, 36, 43

C
Canadian-US Task Force on Archival Description (CUSTARD), 47
catalog records, 40, 116, 124–25
catalogs, 123
CDs, 131
checksums, 135
citation notes, 110
collection guides, 40
collection level, 27–28
collection management systems, 11, 119–22, 125–27
collections, defined, 27
colophons, 151, 193
communication standards, 49
companion standards, 56
computer media, 131
condition, 69–70, 88
conservation, during processing, 89–90

conservation notes, 109
container list, preliminary, 70, 71, 72
container lists, 40, 83
content elements, 100–4
content standards, 46–49
context. *see also* EAC-CPF (*Encoded Archival Context*)
creators, 58–62
in finding aids, 61, 115
importance of, 12, 157
linked data, 147–48
relationships, 62–63
researching, 75, 77
control
administrative, 71–72
intellectual, 71
levels of, 26–29
physical, 69–70, 135
controlled access points, 103–4, 116
controlled vocabularies. *see* value standards
copyright status, 105–6, 138–39
core concepts, 11–14
corporate bodies, 99. *see also* EAC-CPF (*Encoded Archival Context*)
Cox, Richard, 5
creators
describing, 58–62
names of, 97, 98
researching, 75, 76, 99
critical theory, 150–54
crosswalks, 187–91
cultural competence, 151–52
CUSTARD (Canadian-US Task Force on Archival Description), 47
custodial actions, 116

D
DACS, 9
Daines, Gordon, 134
Daniel, Dominique, 150
data
description as, 3, 10, 38–39, 93–94, 157, 196
finding aids as, 113–18
data exchange. *see* interchange standards
databases, local, 119
dates, 97, 116
Describing Archives: A Content Standard (DACS)
about, 47–49
access/use elements, 104–7
acquisition/appraisal elements, 107–8
applying, 94–95

ArchivesSpace and, 119–21
content/structure elements, 100–4
crosswalks, 187–91
descriptive control element, 110
EAD and, 51, 52, 53
identity elements, 95–100
MARC21 and, 50
multilevel description, 57–58, 110–11
notes elements, 109–10
related materials elements, 108–9
description
    arrangement and, 39–40, 57, 93
    audiovisual media, 131–32
    core elements, 111
    as data, 3, 10, 38–39, 93–94, 157, 196
    defined, 2
    of digital materials, 135, 141–42
    history of, 5–11
    levels of, 120, 164
    multidimensional, 147
    multilevel, 48, 52–53, 57–58, 110–11, 117–18, 157
    order and, 64–65
    purpose of, 35, 94, 141, 145
    reasons for, 4
    recommended reading, 195–97
descriptive control element, 110
Descriptive Information Package (DIP), 136
descriptive inventories, 8
descriptive metadata. *see* metadata, descriptive
descriptive standards, 40–41
destruction notes, 107–8
digital archives
    about, 132–34
    accessioning, 137–39
    arranging, 139–41, 193
    describing, 135, 141–42, 193
    original order in, 145–46
    preservation assessment, 138
    processing framework, 134–37
    recommended reading, 203–4
    rehousing, 131
    rights assessment, 138–39
Digital Processing Framework (Cornell University), 134–37
digitization, 10
discovery, 123
diversity, 151–53
donors, documenting, 71–72
Dublin Core Metadata Element Set (DCMES), 56
duplicates, digital, 136

Dutch Manual, 5, 6–7, 14n4, 22, 25, 63
DVDs, 131

E
EAC-CPF (*Encoded Archival Context*)
    about, 10–11, 53–54, 64
    crosswalks, 187–89
    recommended reading, 197, 198
    relationships, 62
EAD (*Encoded Archival Description*)
    about, 50–53
    controlled access terms, 103
    creation of, 113–14
    crosswalks, 190–91
    finding aids example, 176–79
    publishing, 123–24
    recommended reading, 195, 196, 197
    as structured data, 37
efficiency, 3, 32–33, 149, 201–3
encoding standards, 49
European archives, 5, 17
evidential value, 18
Expert Group in Archival Description (EGAD), 146
extent, 69, 97–98, 116

F
families, 99–100
fasteners, removing, 89
Feith, J. A. *see* Dutch Manual
file formats
    analyzing, 136
    web-friendly, 140
file level, 28–29, 82–83, 118
FileMaker Pro, 119
film, 131
finding aids
    creation information, 110
    as data, 113–18 (*see also* metadata, descriptive)
    defined, 35, 40, 157
    digital material, 135
    legacy migration, 199
    linking to catalog records, 125
    as physical/intellectual link, 24
    publishing, 122–27, 136
    purpose of, 36–37
    standards for, 10
    supplemental, 107
finding aids examples
    contextual information in, 61
    EAD-encoded, 176–79

HTML transformation, 180–81
multilevel, container, 166–68
multilevel, file, 171–73
multilevel, item, 174–75
multilevel, series, 168–70
single-level, 165–66
flexibility, 149
fonds, 6, 27
Forensic Toolkit, 145 (more?)
Fox, Michael, 63
fragility, 88
French Revolution, 5–6
Fruin, R. *see* Dutch Manual
functions, describing, 60–62

G
Gilliand, Anne, 133, 152–53
glossary, 159–62
Glossary of Archives and Records Terminology, 2, 22
goals, assessing, 79
Google, 124
granularity, 32–33
Greene, Mark, 148, 149
grooved discs, 131
Guidelines for Processing Collections with Audiovisual Material (McShea), 131
guides, 40

H
handbooks, processing, 199–201
Harvard University, 73
heterogeneity, of archival materials, 12, 13
hierarchical description. *see* multilevel description
hierarchical presumption, 21–22, 26, 33
historical information, 63–64
Historical Manuscripts Commission, 7
historical societies, 7
Holmes, Oliver Wendell, 26, 28, 34n13
HTML files, 123–24
hybrid collections, 134, 139–41

I
identity, control of, 153–54
identity elements, 95–100, 114–15
identity statements, 95
inclusiveness, 151–53
information packages, 135–36
intellectual order. *see* order, intellectual
interchange standards, 49–54
interfiling, 90
An Inter-Institutional Model for Stewardship (AIMS), 133

International Council on Archives (ICA), 11, 42, 44, 121
ISAAR-CPF (*International Standard Archival Authority Record for Corporate Bodies, Persons and Families*), 44–46, 48, 53, 62, 64, 187–89
ISAD(G) (*International Standard for Archival Description, General*), 42–44, 48, 50, 51, 57–58
item level, 29–30, 83–84, 87–88, 118, 146

J
JavaScript, 118
Johnson, Valerie, 152

K
Kaplan, Elisabeth, 153

L
labeling, 86–88
languages (of materials), 106–7
levels. *see also* specific levels, e.g., item level
of arrangement, 81, 85–86, 164
artificial, 30–31
of control, 26–29
of description, 120, 164
of processing, 163–64
Library of Congress Name Authority File (LCNAF), 55
Library of Congress Subject Headings (LCSH), 55
linked data, 53
linked open data, 147–48
loading dock order, 24
location, 69
Lynch, Karen, 25

M
machines, as users, 3
MacNeil, Heather, 151, 152
magnetic media, 131, 132
management view, 149, 199
Manual for the Arrangement and Description of Archives. see Dutch Manual
manuals, processing, 89–90, 163–64, 199–201
manuscripts tradition, 7–8
MARC21, 49–50, 116, 182–86, 190–91
MARC-AMC, 9, 50
Massachusetts Institute of Technology (MIT), 25
McShea, Megan, 131
media. *see* audiovisual materials
metadata, descriptive
about, 111–12
collection management systems, 119–22
for digital materials, 141–42

finding aids, 113–18
  improving, 197
  item-level, 146
  local databases, 119
  publishing, 122–27, 136–37
  sharing, 39, 196
  spreadsheets, 118–19, 120
metadata, technical, 135
Metadata Encoding and Transmission Standard (METS), 56
Metadata Object Description Schema (MODS), 56
metadata schemas, 141
metrics, 201–3
Microsoft Access, 119
Miller, Fredric M., 4, 69
MIT Processing Manual, 90
More Product, Less Process (MPLP), 78, 89, 148–50, 202
moving image materials, 131–32
Muller, Feith, and Fruin, 6–7, 63
Muller, S. *see* Dutch Manual
multidimensional description, 147
multilevel description, 48, 52–53, 57–58, 110–11, 117–18, 157

N
names, forming, 97
National Archives (US), 19–20
necessary order, 25
Nesmith, Tom, 150
neutrality, 150–51
normalization, of files, 136
notes elements, 109–10

O
OAIS (*Reference Model for an Open Archival Information System*), 143n8
ontologies, 146
order, administrative, 64
order, intellectual
  administrative vs., 64–65
  arrangement in, 81, 139–40
  of digital files, 136
  physical vs., 24–25
order, original
  about, 22–23
  absence of, 31–32
  challenges to, 144–45
  in digital archives, 145–46
  origins of, 6–7
  types of, 24–26

order, physical, 24–25, 64
organic, collections as, 12–13, 18–19
organizational culture, 23
original order. *see* order, original
originals, location of, 108, 116
O'Toole, James, 5

P
paleontologist, archivist as, 25
Paradigm Project, 142
PDF files, 38, 39, 96, 123–24, 128n14
Pearce-Moses, Richard, 1
performance objectives, 79–80, 201–203
personally identifiable information (PII), 136
phonodiscs, 131
photographs, 129–31
physical order, 24–25, 64
Pitti, Daniel, 58
Posner, Ernst, 6, 17–18
postmodernism, 150–54
preferred citation, 109, 116
premodern era, 5, 17
preservation, 89–90, 164
preservation assessment, 70, 77, 132, 138
primary sources, 12
principles, archival, 3
privacy, 88–89, 136
processing. *see also* specific formats, e.g., photographs
  accessioning as, 72–74, 203
  conservation issues, 89–90
  as continuum, 33
  defined, 2
  economical, 23, 73
  levels of, 163–64
  principles of, 156–57
processing costs, 202
Processing Digital Records and Manuscripts (Daines), 134
processing management, 79–80
processing notes, 109–10, 116, 118
processing plan, 78–80, 135
processing rates, 202
proprietary formats, 136
provenance, 18–21, 33
provenienzprinzip, 6, 17
Public Archives Commission, 7
publication, of descriptions, 122–27, 136–37
publication notes, 109
published material, archives vs., 12–13

R
real order, 24
record groups, 27
Records in Contexts (RiC), 11, 146–47
reference code, 95–96, 117
Reference Model for an Open Archival Information System (OAIS), 143n8
registers, 8
registraturprinzip, 6
rehousing, 83, 139
related materials, 108–9, 116
relationships, 62–63, 140, 143, 146–47
repository level, 26, 96
reproductions, location of, 108–9
Resource Description and Access (RDA), 50
Resource Description Framework (RDF), 147
respect des fonds, 6, 17–18, *20*, 33
restrictions, 88–89, 104–7, 115–16, 117–18
Revisiting Collections, 152
rights assessment, 138–39
Roe, Kathleen D., 4, 50, 111, 114
Rules for Archival Description (RAD), 47

S
Santamaria, Daniel, 112, 118
Schaffner, Jen, 38
Schellenberg, Theodore, 5, 8, 12, 15n25, 18, 22, 25, 28, 74
schemas, metadata, 141
scope and content, 100–2, 115, 117
scripts (of materials), 106–7
segregation, 28
Selecting and Appraising Manuscripts (SAA), 68
sequencing, 28
series level, 27–28, 77, 81–82, 117–18
Shaefer, Sibyl, 36, 43
Slotkin, Helen, 25
social tagging, 152–53
Society of American Archivists (SAA), 51
sound materials, 131–32
space requirements, 74–75
spreadsheets, 118–19, 120
standardization, 13
standards
    about, 8–9, 10–11
    companion, 56
    content, 46–49
    importance of, 40–41, 157
    interchange, 49–54
    structural, 41–46
    value, 54–56
Standards for Archival Description (Bunde, Shaefer), 36
structural standards, 41–46
structure, lack of, 31–32
structured data, 36, 37–39, 93–94. *see also* EAC-CPF (*Encoded Archival Context*); EAD (*Encoded Archival Description*)
subgroups, 30, 81, 117–18
Submission Information Package (SIP), 135
subseries, 30, 118
supplies, processing, 75
survey, collection, 76–78, 134, 157

T
technical access, 105
technical metadata, 135
technology, 8, 9–10
title, 96–97, 115
topics, identifying, 59
transmission standards, 49
triples, 147

U
unconsciousness of creation, 18
Union List of Artists' Names (ULAN), 55
uniqueness, 13, 49
United States, archival traditions, 7
unnecessary order, 25
use restrictions, 105–7, 115–16, 117–18
user needs, 3, 145–46, 148–49, 156

V
value standards, 54–56
virus scans, 135
voices, multiple, 151–53

W
Wilkinson, Peter, 63
Workbook on Digital Private Papers, 142
workplan, 78–80
workspace, 74–75

X
XML editors, 114
XML schemas. *see* EAC-CPF (*Encoded Archival Context*); EAD (*Encoded Archival Description*)
XSLT, 118

About the Author

DENNIS MEISSNER is the retired deputy director for programs at the Minnesota Historical Society, a Fellow of the Society of American Archivists, and a past president of SAA. Most of his career has focused on the arrangement, description, and use of archival materials, and he has participated in a number of national and international efforts to develop standards and practices in those areas. In 2003–2004, he collaborated with Mark A. Greene on the NHPRC-funded More Product, Less Process research project, which has seen broad adoption within American archives and special collections.